In My Opinion...

Other published books authored by Berel Wein:

HEBREW

Chikrei Halachah
Eeiyunim B'Mesechtos Hatalmud Volume I
Eeiyunim B'Mesechtos Hatalmud Volume II
Chukei Chayim
Bamesilah Naaleh Volume I
Bamesilah Naaleh Volume II

ENGLISH

Triumph of Survival
Herald of Destiny
Echoes of Glory
Buy Green Bananas
Faith and Fate
The Pesach Haggadah
Pirkei Avos
Living Jewish
Tending the Vineyard
Patterns in Jewish History
The Legacy (co-authored with Rabbi Warren Goldstein,
  the chief Rabbi of South Africa)
Who Knows Twelve?
Teach Them Diligently
  (an autobiography)
The Oral Law of Sinai:
  An Illustrated History of the Mishnah
Vision and Valor:
  An Illustrated History of the Talmud
In the Footsteps of Eliyahu Hanavi

In My Opinion...

*Thoughts on Religion, Society, and
Life by a Very Opinionated Rabbi*

Rabbi Berel Wein

Copyright © The Destiny Foundation, 2020
ISBN 978-0-578-63302-2

This book is in copyright. All rights reserved.
Without limiting the rights under copyright reserved above,
no part of this publication may be reproduced, stored in
or introduced into a retrieval system, or transmitted in any form, or
by any means (electronic, mechanical, photocopying, recording or
otherwise) without the prior permission of The Destiny Foundation

Published by
THE DESTINY FOUNDATION
386 Route 59
Monsey, New York 10952
845-368-1425
www.jewishhistory.org

Printed in Israel

Graphic Design: Ben Gasner Studio
Graphic Artists: Rivkie Bookbinder and David Yaphe

Introduction

"Here in Israel..."

- 3   Israel the Beautiful
- 5   Lost Luggage
- 7   Nothing Original
- 9   Taxi Drivers
- 11 Weighty Matters
- 13 Climate Change
- 15 The Inscrutable Future
- 17 Fast Days and Slow Summers
- 20 Disappointments
- 22 Growing Up
- 24 Disconnection
- 26 Rabbi Ovadia Yosef
- 29 Politics as Usual
- 31 Late Rains
- 33 Locked Out

Israel and World Opinion

- 39 A Little Too Jewish
- 41 Christianity and Israel
- 43 Exclusivity and Tolerance
- 45 A Tale of Two Brothers
- 47 Faith and Doubt
- 49 A Stiff-necked People
- 52 Fascinations
- 54 O! Jerusalem
- 56 Revolutions and Mindsets
- 58 Feeling Uncomfortable
- 60 I've Got Your Back
- 62 Praying for Peace
- 64 The Pessimists amongst Us
- 66 Winter Blues
- 68 Twenty-five Years after Oslo

Inspiration in Everyday Experiences

- 73 My Post Office
- 75 Credit Cards
- 77 Answering Machines
- 79 My Keyboard
- 81 Seeing the Big Picture
- 83 On Changing Light Bulbs
- 85 The Broadcaster
- 87 My Orchid Plant

89 Spanning Generations
91 A Sad, Sad World
93 Background Noise
95 My Teacher
97 The Secret of a Happy Life
100 Finding a Parking Space
102 Lost Keys
104 A Sore Back

A Jew in Today's World

109 Eras
111 Departures
113 Rabbis' Business
115 Beliefs and Realities
117 Better Times
119 Rabbinic Responsibility
121 Spirituality
124 Victimhood
126 Charitable Giving
128 Telling the Truth
130 Defining One's Self
132 Stepping Out
134 Loose Change
136 Our Miracle Minyan
138 Unfinished Business

In the Diaspora

143 Ignoring Realities
145 Hostages and Captives
147 Uber
149 A Tale of Two Seats
151 Jewish Education in the Age of a Godless Culture
153 Modern Orthodoxy
156 College Campuses
159 More Soulful
161 "It Could Never Happen Here…"
163 Unity and Disunity
166 An Uncertain Future
168 Jewish Humor
170 My Books
172 Rabbi Meir Zlotowitz

Contemporary Issues

- 177 Hurricanes and Political Storms
- 179 On Being Currently Relevant
- 181 Alcohol and the Jews
- 183 Supply and Demand
- 185 Texting
- 187 Too Much, Too Fast
- 189 Floods and Arks
- 191 On Being a Skeptic
- 193 Price Gouging
- 195 Just Let Go
- 197 Murder
- 199 Prevailing versus Winning
- 201 Is Democracy Jewish?
- 203 Teachers
- 205 The Past and the Future

Human Nature

- 211 Old Magazines
- 213 Oops!
- 215 Confusing Roles
- 216 Extremism
- 219 Certainty and Uncertainty
- 221 Difficult Decisions
- 223 Frustrations
- 225 Doing Favors
- 227 Hypocrisy
- 229 Undoing the Past
- 231 Privileges and Rights
- 233 Optimism
- 235 Rivalries
- 237 Inconsistencies
- 239 Half-Birthdays
- 241 Punctuality

Holidays and Special Days

- 247 Erev Shabbat
- 249 Saturday Night
- 251 Elul
- 253 Our Annual Report – Rosh Hashanah
- 255 Gifts – Yom Kippur
- 256 The Eternal Struggle – Chanukah
- 258 It's Never Too Late – Tu B'Shvat
- 260 Costumes – Purim
- 262 The Fifth Son – Pesach

264 Righteous Women – Pesach
266 Memorial Days – Yom Hashoah and Yom Ha'atzma'ut
268 Days of Fasting
270 Disaster and Rebirth – Tisha B'Av
272 Menachem Av
274 Shabbat Chazon

Lessons from History

279 A Parking Space
281 Eras End
283 Kristallnacht
285 A Family Fight
287 Echoes from the Past
289 Government and Religion
291 It's the Zhids
293 Europe Is Gone
296 Promises
298 Individuals and History
300 Regressing
302 Infanticide
305 Ideology and Reality
307 Rabbi Isaac Halevi Herzog
309 Jewish Mail

Jewish Heritage

315 The Universal Jew
317 Back to School
319 Gratitude
321 Civil Argument
323 On Being a Rabbi
326 Prayers – Answered and Unanswered
328 My Unseen Minyan
330 Charity
332 Half-Empty
334 Good Fortune
336 Spring Ahead
338 Career or Calling?
340 Sermons
341 Poetry
343 Head Checks

This special book by Rabbi Berel Wein
is dedicated in memory of our dear friend,

PETER WEINTRAUB
Pinchas Meir ben Herschel Avraham HaLevi, z"l

Peter lived his life with passion, spontaneous joy, integrity, respect, and warmth towards all. He had the ability to make everyone feel like they mattered. He lived deeply, while giving of himself generously, and his oxygen was connecting to people. He made what was important to them, important to him, especially with his wife.

Peter greatly enjoyed music. His light and "boy" in him would shine as we sang for hours at the piano in his living room. His life was a series of beautiful songs, each composed of notes melding into unique melodies, rhyme, beat, tempo, rhythm, and verse....

He had a family song, a father of Lauren song, a father of Ariela song, a step-dad to Jennifer song, work songs, friend songs, a son song, a husband song and, most important, his special love song for his beloved wife, Sarah. They made unique, beautiful music together.

We miss Petey, and were blessed to know him.

And
in loving memory of

IAN SHAPIRO
Haim ben Yitzhak, z"l

who left us too soon.

He blessed us all with his gentle kindness and caring attention.
Loving son, brother, uncle, and friend.
He honored his parents beyond words.

May he live in our hearts and through our deeds in his memory.

DEBRA AND DENNY BERMAN

Dedicated to the memory of our father and grandfather

WILLIAM M. DAVIDSON
Velvel Moshe ben Refuel

To paraphrase Kesubos 50a,
"He who writes scrolls and lends them to others,
his charity endures forever."

Ethan and Gretchen Davidson
Asher, William, and Levi

This insightful and thought provoking collection
of essays by Rabbi Berel Wein
is dedicated to our greatest influencers and motivators

Our Parents

Rabbi Mordechai Joseph Kronenberg *z"l*
הרב מרדכי יוסף בן ר' עזריאל זעליג ז"ל

Rabbi David Isaac Bergstein *z"l*
הרב דוד יצחק בן הרב שמעון מרדכי ז"ל

HaRabbanit Reba Bergstein *a"h*
הרבנית רבקה בת הרב שמעון אשר ע"ה

Who dedicated their lives not only to their families but also to
the nurturing of thousands of impressionable Jewish children,
adolescents and adults from all segments of Jewish society.

Through their teaching, wisdom, and guidance they not only inspired
and impacted the Long Beach/Far Rockaway/Five Towns and Greater Queens,
New York, communities, but also the future generations that now
flourish throughout the United States, Israel, and global Jewish communities.

And in honor of our Matriarch and dear Mother

Mrs. Pearl Kronenberg Shafier
מרת פעריל פריידא בת ר' יצחק שתחי'

Who shared and contributed in all aspects of our father's
noble and holy endeavors and initiatives on behalf of Klal Yisrael

And in grateful appreciation of our esteemed
and revered Mara D'Asra for four decades

Rabbi Berel Wein שליט"א

For the immeasurable influence and guidance he had
and continues to have on us and our family.

May ה' יתברך grant him the sustained good health and strength to continue to educate,
influence, and inspire the countless number of people throughout the Jewish world.

Michael and Sharon Kronenberg
משה אהרן ושרה מרים קרוננברג

And their family

Introduction

People are fascinating creatures. As the Talmud points out, no two people are the same, and each of us possesses a different opinion and a different viewpoint on life and society. Naturally, we all believe that our opinion is the correct one, and we are incredulous if we discover that many other people do not agree with us, or even that they are vehemently opposed to our opinion.

But the fact that there is no unanimity of opinion in the world generally, and among the Jewish people particularly, is in its own way a blessing and a positive thing. All progress – whether it be in spiritual or physical matters – is a result of differing opinions. It is no accident that the Talmud is a record of the debates of the great rabbis over spiritual and practical matters. It was this give-and-take of ideas and personalities that has formed the basis of Jewish life for millennia. There is no doubt in my mind that if everyone agreed on everything and would not cross-pollinate the Jewish world with different opinions, Judaism and the Jewish people would not survive.

Like everyone else, I am a very opinionated person. I have opinions on many subjects in life. Some of those subjects are truly important, while others may be seen as trivial. Nevertheless, I have an opinion regarding all of them. Over the past many decades I have written numerous essays and newspaper columns expressing my opinion on issues – current, past, and future. These essays were written mainly for the readership of my congregation here in Israel, and for a number of years I was a fairly regular columnist for the *Jerusalem Post*. My editor and friend, Charlotte Friedland, suggested to me a year ago that I should collect all of those essays and put some of them in book form so readers could review them at their leisure. The Lord has blessed me with generations of intelligent descendants who humor me by often asking me my opinion on past and present issues. So I thought that compiling some of my essays and putting them into a book could be an acceptable idea for my family and me, and perhaps for the broader community as well.

I have spent many months reviewing past essays online. Sometimes I was amazed that my opinions so radically changed since I wrote some of those essays, so most of those have been omitted from this book. Nevertheless, believe it or not, there are essays in this book that represent opinions that I am no longer quite certain of being correct, and they may not reflect accurately my current views. Yet I have included them to offer diversity of thought.

I know that there is a touch of hubris and arrogance in publishing my personal view on so many topics. The assumption is that other people will be interested in reading my ideas and opinions. But I have never suffered from false modesty; so I am more than satisfied that I have taken the plunge and actually helped compile and publish this work. I hope that it will find acceptance among those who read it, and that it will help prod intelligent comments, thought, and debate on many of these issues that are represented in this book. King Solomon stated that there is no end to the number of books that are written. I therefore do not feel too guilty adding to the pile.

Mrs. Friedland has done most of the heavy lifting on this volume. I am enormously grateful to her for her talented work, making this a readable book. My thanks go to Ben Gasner, one of the great book designers of our era, for his help and talents in making this book presentable and pleasing to the eye. I am also naturally indebted to all of my colleagues at the Destiny Foundation for their support in this project, and in all of the other areas that we have worked together to further Jewish knowledge and thought. And I certainly thank the God of Israel, Who somehow has allowed me now, in my eighty-fifth year, to live in Jerusalem and continue to serve to my limited ability as a teacher, author, and rabbi for the Jewish people.

Berel Wein
Jerusalem, Israel
5780/2020

Israel the Beautiful

As a city dweller, I rarely leave Jerusalem, so I do not get to see and appreciate the natural beauty of our wondrous country. But every summer the Destiny Foundation hosts its annual retreat at Kibbutz Lavi in the Lower Galilee section of Israel. The journey to and from Lavi (by different routes) affords me the opportunity to again witness the innate natural magnificence of Israel.

The Land of Israel is basically a land of desert and rocky ground. And that is what it appeared to be through many centuries of neglect and barrenness. As recently as the beginning of the twentieth century, visitors always commented upon the country's desolation, poverty, and drabness. Yet today, from the northern (and parts of the central) Negev to the northern and eastern reaches of Israel's current borders, the country is green and lushly forested.

This feat was accomplished by intensive, self-sacrificing human labor and the ingenious ability to distribute water plentifully and efficiently to all parts of the country. Developing and exploiting the country's national aquifers, drawing on the waters of Lake Kinneret, and building major desalination plants have all combined to make our country a green place. Waste sewage water has been purified and supplied for agricultural purposes. An astounding 70 percent of Israel's drinking water comes from desalination methods. What a strategic blessing!

4 In My Opinion …

God promised us a land that flows with milk and honey and all sorts of bounty and blessings. As well as supplying our country's basic food needs, Israeli agricultural products, machinery, and crop production efficiency help feed millions of people worldwide on a daily basis. Jews have returned to their agricultural roots (no pun intended, but compliments nevertheless will be graciously accepted) and are expert vintners and producers of olive oil, exotic cheeses, and every imaginable fruit and vegetable.

Flowers of every conceivable color, shading, and hue dot our country's landscape and appear regularly on our tables and in our homes. I have no recollection that as a child I ever saw flowers in our home, or for that matter in any of the homes of my friends. Even on Shavuot, the synagogues of my youth boasted no flowers on their premises. That may have been because of the cost of purchasing flowers in a much less affluent society than today's Jewish world, or of the lack of an Eastern European flower-friendly mentality, or for other reasons. But there is no question that today flowers are commonplace, and they help dispel a feeling of drabness and ordinariness. Israel has created itself as a major producer and exporter of flowers. The flowers of Israel confirm the feeling of natural beauty that one feels when viewing the landscape of the country today. Our little country is not only booming, it is blooming as well.

Yet there is a beauty to the Land of Israel that cannot be seen physically but must be experienced internally and spiritually. The Talmud poses the question: "Why are the hot springs of Israel located in Tiberias and not in Jerusalem?" Why, indeed, does Jerusalem not contain any natural wonders – no rivers or lakes or sunsets over the sea? The lack of any natural wonders in the Holy City is puzzling. After all, Judaism always preached the necessity of visiting Jerusalem, so why was it not made to be physically wondrous and naturally inviting?

The Talmud answers that Jerusalem's beauty is so rare and holy, so naturally spiritual and eternal, that physical and natural phenomena would prove distracting – perhaps even demeaning to the true essence of its beauty and grandeur. Jerusalem has to be appreciated not only with one's eyes and physical senses, but also with one's soul.

The same is true of the Land of Israel generally. Even though the country is outstandingly beautiful in every physical and natural sense, its true beauty exists in the soul of the beholder. There is so much history and purpose hidden in every inch of the land that to deal only with the surface and the obvious really does a disservice.

Perhaps that is what is meant in our daily prayers when we hope "for a new light to shine on Zion." The new light should emanate from our souls and hearts so that we may be privileged to see Israel the beautiful in all of its splendor.

Lost Luggage

There are many discomforting, even unpleasant, experiences that await those of us who travel by airplane in our current world. Travel was once considered a luxury vacation in itself, no matter what the destination. Not today. The combination of terrorism, stringent security measures, crowded planes, narrow seats, surly service, and other sundry annoyances have turned air travel into a chore, at best. But perhaps the most dreaded of mishaps on arrival is the sinking feeling that you have standing at the baggage carousel – and your luggage does not appear.

The airlines claim that almost all luggage eventually *does* appear and is delivered to its intended destination and recipient. They also claim that their record of luggage being correctly placed on the carousel at the end of the flight is 95 percent. This may be so, but it is of little comfort to the 5 percent who stand patiently and forlornly at the baggage carousel waiting for bags that may have now been shipped halfway around the world. This is one of the most depressing emotions that humans can experience.

I recall that once I arrived at my daughter's home in the United States and she was not home, so I left my luggage on the front porch and circled around to the back entrance to see if I could gain entry there. When I could not, I returned to the front porch and, to my horror, my luggage was gone! I was beside myself. Eventually, the cleaning woman in the house noticed me on the front porch and allowed me in, and I saw that she had efficiently brought in my luggage. My feelings of relief matched those of the frustration that I had experienced just a few short moments earlier.

This experience, long stored away in my memory bank, surfaces every so often when I think about the situation of the Jewish people currently, especially those of us who live in Israel. The Jewish nation has returned from being almost annihilated by the events of the past century. In the Diaspora, most Jews have become successful and prosperous. Here in Israel, we have been successful in building a first-world state and society, a home for all Jews who wish to come. Yet, undoubtedly, not all of our luggage has arrived with us.

For many Jews, any sense of tradition or Jewish history has been misplaced or lost entirely. For many, if not most, of the Jewish people, family traditions and long-held value systems have been eroded by secularism, assimilation, and the pressures of modern society. But many of these Jews still stand beside the baggage carousel, in their hearts and minds waiting for their lost luggage to appear, even if they would be hard-pressed to identify it if it somehow came tumbling down the chute of history.

Jews who live without tradition, without an attachment to Torah or to the Jewish people, sense within themselves that something is missing. Few are willing to go to search for their lost luggage, but somehow if that luggage does appear, they are drawn to it; and there is an inner sense to claim it. There is a real awakening today, a search for tradition and Jewish values in parts of the Jewish community here in Israel, and even in some places in the Diaspora as well. Piece by piece, some of those bags are being reclaimed.

This past century has been a very long and tiresome trip for us. We are severely jetlagged by the agonizing journey that we have been forced to traverse. It is understandable, therefore, that some of our luggage – long treasured and valuable as it was and is – got lost on the way. But we should never despair, because even the airlines say that eventually all luggage will be delivered to its proper destination and owners. There are many signs of change in much of Israeli society and its attitude towards tradition, Jewish values, and even to certain observances and customs.

I have no doubt that this trend will continue in the future, and that just as there has been the fulfillment of the prophets' prediction regarding the ingathering of the exiles, so there will be an ingathering of our values, traditions, hopes, and aspirations. None of our luggage will be lost forever.

Nothing Original

I imagine that most blogs and commentary articles in the Jewish world this week will concentrate on the tragic and difficult events that occurred in Israel: the firebomb murder of a Palestinian infant and the slashing attack by a religious fanatic upon participants in a Jerusalem parade. It certainly makes sense that these events should be written about and commented upon, for they expose the dark fringes that exist in human society, and point out to us again that we may be the "chosen people," but, in many respects, we are no different from others. The combination of political or ideological extremism with religious or national fanaticism is a witches' brew from which no good can ever come.

There will be a great deal of "I told you so" commentary regarding these events, and there will also be the pious and partisan political comments from the leaders of our various factions. There is no need for me to echo their sentiments or to explain the underlying ills of our society, all of which are well known to all of us, even though we are loath to admit their existence.

The truth of the matter is that the world is a violent place and violent behavior has been the accepted norm in societies, Jewish and non-

In My Opinion…

Jewish, religious and secular, for much of the past half-century. It has been condoned, if not even encouraged, by religious and political leaders who should know better. In such an accepting society, violent people and violent acts flourish. When combined with religious/ideological belief, acts of violence are raised in the eyes of the perpetrators to become holy and completely justified, even necessary.

It must be stated that the value of human life has been denigrated over the past century. World War II consumed tens of millions of lives, most of which were those of innocent civilians. The purpose of winning the war at all costs overwhelmed the moral consideration of sparing human lives in the process. Mass industrial murder such as the Holocaust and the Gulag became almost normal human behavior instead of being seen as exceptional aberrations. The State of Israel has been forced to fight numerous wars in order to survive. Almost 60 to 70 percent of the Israeli population has served in the army, knows how to fire weapons, and is therefore accustomed to violence, justified as that may be.

In the religious Jewish world, all of us know that over the past decades, acts of violence against other Jews by small fringe groups of zealots occur on a regular basis. No one speaks about it, and in reality no one takes any action against it. But the spirit of violence is alive and well even among those who profess their loyalty to the Torah and to its values of harmony, tolerance, and goodness. Violence is somehow an accepted form of behavior against those who denigrate Jewish tradition and practice. The silence of the religious Jewish world over the past decades to this atmosphere of violence and antisocial behavior has been deafening and depressing. The events of last week only pour more fuel on this destructive fire that rages within our camp.

There is nothing new or original in the words that are being written here. As long as we are satisfied with allowing violence to be an integral part of our religious community, these types of events will continue to occur. Simply because a Jew is observant of certain commandments of the Torah or wears visibly Jewish garb, his antisocial and anti-Torah behavior is ignored. This is a sure recipe for future tragedies.

Though governmental action will try to stem it, the effort will probably be ineffective in the long run. Societal changes are needed, and that has to come from the inside and not from the outside. Our spiritual and rabbinic leaders, our educators and schools, need to address this issue in a strong and continued manner. Of what value is all of our knowledge and seeming accomplishments if our society shields murderers, violent people, sexual predators, thieves, and charlatans?

We are taught in Psalms, and throughout the words of the great prophets of Israel, that peace and social harmony require constant attention and pursuit. Being passive in the face of our weaknesses certainly will not help to correct them. Again, nothing that I write here is new or original. But I do feel that it is important and vital.

Taxi Drivers

One of the storied professions in Jewish lore is that of the *baal agalah* – literally, the owner of a wagon. Until the advent of the automobile and its attendant spinoffs – buses, motorcycles, all-terrain vehicles, etc., a horse or donkey and wagon was the common means of ground transportation. The other alternative was to walk, one used by most of humanity most of the time. Throughout the Talmud, we find references to long journeys on foot undertaken by the rabbis of the time. Rabi Yochanan, even at a rather advanced age, walked from Tzipori to Tiberias with his disciples accompanying him, no mean feat for any present-day hiker.

But in Eastern Europe, the heartland of Ashkenazic Jewry for centuries, the *baal agalah* reigned supreme as the provider of ground transportation. As such, he eventually entered Jewish life as an almost mythical character. At times, he was portrayed as the simple, intrinsically pious and holy Jew, who discussed weighty theological questions with God, his passengers, and sometimes with his horse. In other forms, he was an intrinsically wise man whose advice and counsel was to be sought and followed. In other portrayals, the *baal agalah* was depicted as the ultimate boor and ignoramus, uncouth and ill-mannered, almost without any redeeming social values except for the necessity of using his horse and wagon. These different portrayals were undoubtedly all true, depending upon which *baal agalah* one met. People remain who they are no matter how they earn their livelihood. But the *baal agalah* remained a popular folk character in all of his forms and guises.

The day of the *baal agalah* has departed from us, as has Eastern European Jewish life. While Eastern European Jewry has yet to find its replacement either quantitavely or qualitatively, the *baal agalah* has once again emerged in the form of our beloved taxi drivers. And just as with their predecessors, the horse and wagon drivers, the taxi drivers come in all different sorts and shapes, moods and characteristics. Some are wise and pious, some are boors, some are simple, and others are complex. But they are rarely boring. One hears great political wisdom and analysis from them. Theology, as well as the nature and future of Judaism, are subjects that almost always eventually arise in their conversations.

The opinions expressed on any and all subjects are almost as freewheeling as the way they drive their cars. It is hard work driving twelve to fourteen hours a day on the streets of Israel, so like the *baalei agalah* before them, they demand attention and consideration. Whatever the destination, a taxi ride in Israel is almost always an interesting experience. If one is fortunate enough to find the "right" (no political pun intended here) taxi driver, it can be an enlightening and educational one as well.

I am certain that everyone has his own favorite cab driver stories. Here are two of mine.

When my wife and I visited Israel in the late 1960s, we took a taxi from the airport (ah, the old, old Ben Gurion Airport – what nostalgia!) to Jerusalem. The car was a rickety old DeSoto that must have been twenty years old. Not surprisingly, the car blew a tire on the ascent to

Jerusalem. The driver and I unloaded all of our luggage, jacked up the car, and he changed the tire while I supervised this delicate operation. As I commiserated with him, he turned to me and said: "What do you think, it is easy to go up to Jerusalem?" That comment, representing the Jewish wisdom of the ages on this subject, helped put our tourist trip to Israel into the proper perspective of appreciation, wonder, and thankfulness. Going up to Jerusalem has never been easy, nor was it ever meant to be.

My second story concerns a cab I was in that was stopped by a policeman for a minor traffic violation (turning left from the right-hand lane) in front of a synagogue. As the cabdriver and the policeman were debating the finer points of traffic law, someone ran out of the synagogue and shouted that they needed three more people for the *minyan* immediately. Dutifully, the three of us trooped into the synagogue for the *Minchah* prayer service. After it concluded, the cabdriver said to the policeman: "Now that God has forgiven my sins through my prayer, you certainly can do so as well." He got off with a warning.

Weighty Matters

Some time ago, I was standing in a long line before the check-in counter at an airport in the United States. There was quite a delay, as a young woman already at the counter was having a great problem because her suitcase was overweight. The airlines are very strict in enforcing weight limits on luggage, especially since charging for luggage and overcharging for overweight luggage has proven to be very profitable. In any event, her suitcase was apparently four or five pounds overweight. She immediately began to unpack it before a crowd of overly curious people, looking for space in her carry-on or on her person for those extra items. I felt very sorry for the young woman because of this public humiliation that was being visited upon her. She ended up wearing two jackets and an overcoat inside an airport terminal building where the temperature was at least 72° Fahrenheit.

Of course, the lesson here is that one should think ahead and pack wisely before coming to the airport. But that is not the usual way that human beings function. No matter how repeatedly we are warned against overweight luggage, we are all convinced that a few extra pounds won't matter. Yet the airlines will be scrupulously exact in weighing the luggage. And this impasse with human nature can be witnessed on a regular basis at any airport check-in counter in the world.

Over the past century and a half, Jewish people, individually and as a whole, slowly but steadily began their return to the Land of Israel. Like all travelers, these Jews came with their luggage. And like all travelers, their luggage contained things that are completely unnecessary and irrelevant to the new situation of a resurrected Jewish homeland and national state. And just as at airline check-in counters, so too there has been a price to be paid for the overweight national and personal luggage of the Jewish people returning to the Land of Israel.

All of the difficulties, disputes, mindsets, and distortions of life that the millennia-long exile inflicted upon us has been packed into our luggage and brought here to the nascent and miraculous Jewish state. And here we have begun to unpack our luggage in front of the entire world to see. Some of this unnecessary – and in many cases, unwanted excess – baggage thankfully has been discarded. But much of it has been simply repacked; and we resemble that poor young woman wearing two jackets and an overcoat, marching through a warm airport.

Bitter ethnic divisions still exist here in our wonderful little country. The old discriminations and divisions that marked Jewish Eastern European life and society have not completely disappeared from our midst. The current fracturing of Israeli society as represented by the plethora of political parties competing for office is only a replay of Jewish life in Eastern Europe almost two centuries ago.

In the Diaspora, it was rather easy for everyone in the Jewish world to beat his own particular drum, for there was no such thing as a united

Jewish community that controlled the life and society of our ancestors. The czars, kaisers, and emperors of Europe saw the Jewish people as monolithic and capable of assimilation into their general society. The Jews, however, saw themselves as individuals; therefore everyone had the right not only to his opinion, but also his own mindset and behavior.

The idea that a national mindset with a sense of responsibility for the whole, and not just for the individual, was not and is not present in Jewish life in the Diaspora. But the Jewish state can ill afford not to have such a national mindset. The success of our national entity demands that our suitcases must be packed cleverly, with an eye to the dreaded scale that will measure whether it must be unpacked once more.

Climate Change

The recent furor over the *chametz* court ruling and subsequent attempt to legislate a ban on publicly displaying *chametz* on Pesach suggests an issue that is far different and deeper than the relatively narrow (though vastly important) one of *chametz* itself. That issue is one of climate change – not the weather, but rather the mindset of secular Israeli society, our courts and governmental systems.

Observance of traditional laws and rituals is a personal matter and always has been a personal matter. The Talmud taught us long ago that "all things may be in the hands of Heaven except for the fear of Heaven itself." Judaism is based on the supreme idea that humans have free will and the power to choose (without heavenly coercion) one's actions, behavior, and belief, according to one's own lights. However, since no person is an island, we all live in a general society that surrounds us; so there are certain norms that prevail and, therefore, to an extent restrict our behavior and choices. Justice Oliver Wendell Holmes, in a famous United States Supreme Court decision on the issue of freedom of speech, opined that no one has the right to shout "fire" in a crowded theater when, in fact, there is no fire. There is a certain mindset, a climate of civility and accepted respectfulness that rules a society.

Naturally, over time and circumstance, this climate and mindset may and will change. The question is whether this change is warranted and beneficial to the society or if it is merely divisive, temporary, and eventually destructive to the very nature of that society. Not every climate change can be seen as being beneficial.

There were certain norms of respect that once governed Israeli society, even though that society was perhaps even more secular in its lack of observance and in its anti-religious ideology than it is today. Marxism was a powerful influence in the Jewish world then, as was its attendant atheism. Nevertheless, there was a general consensus of a modicum of respect towards traditional Jewish norms. Maybe it was nostalgia, or just good, hardheaded common sense, that the climate in the country marked Yom Kippur without traffic, Pesach without public displays of *chametz*, Tisha B'Av without restaurants being open for business. Such was the climate of the times – not one of religious observance, but rather one of respect for Jewish history and tradition, and for the great section of Israeli society who held these concepts and observances dear.

But the estrangement of Israeli society from this type of public climate has been taking place gradually over the past few decades. Respect for tradition and knowledge of the Jewish past are certainly not emphasized – and in many cases, not even taught – in the Israeli public educational system. Religious Jews are demonized, albeit subtly, but nevertheless constantly, in the main media channels. Sensitivities to neighbors and fellow citizens have become nonexistent. Public Shabbat desecration abounds, and no one takes into account the damage – spiritual, social, and generational – that springs from this source. The climate has changed: there is no respect for our tradition, for our past, or for the sensitivities of a large and ever-growing section of Israeli society.

So it is not the individual issue of the public display of *chametz* on Pesach that is so hurtful. It is rather the indication of how severely the climate regarding Jewish tradition has changed. There are many Jews who are not observant, but who nevertheless respect the prohibition of *chametz* on Pesach. The court's ill-advised decision, which concentrates on the legal tree in front of it and does not take into account the general societal forest that exists, weakens the public's resolve of respect for tradition and sensitivity to generations and to other sections of society. If *chametz* on Pesach were a Christian or Moslem religious tenet, I am confident that the court would have ruled otherwise. It is ironic in the extreme that in the Jewish state, Judaism is the least respected of all religions.

Unless that public climate is now changed through education, political leadership, common sense and goodwill, in years to come there will be further divisiveness, erosion of respect for one another, and a greater atmosphere of social discontent. We worry about and debate the problem of environmental climate change – global warming – endlessly. But certainly not enough attention is being paid to the social and spiritual climate change that is so dangerous to the homogeneity of Israeli society and to its unity and future destiny. Global warming may be a climate change that defies our attempts to govern it. But our social climate change is certainly subject to rectification and improvement.

The Inscrutable Future

There is no question that world history would read far differently if only the assumptions of the present could be tempered by the realities of the future. As human beings, we are limited drastically by our inability to forecast the future. In the autumn of 1914, the German army stood at the gates of Paris, Kaiser Wilhelm II believed that victory was at hand, and that his troops "would return home before the leaves fall." His assumption was that the war could be won by a relatively short and swift campaign. Had the Kaiser and his generals been able to peer into the future and see that the war would last for more than four agonizing years and consume millions of people – soldiers and civilians alike – perhaps he would not have entered into his alliance with Austria-Hungary that touched off the Great War.

But his arrogance betrayed him. Convinced of his imminent success, he set in motion a chain of events that would destroy Europe over the balance of the century. Not being able to foresee that he would plunge the world into a bloodletting of unimagined proportions and destroy his empire, the Kaiser was convinced that the present reality – that the German military was the strongest force in Europe – would prevail in his favor. He could not imagine that in four years they no longer would be the strongest army in Europe.

Though the German army had been repeatedly victorious, after the Second Battle of the Marne in July/August 1918, the situation was radically different: General Erich Ludendorff and Field Marshal Paul von Hindenburg informed the Kaiser on September 29 that, in their opinion, the war was lost and that Germany should seek the best terms possible in an immediate settlement. The turning point of the war had come, but the Kaiser refused to believe it. Germany continued to fight until it ultimately lost the war, and the Kaiser was forced to abdicate.

I have often wondered what our part of the world would look like today if the Arab nations would have taken advantage of the peace offers made to it by various governments of Israel over the past seventy years. In 1948, before the War of Independence, the fledgling Jewish state had agreed to accept partition lines that were enormously favorable to the Arabs. Instead of consenting to those lines, the Arab nations attempted to destroy Israel completely, and thereby lost territory and resources. After the War of Independence, the parties agreed to armistice lines that were more favorable to Israel, but still overwhelmingly much more favorable to the Arab population. Again, the Arabs refused those advantageous terms and the possibility of building a future for their people; rather, they concentrated on fomenting successive wars in an attempt to destroy the Jewish state.

After every war, they found themselves in a worse position than they had held before the war. Egypt and Jordan came to this realization and eventually agreed that the best hope for their future was not the destruction of Israel. It would be better to accustom themselves to the reality of the State of Israel. Unfortunately, the rest of the Arab world still does not see the future in those terms.

The actions of the present shape the world of the future. In the seventy years of the existence of the State of Israel, actions and policies taken at one time make for difficulties in arriving at a permanent, fair, and equitable peace arrangement in the future.

Many mistakes have been made by both sides over the years. Most of Israel's mistakes were based on rosy assumptions and wishful thinking. There is no other explanation for the Oslo Accords and other interim agreements that have been made over the past decades. The Arab mistake is a fundamental one: believing as a matter of faith and religion that the Jewish people have no right to a state in the Middle East, and that all sorts of tactics – diplomatic, terroristic, propaganda, etc. – will eventually grant their wish that Israel will disappear. This is a terrible misreading of the future and only serves to prolong the conflict, the pain, and the cost to all concerned.

Fast Days and Slow Summers

Here in Israel, summer is the time for Saturday night demonstrations. Most of the time the demonstrations are gatherings looking for a cause rather than a cause inspiring demonstrations. It is just the thing to do on the warm Saturday nights in Tel Aviv. For many years the demonstrations concentrated on the peace process with the Palestinians. But it has become clear to the vast majority of Israelis that the Palestinians are not interested in any sort of peace process that would accommodate the security, or even the existence, of a Jewish State of Israel. So the "peace process" can no longer inspire demonstrations despite the protestations of the hard-core Left that the lack of peace with the Arab world is all the fault of Israel and the settlements.

Last summer it appeared that the demonstrators had found an issue that would resonate within the general Israeli public: social and economic equality. But this issue has also petered out with the politicians paying lip service to it and appointing commissions to study it. (The price of cottage cheese was temporarily lowered, but has started to creep up again.) But very little has been truly accomplished on this front. The fact that agitators and anarchists have used the social equality demonstrations to wreak violence and havoc has seriously dampened any enthusiasm for further popular participation in demonstrations on behalf of this seemingly worthy cause.

So this year's rallying point is one of the favorites of Israeli society: bashing the Charedim and forcing them to do military or national service. To put it mildly, Charedi society is not very popular nor respected by the general Israeli public. There are many reasons for this, some of them justified by the behavior of some Charedim, but most of them are imaginary and unjustified.

Nevertheless, Charedi society has never seen fit to engage and enlighten its adversaries regarding any of the core values and lifestyle systems that govern it. And the fact that it allows itself to be run in a de facto fashion – not by its rabbinic leaders, but rather by handlers, politicians, and *machers* only further beclouds and besmirches its image in the eyes of the Israeli public. Thus Charedim and service in the army is the natural default issue for Saturday night demonstrations when all other public issues are no longer troubling enough to attract thousands to come out on the street.

But all logic and common sense tells us that bringing the Charedi public into general Israeli society and to achieve its participation in military or national service is an evolutionary process – one that will require time, patience, tolerance, education, compromise, and goodwill on behalf of everyone involved. Coercion, mandatory prison sentences, fines, etc. are populist solutions that will have no significant effect in the real world that we currently inhabit. Equal distribution of national service is a great populist electioneering issue, but like the social equality issue it will not be solved by government fiat or political bombast.

Last Sunday we commemorated the fast day of the Seventeenth of Tammuz, a day of many tragedies in Jewish history. Some of these tragedies were due to outside forces – the breaching of the defensive wall outside Jerusalem, the burning of the Torah by a tyrant. But some were self-inflicted by the behavior of the Jewish people, such as the shattering of the tablets of stone by Moses at the sight of Israel worshipping the Golden Calf. Even though the "outside" tragedies occurred to us also because of our spiritual shortcomings, at least we can accommodate our thinking to the fact that we have bitter and powerful enemies in the world who sometimes are successful in prevailing over us temporarily.

However, the destructive nature of our inner self-inflicted tragedies can never be rationalized or excused. Demonizing and coercing an entire large population of Jews into doing what others wish them to do is counterproductive and ultimately doomed to failure. Those who danced around the Golden Calf proclaimed: "This is your God, Israel!" They were unwilling to tolerate a different opinion or lifestyle – everyone had to worship the Golden Calf. This led to civil war, thousands of Jewish deaths, and the destruction of their precious idol itself.

It is ironic that here in Israel those who continually rail against religious coercion are now in the vanguard of enforcing real coercion of others. Summer evening demonstrations won't accomplish much in this area. Only a gradual and tolerant program of integration over time will lead to a solution to this most nettlesome problem.

Disappointments

Disappointments are almost always based on the failure of people, technological gadgets, or public policies to live up to expectations. The higher the expectations, the greater the disappointments. Because we invest so much confidence and hope in our political leaders, we are invariably doomed to disappointment and frustration when they turn out to be fallible human beings. We are always looking for that great infallible leader able to justify our outsize expectations. The greater the electoral victory, the harder it will be for that victor to justify his or her electoral success.

So the best solution to ameliorate our frustrations and disappointments is to not set our expectations too high. The companies that manufacture and market all of our new electrical and communication wonder devices advertise them in terms of perfection and ease of operation, only causing disappointment when those exaggerated claims do not match up with the reality of the product itself. So we are constantly searching for the next iPhone that will achieve the perfection we expect. And thus we come to resemble the racing greyhound dog chasing the mechanical rabbit around the track.

I have found in my years of rabbinic experience that unrealistic and exaggerated expectations of one another often lie at the root of family dysfunction. Never believe the sales pitch of the well-meaning *shadchan*. Except for certain rabbis, no perfect people exist. Realizing and accepting this as a reality of life will go a long way in reducing the unnecessary disappointments that we often bring upon ourselves.

The great cities of New York and Chicago suffered only minor disappointment when their respective baseball teams did not win the ultimate championship in the World Series. I happened to be in both cities when their respective teams finally lost the playoff rounds for the championship. The mood in both cities was less of disappointment and more of pride – even wonderment – that their teams had unexpectedly achieved so much and made it so far. Nobody in either of these two cities at the beginning of the baseball season had any expectations that the teams would be able to contend for the championship. Since the expectations were low, the disappointment at the failure to win the championship was muted and easily taken in stride.

In the broader and more important areas of life, it is clear that people should not expect that marriage, a new job, or a new face in politics and government will somehow solve all of our problems and bring us to paradise on Earth. We must have a proportionate and realistic view of people and events and not give in to wishful thinking, boastful hopes, and completely unrealistic scenarios.

The creation of the State of Israel was, and is, a great historical and spiritual event. However, those who thought that somehow it would be the end of all problems in the Jewish world raised expectations that cannot be fulfilled. And that is why so many utopians today express disappointment in this wonderful state, despite its unbelievable achievements.

We had very high expectations after the Six-Day War, so we had enormous disappointment after the Yom Kippur War. We repeated this cycle of euphoric expectation followed by depressing disappointment regarding the decades-old "peace process" that began with the Oslo agreements and continues until today. By giving in to our hopes and wishes and not looking at our adversaries realistically, we are always surprised by the recurring waves of terror that have accompanied all efforts at mutual understanding and respect. I think that by now almost all of us have lowered our expectations regarding this issue of peace with the Palestinians. So the level of disappointment has also been tempered; and most Israelis, if not most Jews the world over, have adjusted to the tensions of our situation here in the Land of Israel.

We wish things were different, but we realize that we simply have to make the best of a very difficult and dangerous situation. We should not expect any magic bullets or great political initiatives that will solve our problems in one fell swoop. A gradual change of mindset and an acceptance of reality by all concerned is required to move forward in the attempt to build a more stable and peaceful relationship. I have no doubt that this will eventually occur.

Growing Up

All children grow up and hopefully mature into independent, self-sufficient, and productive adults. The Torah advocates this process when it states that "therefore every man shall leave his father and mother" in order to marry and build his own home and family. Growing up is often a painful process for both parents and children. I have often suggested that everyone should be born twenty-one years old, educated, and with the necessary skills to manage in life successfully. However, somehow Heaven has not adopted my scheme of things, and thus the process of growing up remains as vital and difficult as ever.

Unfortunately, many a failed individual and dysfunctional families are the products of not ever growing up. Remaining an eternal adolescent when one's hair has already turned gray is a sure recipe for personal and family failure.

The advantages of growing up are many. We no longer look for monsters hiding under the bed, nor are we as fearful of the vicissitudes of life as we once were. In short, growing up and becoming an independent and mature adult creates a sense of self-confidence, self-identity, courage, innovative spirit, and a broader outlook on life, even with all its attendant problems.

When we are children (and even adolescents), we are completely dependent upon others for our sustenance and achievements. Parents, teachers, schools, yeshivot, seminaries, colleges, and universities rule all our lives and shape our attitudes and behavior. We are always subject to peer pressure as well, and most of the time bending to such pressure is very detrimental to our later life. To put it mildly, it is vitally important to be able to grow up properly.

This is not only true for individuals, it is true for nations as well. For two millennia, the Jewish people were never allowed to grow up. The Exile robbed us of any sense of independence and of national maturity. We were always subject to the whims of inimical governments, rapacious noblemen, and the vagaries of ever-changing rules, societal revolutions, and temporary vogues of thought and behavior.

We developed a mentality of dependence upon others: in the Exile we had no other choice. We could never stand up to anyone in a meaningful fashion, and so we were unable to absorb necessary criticism and change. We remained the eternal adolescent in human society, never having a chance to mature and stand on our own, never able to achieve success without the help of others.

Even after the State of Israel was founded, this mindset of dependence remained in place. We were dependent upon others for monetary help, military weapons, and diplomatic protection. Because of the reality of this dependence, despair descended upon us whenever we felt that our patrons and benefactors would perhaps desert us. We were simply afraid of being independent, of growing up in a national sense.

Those of us living in Israel now are able to sense a change in this attitude. We are beginning to stand up openly to our erstwhile friends who always profess that they mean our good while their advice and policies have a history of being wrong and dangerous to us. National maturity is beginning to seep into the Jewish people living in Israel. It took us a long time to grow up, but we are certainly growing up now.

There are parts of our society that still need to grow up. Much of the religious community still feels itself completely dependent upon others for its survival and well-being. Whether it be dependence upon governmental largesse, the donations of others, or the benevolence of society at large, there is a mindset in much of the religious community that it is imperative for its survival that others somehow take care of its needs and problems. It is apparently uninterested in growing up. As such, it dooms itself to poverty, increasing family dysfunction, as well as societal discrimination and conflict.

We are no longer subject to arbitrary and prejudicial rule over our lives. A great contribution of the State of Israel to the Jewish world is that it has helped us to grow up and mature as a people and as individuals. As mentioned above, growing up is painful, and many mistakes can be made (and usually are) on the way to successful maturation. Nevertheless, one can never agree to a program that perpetuates adolescence and dependency into later years of existence. We are in the midst of growing up as a people and as a nation. We should attempt to include all sectors of our society in this process.

Disconnection

One of the problems that faces religious leadership in the Jewish world, especially the leadership of the great scholars and heads of the leading educational institutions in Israel, is that there is a chasm of disconnect between them and the masses that they wish to lead and influence.

When I was a rabbi in Miami Beach many decades ago, a noted Israeli Talmudic scholar asked permission to speak in my synagogue on Shabbat. I immediately arranged for him to do so, but I spoke to him in advance and told him that the makeup of the synagogue would not allow for an intricate Talmudic lecture; it would not be understood nor appreciated. Ignoring my advice (a situation to which I am well-accustomed), the scholar proceeded to deliver a thirty-five-minute discourse on a very esoteric Talmudic subject. Naturally, his words were ill-received and I suffered the indignities of being reprimanded by many in the synagogue for allowing him to speak. I asked him why he had ignored my advice and chosen to speak about a subject that had no relevance to the audience. He facetiously (or perhaps seriously) answered: "I was trying to raise them to a higher level of Torah knowledge." I said to him that I thought his goals were admirable, but that his methods were deplorable. I explained to him that, in my opinion, a speaker – and certainly a religious scholar who views himself as a person of leadership and influence in the Jewish world – cannot afford to have a complete disconnect with the people to whom he is speaking and trying to lead.

The Torah teaches us that our teacher Moses "descended to the people." That is not only a physical description of Moses coming down from Mount Sinai; its broader implication is that Moses had connection and empathy with the people of Israel. He could not lead them from the heights of Sinai. He could do so only if he was willing to descend from the mount, so to speak, to the level of the people.

Much of the struggle, both within and without the religious Jewish world here in Israel, is over this issue of disconnection. For various reasons – some of which are true, but most of which are exaggerated or based on ignorance – the Israeli public has little confidence in, respect for, or adherence to its rabbinic leadership. This is not only true regarding the sorry state of the official Chief Rabbinate. Even in those sectors of religious society that claim to follow the wishes of the great scholars of Israel, their influence at ground level is minor. This failure is because of the enormous disconnect between the environment in which the scholars live and the true environment of daily life, with all its challenges and problems, that the masses reside in. Raising the level of knowledge and spirituality amongst people is a lengthy and arduous process. It can only be done if the leadership truly understands and appreciates the situations and difficulties that the public faces.

The Talmud stated that religious leaders should not establish decrees that most of the public will find impossible to abide by. Yet on a regular basis we are witness to the utterances and decrees of great scholars that, if followed, would make it impossible for most Jews in Israel to survive. This disconnect is apparent to all – it is the elephant in the room that is ignored by both the leadership and the masses. So we are forced to live in some sort of fantasy land of theoretical obedience to the scholars coupled with the practicality of ignoring their pronouncements.

Disconnect eventually breeds disrespect. There are currently a number of initiatives to try and bridge this disconnect to rebuild the authority of the rabbinate and the scholars here in Israel. All of these initiatives are being fought tooth and nail by the established powers and political interests that are so embedded in Israeli public and religious life. The struggle to create a rabbinate that can understand and speak to the people, gain the respect of the public, and restore itself to spiritual and moral leadership has been ongoing for the past century. It does not appear that this struggle will be won in the very near future.

The problem will not disappear, nor will it be solved by benign neglect. It is one of the major issues that we must think about and act upon in order to initiate a process that will eventually lessen, if not even eliminate, this disconnection.

Rabbi Ovadia Yosef

I was not in Israel when Rav Ovadia Yosef passed on to his eternal reward. However, even in Brazil – where I was at the time – it was front-page news, and pictures of the enormous funeral procession accompanied the obituary article. Rarely has one person had such an imposing effect upon the lives of millions of others. His greatness in Torah knowledge was unquestioned, even by those who may have disagreed with some of his policies and halachic rulings. Possessed of a photographic memory coupled with an encyclopedic knowledge of thousands of rabbinic works and writings spanning the ages, his own volumes of halachic rulings and Torah insights became a staple in every yeshiva and rabbinic library the world over.

But as impressive and noble as his scholarly accomplishments were, they pale, in my humble opinion, to his achievement in raising an entire section of the Jewish people from intellectual poverty and a despised social status. One of the more sordid chapters in Israel's history was the treatment of Sephardic Jews by the leaders – both religious and secular – of Israel's government and society. The Sephardim were discriminated against in all walks of Israeli life and education, and were treated with contempt and derision by the Ashkenazic intellectual, religious, and educational elite. The Sephardic chief rabbi of Israel – the *Rishon L'Tziyon* – always seemed to be subservient to his Ashkenazic counterpart. All of this began to change when Rabbi Ovadia Yosef became the Sephardic chief rabbi. His agenda was to revitalize Sephardic Jewry and give it its due. And he succeeded in so doing.

He was the driving force and spiritual leader behind the Sephardic political party, Shas. In effect, he controlled the levers of its leadership and policies. Because of this role, he was seen as a kingmaker in Israeli political life, and he profoundly influenced the policies and directions of Israeli governments. He was a very outspoken person, and often his comments and words caused controversy and brought criticism upon him. But he never shied away from the struggle and always had his public say on the issues of the day. The public power and influence of the chief rabbis of the past few decades dimmed in comparison to his influence, political power, and halachic rulings.

Even when he no longer bore any official public title, aside from being the head of the high council of Sephardic rabbis, he dominated the religious world of Israel and achieved the respect – begrudging as it may have sometimes been – of vast sectors of Israeli society. Rav Ovadia created a vast Torah school system that has raised a generation of observant, traditional, and vitally successful Sephardic citizens of an increasingly traditional Jewish state. There are many more Sephardic yeshivot present today in Israel than ever before, and the continuing push towards Torah greatness and community leadership in the Sephardic community is Rabbi Ovadia Yosef's lasting legacy to the Jewish people in Israel and the world over.

His influence was felt not only in Israel but also wherever communities of Sephardic Jews resided in the world. Even though it would be an error to view Sephardic Jewry as a monolithic whole, Rabbi Ovadia Yosef served as a magnetic core that bridged communities, differing customs, and varied historical and social experiences and events.

It is very hard to categorize his views except regarding Torah learning and observance as well as the restoration of Sephardic pride and relevance in the broader Jewish world. He was neither tolerant nor intolerant, temperate nor intemperate, forceful nor gentle. He was all of the above and yet none of the above. I think that this was part of his talent and influence over so many people and events. He was truly a special person who single-mindedly, and almost single-handedly, shaped a new Sephardic and a new Jewish world.

The hundreds of thousands who attended his funeral testified to his uniqueness and to his contributions towards the strengthening of Torah, the State of Israel, and the Jewish people. He was not an orator of note, but everyone paid attention to what he had to say. Great people are almost always complicated people. I do not know what his inner persona was like, but his goal in life was simple – "To restore the glory of Torah and of Sephardic Jewry to its original luster." He was eminently successful in achieving that lofty goal.

As time passes, Rabbi Ovadia Yosef's reputation and status continue to grow. He was genuinely as his name indicated – a true servant of the God and people of Israel.

Politics as Usual

The national sport in Israel is politics. Everyone engages in it and it is played at all levels of society, the workplace, the family, the synagogue, and especially in local and national governments. Elections are held frequently and are conducted in a vigorous and contentious manner, with no holds barred. No Israeli government coalition has ever served its entire mandated time and we are treated to national elections approximately every three years. Elections are expensive and divisive, but everyone enjoys them because they are the field on which our national sport of politics is played.

So it should come as no surprise that we are due for another national election sometime in April of this year, and that everyone in the country is gleefully preparing for the event. Politics allows for personal ambition to be engaged, on display for all to see. Reticence, embarrassment, and restraint are not tools employed when running for office nor in Israeli politics generally. By their nature, elections presuppose that the citizens of a country know what is good for them and who is best to be their leaders. This presumption has been tested severely over the course of centuries of elections and democratic processes. Nevertheless, we are convinced, as Winston Churchill once said, that democracy is a very inefficient and ineffective way of governing, but it is the best way that human beings have devised so far in their long history. It's a messy way of trying to decide things, yet we have to adjust to the constant presence of elections in our communal life.

There is no question that ego plays an important part in all elections and in the candidates running for office. However, someone who has no ego is not really fit for leadership, nor can that person ever achieve success in our current electoral world. Calvin Coolidge, who had perhaps the smallest ego of any president of the United States, did not even bother to campaign away from his front porch in the 1924 election. And he won the election very convincingly. Such tactics and procedures would be doomed to disastrous failure in today's world. Modesty and humility are in short display in the season of elections.

It is noteworthy that the greatest leader of the Jewish people, our teacher Moses, was described in the Torah as being the most humble of all human beings, the paragon of modesty itself. Yet he was a very strong leader and, in fact, became the role model for all future leaders, political and religious, of the Jewish nation. So it is possible to exercise great leadership qualities without having to resort to overweening ego and arrogance. I will admit that it is truly a fine line, not easily recognized or observed. But ultimately ego certainly is a necessary quality for leadership to function properly and be of benefit to the people at large.

Rule of the majority often turned into tyranny of the minority. Especially in elections as they are now held, very rarely do we find an overwhelming and convincing majority from one side or the other. Here in Israel, this reality always forces government to be composed of a patchwork of differing political parties and political leaders, each of whom has a differing view of the future of the country and the direction it should take. Because of our system of proportional representation in the Parliament, smaller parties are always represented in the government coalition. These parties usually have a limited objective and view the entire country through the prism of their basic electorate. This system is democratic to the core, but it causes a constant feeling of instability in the makeup of the government.

As I pointed out earlier, it is the reason that no Israeli coalition government has ever been able to serve out its entire term in office. Parties become antsy after a few years and hope to improve their position by dissolving the government and going forward to new elections. Political parties here rise and fall as the seasons change. But one can be certain that whenever a party does disappear from the electoral map a new one will arise to take its place. So let us all sit back, enjoy the spectacle, and hope that the result will be positive for the future of our state and the Jewish people.

Late Rains

This past week, we in Jerusalem had the experience of late rains falling upon our protected or unprotected heads. In the Torah, these rains at the end of the winter season are called *malkosh*. Late rains are seen as a blessing, fortifying and nurturing the soil for the long, hot, dry summer that lies ahead. Rain in our part of the world is an especially treasured commodity. Coming from the United States, where rain is pretty much a weekly event, or from England, where it is almost a daily event, we Anglos are always surprised by the fact that it does not rain here from May till October.

The great prophet Samuel impressed his Godly message on the people of Israel by having it rain upon them in the midst of the summer wheat harvest. So the late rains that we experienced served to remind us of what a gift rain is and how dependent we are on it for food and life itself. From the way the Torah writes about *yoreh*, the first rains of the fall season, and *malkosh*, late rains, it seems that these rains are viewed as an extra and special blessing from God. The recent late rains come to fill the deficit of a below-average rainy winter season. It is symbolic of the truism that it is never too late to be a recipient of God's blessings.

In describing the Land of Israel to the Jewish people before their actual entry, the Torah warned them that the Land of Israel is not like the land of Egypt which they had left forty years earlier. Egypt has the great Nile River that waters its crops and provides irrigation to its fields. Egypt was not directly beholden to rains for its prosperity and survival. Primitively, the Egyptians worshipped the god of the Nile to thank the river for its sustenance of Egyptian life. The Torah points out that in contradistinction to Egypt, the Land of Israel possesses no great rivers. The Jordan is no comparison to the Nile in size, water content, or volume, nor does it overflow its banks. The Jews would have to rely upon rain for the sustenance of their land. And relying upon rain meant relying upon God. Not the god of a particular river, but upon the unseen and unfathomable God that sustains the universe and all that it contains.

As Jews turned their eyes to search for rainclouds, they looked heavenward to the God that alone would sustain them and their land. The Mishnah makes this point clear when it discusses how the Jews triumphed over Amalek when Moses raised his hands. It was not the upraised hands of Moses that sealed the triumph; rather, it was the fact that the Jews looked heavenward, higher than the upraised hands of Moses that brought them God's aid and eventual victory. The same idea is true regarding Heaven-sent rain. By looking upward to the Creator Who is the source of all blessings and realizing what a blessing the rains are for us, we place otherwise natural phenomena in the proper perspective.

Every season has its blessings that are particular to it. In Jewish tradition, Pesach is the swing time when we cease praying for rain and instead ask for the blessings of the morning dew to sustain our land during the summer. The beautiful prayer of *Tal* – the prayer for dew – is an integral part of the Pesach liturgy. It acknowledges once more our realization of our reliance upon God's bounty and special care regarding the welfare and prosperity of the Land of Israel. While rain and dew can be taken for granted as natural events in many parts of the world, not so in the Land of Israel. Here, prayer and belief are necessary requirements for sustenance and prosperity.

Nature alone is very stingy with its blessings in our country. The additional ingredient of God's special blessing is necessary for us to enjoy the blessings and bounty of our blessed land. The late rains that fell remind us of all of these truths. They should be seen as a timely message about our duties and responsibilities and about our relationship with the source of all of our blessings, the Creator Himself.

Locked Out

Last week, the latch to the formidable front gate of my building broke, so we could not enter or leave through it. As resourceful people (otherwise, why would we be living in Jerusalem?), all of us living in the building developed an alternate form of gaining access to our homes and to the street by using a circuitous route, going through the parking entrance whose gate had to be left open at all times. It is a queasy feeling to be locked out of one's own dwelling. On reflection, the situation represented to me the crux of the current contempt regarding Charedi society here in Israel.

Basically put, both the Charedim and the rest of Israeli society were very satisfied until now with the status quo: Charedim were locked out of meaningful participation in general Israeli life. The Charedim were to be kept in their study halls and neighborhoods, subsidized to the hilt by a benign but destructive welfare state system; their educational system was supported minimally and grudgingly by the state as long as they agreed to be locked out of general Israeli life. For various reasons, which I will not now detail, the leaders and rabbis of the Charedi public acquiesced to this eventually unsustainable situation, and for decades this practice became the norm.

But this arrangement was doomed to collapse. It was caused by the demographic growth of the Charedi community, government austerity measures that could no longer support the level of subsidies and welfare to that community, and the arrival of a new generation of Charedim who were no longer willing to be permanently locked out of opportunities for personal advancement and economic independence.

The situation began to change over a decade ago when government grants to large families were severely diminished. This has led to a decline in the birth rate among the Israeli Arab population, but the Charedi birth rate remained unaffected. The Charedim have had to expand their neighborhoods and move to cities where they never before appeared in major numbers.

But, to put it mildly, the Charedim did not feel welcome in their foray into Israeli society. Parts of that society were determined to keep them locked out and not accommodate them with an alternate path through the parking lot gate, so to speak, to enter the general community. In effect, the op-ed writers in *Haaretz* and other anti-Charedi media have said: "You can only enter our society, you can only serve in the army, you can only hold a job in our economy if you will change your appearance, your lifestyle, and eventually your beliefs and traditions."

Since this is an unreasonable, unfair, anti-democratic, and spiteful demand, the Charedim rightfully reacted negatively to its tone and message. Yet the Charedim continue to use side paths to enter Israeli society, and this phenomenon has caused panic in certain circles.

The government follows a contradictory set of policies regarding the integration of Charedim in the general society of Israel. It builds Charedi-only cities such as Beitar Ilit and then complains that the Charedim want to live only with their kind. Years ago, it claimed that it wanted Charedim to serve in the defense forces, but conditions there rendered it nearly impossible to serve. What in the world does ordering male soldiers to attend events with women singing have to do with defense of the country?

I'm glad to report that in this area conditions have improved. Relatively new programs such as Nachal Charedi – units for Charedim serving in the Israeli army – have opened the door of military service to those who choose to avail themselves of them. The military authorities have tried to accommodate the special religious needs of Charedim, and are trying to make military service more attractive to them. I am told that there's even a TV program about Chareidi soldiers in which they are depicted as normal, even heroic, people.

Charedi colleges and universities for women and job training, especially in computer-related fields for Charedi men, have emerged as well. These innovations have begun to make an impact both on Charedi and general Israeli society.

Yet there are still hurdles to be overcome. Why should Charedi men entering the workforce find hostility among their coworkers and the commercial world generally? And why should the misdeeds of certain Charedim – of which there are unfortunately manifold examples – be used to tarnish an entire group and, in fact, religion and Judaism itself?

I have written before about the failings of the leadership and society of the Charedim and this is no apologia for that society and its sometimes self-destructive behavior. But is it not the policy of good government and sane society to help correct those faults, and to accommodate the necessary changes in attitude and perception that will facilitate inclusion instead of permanent exclusion? No one feels comfortable being locked out.

Israel and World Opinion

A Little Too Jewish

There were a number of articles written in the Israeli newspapers about the determined opposition of Reform Jews in America to the appointment of David Friedman as the American ambassador to Israel. The shameful behavior of a number of Jews at the Senate confirmation hearing of Friedman only points out the great fault line that exists in American Jewish society today. The century-long erosion of Jewish life, practice, and observance has led to the appalling rate of assimilation and intermarriage that numerically threatens the very existence of the American Jewish community. It is tearing out the heart of American Jewish society.

President Trump, whether we voted for him or not, is the president of the United States of America. He has the mandate to choose the person that he wishes to represent the United States to the State of Israel. He chose David Friedman because of personal, and perhaps even ideological, reasons. There is no question as to Friedman's abilities or credentials. The problem with Friedman is that he is too openly Jewish. He is an Orthodox Jew, a Sabbath observer, and in his civilian private life an advocate for the State of Israel. As ambassador, he will follow the directives of the president and of the State Department who will set policy and tell him what to say and how to say it. So it is hard to understand all of the tumult over his nomination. His main fault is that he is a little too Jewish for the liberal, assimilationist, intermarried establishment, which Reform Jewry in America represents and supports.

If we are but honest with ourselves, this discomfort is probably the main problem why there are Jews who are constantly critical and destructive of the Jewish state. The problem with Israel is that, in spite of all efforts, internal and external, to make it resemble Switzerland or Sweden, it still remains a little too Jewish for the taste of the world generally, and for the tastes of certain sections of Jewry particularly.

It is not really settlements that are difficult to defend in a world of hypocrisy and selected values. It is the fact that El Al does not fly on the Sabbath that makes it difficult for Jews who have long ago abandoned the Sabbath to accept and appreciate Israel's airline. It is just a little bit too Jewish.

Within Israel, there is the mantra that the state is democratic and Jewish at the same time. However, no matter how equal we want things to be, no two things are ever completely equal. So the question arises: is Israel a Jewish state primarily and a democratic one secondarily? And when the Jewish and the democratic occasionally clash, should the Jewish prevail, or is it primarily a democratic state – and only privately and secondarily a Jewish one? So when the inevitable contradiction will arise, the secular democratic idea must prevail.

This latter opinion has certainly been that of the Israeli Supreme Court over the past number of decades. The court is now being subjected to ever harsher and continued criticism from that section of Israeli society – which no one can argue represents a majority of its citizens – that sees Israel first and foremost as a Jewish state with all that connotes. This struggle is being played out in the political, legislative, and social arenas of Israeli life. It is a problem, like all problems confronting Israel, which does not have any immediate or clear-cut solution. The State of Israel, which is already a little too Jewish for some tastes, may yet become even a little more too Jewish in the future.

Christianity and Israel

It is well known, though hardly discussed in public, that the creation and existence of the State of Israel has created serious theological problems for sections of the Jewish community. But the creation and existence of the State of Israel has created even greater theological and emotional problems for much of the Christian world. The recent visit by Pope Francis to Israel both soothed his relationship with the Jews, yet exacerbated the theological, almost irreconcilable, issues that separate Judaism from Christianity.

The main problem that the State of Israel poses to Christian thought and tradition is that it was never to have happened. A large part of Christian tradition condemns the Jews to endless exile and to an eternally subservient role to the Church and Christian civilization. That the Jews should somehow possess an independent state of their own – not only that, but in the Holy Land itself – was an event that Christian doctrine deemed to be enormously improbable, if not impossible. For many decades, the Church of Rome did not maintain diplomatic relations with Israel and found it difficult to reconcile itself to Jewish domination and control, no matter how benign and fair, of the Christian holy places in the Land of Israel.

This attitude is slowly changing and great strides towards reconciliation and cooperation between the Vatican and the Jewish state have been made over the past few decades. This is certainly to be seen as a positive development after so many centuries of hatred and violence sponsored by the Church against a hapless Jewish people.

The situation with mainstream Protestant denominations is murkier. The vote of the Presbyterian American church encouraging divestment of investments in companies that provide Israel with machinery, building supplies, and technologically advanced capabilities is an example of the latent anti-Jewish theology and attitude that has dominated much of the Protestant church over the past centuries. As the Anglican and Presbyterian churches have become the cutting edge of the new culture and permissiveness of Western society – supporting gay marriage, for instance, and thereby reversing the tenets of their own Bible – they have adopted the mantra of the Left in becoming openly anti-Israel.

The existence of the State of Israel and whether it should be supported or damned is a deeply divisive issue within the Protestant movements. The extremely "progressive" leadership of certain Protestant denominations is not necessarily representative of the mass body of church members and believers. Nevertheless, it is deeply disturbing that the Presbyterian Church can take upon itself the responsibility of telling the Jewish people, who are embroiled in a life-and-death struggle with a Muslim enemy sworn to its destruction, that they are not entitled to build and protect themselves in their own homeland. Speaking out of both sides of their mouth at once, the Presbyterian Church supports the right of the State of Israel to exist but does not want it to have the material tools necessary to guarantee that existence.

There is a significant section of Protestant denominations that wholeheartedly supports the State of Israel and has donated very large sums of money to Jewish charitable and educational organizations operating in Israel. Since many of these denominations also sponsor widespread missionary and proselytizing activities, there has been a determined campaign mounted here in Israel to refuse the acceptance of these monies, no matter how worthy the causes they apparently support.

There is a great split in the observant Jewish community on this issue. There is rabbinic opinion on both sides of the question, and there is no doubt that this flood of Christian money given to Israeli institutions has had beneficial educational and social results. Nevertheless, lurking behind all of it is the increased missionary activity of many Christian denominations in Israel. These activities are aimed at Jews, mainly new immigrants from very poor families. The laws against Christian missionaries and their activities in Israel are not enforced because of diplomatic reasons and international consequences. So the question remains as to the true intent of the Christian supporters of the State of Israel.

Nevertheless, in a world filled with enemies and with those who wish us no good, it would be cavalier and almost foolish to cast away the hand of friendship which these Christian denominations have extended to Israel and the Jewish people. How to square this circle and arrive at a wise decision remains a troubling issue for us. Thousands of years of enmity are not easily forgotten, but in the world that we inhabit, friends are hard to come by. Wiser and greater minds than mine will decide what is a reasonable policy and solution to these issues.

Exclusivity and Tolerance

One of the main differences that separates Judaism from the other major monotheistic religions – Christianity and Islam – is the matter of exclusivity. The rabbis of the Talmud long ago reiterated the traditional Jewish position that "the righteous of the nations of the world all have a share in the World to Come." This means immortality of the soul and Heavenly reward once one passes on from this life. One need not be Jewish to gain holiness, immortality, and eternal reward. I am reminded of the famous bread advertisement so popular in New York City decades ago which loudly proclaimed, "You don't have to be Jewish to love Levy's real Jewish Rye." Well, immortality and Heavenly reward aren't rye bread – but you get the idea.

The seven Noahide laws, which for all practical purposes are the basis of Western civilization, are the guidelines for determining "the righteous of the nations of the world." Because of this inherent nonexclusivity, Judaism allows for tolerance and diversity in a world of different faiths, societies, and peoples. (One should always be sophisticated enough to differentiate between the behavior of Jews and Judaism itself.)

Our father Abraham was so named because of his ability to be the "father of many nations." Judaism and the Jewish people were meant to be the catalyst for bringing the ideas of monotheism, goodness, concern for others, and the recognition of the universality of the Creator to all of humankind. To a large extent, it has succeeded in this mission for, as I mentioned above, its worldview has become pretty much that of Western civilization.

The Jewish people are very small in number, especially compared to other major faiths that count their adherents in many hundreds of millions. The Torah told us in advance that we were destined to be small in numbers. "I have not chosen you because of your great numbers, for you are the smallest of all peoples," God told us in the book of Devarim. Being small in numbers and obviously never aspiring to be the majority faith in the world – for God had foreclosed that option to us at the dawn of our nationhood – Judaism could never take the position that all of the other billions of humans were automatically doomed to eternal damnation and destruction. Our understanding of the God of Israel, the all-merciful and gracious One, would not countenance such an attitude towards His creatures. Our very meagerness in numbers forces us to accept the religious axiom that "the righteous of all nations have a share in the World to Come."

God's statement that we will always be the smallest of all peoples renders us bound to be the most tolerant and least proselytizing of all faiths. (Again, please don't confuse Jews and their behavior with Judaism.) An openness towards others – *darkei shalom,* the ways of peace and harmony – have been the hallmarks of Judaism's attitude towards "the righteous of all nations."

Unfortunately, all of this has been in sharp contrast to the exclusivity that the theological doctrines of Christianity and Islam force upon their adherents. Without belief in Jesus or Mohammed, as the case may be, no matter how "righteous" one may be in terms of personal behavior, one is automatically doomed. Because of this exclusivity doctrine, Jews throughout history have been the eternal outsider and infidel, doomed from the start of life to damnation if they did not convert to the "true faith."

This religious belief lies at the heart of anti-Semitism and the persecution of Jews and Judaism by both major faiths throughout our long and bloody history. Many times, the persecution of Jews and the banning of Jewish practice was perversely seen as a favor to those persecuted, for it would hurry them along to the baptismal font or to donning the fez, and thus to eternal reward. Realistically speaking, there is little likelihood that these religious doctrines of Christianity and Islam will undergo radical modification in the foreseeable future.

Jews like to project their own feelings of tolerance and liberalism on others. But not recognizing the fundamental difference between Judaism and the other monotheistic faiths – our deeming others worthy for their righteous behavior versus their exclusivity of belief – only serves to widen the gulf of misunderstanding between "us" and "them." A clear appraisal of the true situation and a recognition of the fundamental differences in worldview can help us deal with our neighbors in the world in a more honest and open fashion. Pretending that there are really no major differences between the faiths only increases the tensions, enmities, and dangers for all concerned.

A Tale of Two Brothers

On a trip to the United States a number of years ago, my wife and I had occasion to use private car services. All of the drivers were courteous, respectful, and skilled at their chosen line of work. One was a young Jewish man, a college graduate who told us that he was raised "Reform" by his family. He said that he had a younger brother, a current college student, who had just returned from a visit to Israel on a Birthright program. He said that his brother was very impressed by his visit and now was starting to look into Judaism and his heritage more seriously. He had enrolled in a number of Judaic studies classes and had told his family that upon graduation he intended to move to Israel, marry, and make his future there "with the rest of the Jews."

We naturally gushed over this news and asked him if he himself intended to also visit Israel. He told us that since he had already finished school he was not entitled to a Birthright trip and doubted that he would ever visit Israel. Even though he bragged about how successful his car service was, he apparently never considered spending any of his own money on a visit to Israel, even though he did tell us about expensive vacations that he had taken to South America.

He then informed us that he had recently become engaged to a non-Jewish woman and that they were going to marry soon. He said that his family wanted the woman to convert to Judaism and he broached the subject to her. The woman was an atheist and she stated that becoming Jewish would in no way compromise her beliefs or non-beliefs, since most of the Jews she knew had no firm beliefs about God or any theology. He said that he brought her to his Reform rabbi, who agreed to perform the ceremony even prior to her conversion. The rabbi was very impressed by the sincerity of her atheistic beliefs. Nevertheless, he said that he would not perform the wedding ceremony in the sanctuary of the temple but only outside on the lawn, since the woman was not yet officially converted. The driver said that he was "praying for nice weather." I wonder if his bride was "praying" and to whom for a fair weather day.

The cavalier attitude towards the whole matter by the young man, and apparently by his Reform rabbi, saddened me deeply. It provided me with a microcosm of what is happening to the American Jewish community, which is rapidly disappearing – abetted by the laxness and failure of Reform, and to a somewhat lesser extent, of Conservative rabbis in stemming this tide of disaster. It was a very depressing car ride for me, for I knew that this scenario was no longer an exceptional case in Jewish America.

The influence of the State of Israel is crucial to the survival of Jews and Judaism in the Diaspora. Even those pockets of Orthodox religious life in America that had previously convinced themselves that Israel is not a key ingredient in their lives are beginning to see things in a different light. Many Jews in Europe, suffering intensely under growing open anti-Semitism – private, public, and official – view Israel as an insurance policy. It is an escape haven if and when the necessity arises.

American Jews still feel much more secure, so their attitude towards Israel is more guarded and ambivalent. Hardly more than 20 percent of American Jews have ever visited Israel, and the more assimilated American Jews become, the more distant their relationship with Israel becomes. The key to helping American Jews counter assimilation and alienation from Judaism is helping them feel more Jewish by establishing a strong sense of Jewish self-identity within themselves and their families.

One undeniable fact about visiting – and hopefully, eventually living – in the Land of Israel is that it certainly makes one feel more Jewish. People who feel they are Jewish eventually begin to search and find a way back to Jewish life and Torah values. The story of the two brothers I outlined above shows how true this is – how crucial is the relationship to Israel for Jewish communities in the Diaspora that are threatened with assimilation and eventual extinction.

Faith and Doubt

Since the Talmudic era, the rabbis have always maintained that the stories of our fathers – Abraham, Isaac, and Jacob – and our mothers – Sarah, Rebecca, Leah, and Rachel – are not only past history but are also guideposts and predictions regarding the future of the Jewish people. In effect, we are imbued with the spiritual DNA of our ancestors and that DNA influences our attitudes and behavior today, as it has throughout our history.

The Torah compliments our father Abraham for his faith and trust in the Lord. It states: "And he [Abraham] had faith in the Lord and the Lord reckoned it for him as an act of righteousness." Yet the rabbis of the Talmud pointed out that regarding one matter Abraham's faith was found wanting, so to speak. And that was regarding the promise made to him that his descendants through Isaac would inherit and control the Land of Israel. On this issue Abraham questions God and asks him: "How can I be certain that I will inherit and control this land?" And God answers him that only through sacrifices and disappointments, troubles and travail, will your descendants come to inherit this land. Abraham's doubts on this subject affected the future of the Jewish people and its connection to the Land of Israel in the short run – the Egyptian exile and forty years in the desert – and in the long run of Jewish history as well. The doubts raised by Abraham made the achievement of Jewish sovereignty and settlement of the Land of Israel much more difficult than it originally should have been.

Even when he is already one hundred years old and Sarah is ninety years old, Abraham is of perfect faith that they will have a son. He is of serene faith when he goes to war against overwhelming odds to rescue his nephew Lot in the great struggle between the kings and empires of his time. He has faith that the Lord will save him and Sarah from the clutches of Pharaoh, and later from Abimelech. He has faith that his message of monotheism will somehow be heard in a society of rampant paganism and that he will survive all attacks against him. He even has faith that God will hear his pleas on behalf of the wicked people of Sodom. And yet when the issue of the Land of Israel and of Jewish sovereignty and entitlement over it arises, his faith flinches and he demands proof from God that this will occur. And to a certain extent, this particular doubt has been transmitted throughout the Jewish generations till our very day.

The Jewish people have weathered every storm with firm and unwavering belief in the Torah, in the God of Israel, and in His Providence. In spite of the enormous price exacted from us for remaining Jewish, despite all coercions and enticements, the Jews have believed and remained loyal.

Yet the issue of Jewish entitlement to the Land of Israel was always and certainly is today the litmus test of Jewish loyalty and belief. There are elements in Jewish society that deny this right of ours. There are others who ask Abraham's question: "How do we know that we are supposed to be here? Is the land really ours?" This element of doubt weakens us greatly. It leads to depression and recrimination, foolish policies and grave errors. And it certainly makes the eventual price that we are paying, and will continue to pay, for our right to exist here as a Jewish democratic state much steeper than it really need be.

The rabbis of the Talmud were certainly on to something important when they noted that only regarding God's promise to Abraham concerning the Land of Israel did an element of doubt blemish Abraham's perfect record of faith. How to overcome this structural weakness in our spiritual genetic makeup is the daunting challenge that faces our generation currently. A better education about the Jewish past and about our faith and its values will certainly contribute to an improvement in this situation. But in the final resort, it is up to each and every one of us to overcome doubts and strengthen our faith in our cause and in the promises of God and His prophets to us regarding the undoubted redemption of our people in the Land of Israel.

A Stiff-necked People

The Jewish nation is described in the Torah as being a stiff-necked people. In the context of that particular Torah discussion, this description is not a complimentary one. It refers to the stubbornness of the generation of the Sinai desert and its rebellious nature in constantly refusing to abide by God's will and to accept Moses's authority. Neither plagues nor wars, natural disasters such as poisonous snakes nor supernatural punishments seemed to break their stubborn nature. That generation –

those who left Egypt, stood at the Revelation of the Torah at Mount Sinai, survived on manna from heaven and water from the rock – still never lost its attachment to the culture and slavery of Egypt.

At every turn in the desert we read that they complained and said: "Let us turn around and go back to Egypt." Part of the nature of stubbornness is the inability to admit past error and to recalculate decisions, attitudes, and policies. In the case of the generation of the desert of Sinai, this trait of stubbornness led to tragic consequences. This generation, which possessed such greatness – the rabbis characterized the Sinai generation as one of great knowledge and superior potential wisdom – doomed itself to destruction because of its stiff-necked stubbornness and preconceived negative attitudes. Because of this history of Jewish stubbornness, the phrase "a stiff-necked people" has entered the Jewish lexicon as a very negative trait.

Yet, in the long view of Jewish history – over the millennia of our troubles and travails, exiles and persecutions – it is clear that it is this very nature of Jewish stubbornness that has preserved us until this day. Only a stiff-necked people could have survived and retained its identity, its faith, its culture, and its vision of eventual destiny over so many years and obstacles. We are alive simply because of the fact that we are a very stubborn people. Only a stubborn people would have survived the destruction of its Temple and exile from its land, and still return to it and build it anew after centuries of absence and distance.

A stiff-necked people refuses to succumb to passing fads and political correctness. A stiff-necked people realizes that a small minority can hold correct views and beliefs, while more often than not overwhelming majorities are wrong in their policies and beliefs. The great Rebbe of Kotzk phrased this concept succinctly: "Truth can never be outvoted."

So the trait of stubbornness and being stiff-necked has enabled the Jewish people to survive long and bitter centuries of exile and to restore itself to its land, to independence, and to influence. It certainly has served us well through our travels in world history.

The Jewish people here in Israel exhibited tremendous fortitude, determination, and resolute stubbornness during our struggle with Hamas. Innumerable rockets have fallen on the Jewish population in the Land of Israel without breaking our spirit or crippling our justified response. It is not only the Iron Dome antimissile system that has protected us – though one should be awestruck at its efficiency and capabilities – but the *iron will* of the Jewish people that has also protected us in this hour of need.

Other civilian populations have succumbed to such bombardments. In World War II, Poland and the Netherlands were broken by the Luftwaffe. A determined Great Britain, on the other hand, survived the Blitz and later the V1 and V2 rocket attacks, even though it suffered more than sixty thousand civilian casualties. But this ability is currently waning, at least in the eyes of this observer of the current world. Little such fortitude remains in Western society today. There are very few stubborn people left on the globe.

But the healthy trait of stubbornness has survived well in the people of Israel. It is undoubtedly part of our DNA makeup. Applied correctly and in proper measure and fitting circumstances, stubbornness can be a great virtue, a most positive national character trait.

The world looks at us as being too stubborn and unreasonable. In a culture where moral equivalency prevails and there is no right or wrong, the world is disturbed by our stubbornness and by our refusing to just let things be when our very existence is challenged by the actions of a murderous enemy. If our enemies (and our friends, as well) would but look at our history and our accomplishments, they would realize the positive nature of our stubbornness and respect us for it, instead of criticizing us. We have always been a stiff-necked people and will undoubtedly continue to be so.

Fascinations

Parts of the Muslim world are currently experiencing a morbid fascination with death – their own and that of others. There is no long-term strategy to the terror that grips Western countries as well as here in Israel. Stabbing a soldier or running down a policeman or pedestrian with an automobile has no strategic value, and in reality accomplishes nothing for the cause of the perpetrator. Killing 129 innocent people in Paris in no way induces France to be more lenient or accepting of any Muslim caliphate. In fact, as we are witness, it does just the opposite, only hardening French opposition to the idea of a caliphate and to the acceptance of more Muslims into France itself.

The same thing is undoubtedly true here in Israel. The murder of innocent Jews by people who are well aware by now that they will probably die committing that act of murder has no strategic value and gains nothing substantial for the Palestinian cause. Yet logic plays no part in any of this. Constant religious incitement, demonizing the "other," and promising eternal reward all play in to this current wave of terror. Why should children who are barely teenagers attempt to kill people whom they do not know and who have never directly harmed them?

It is part of this mental and spiritual fascination with death that helps drive this phenomenon. The killers are not soldiers, after all, who are trained for war and killing. In the famous words of General Patton in World War II, "The object of war is not to die for your country; it is to make the enemy die for his country." But that type of logical thinking wanes in the face of this utter fascination with death and expected rewards in the hereafter.

Part of the task of religion is to teach a person how to live a meaningful life in this world coupled with an understanding that there is a spark of eternity within all of us that will exist after our physical demise. The Torah is a book of life, and living remains the supreme value in Jewish thought and law. Though the Jewish people have a long history of martyrdom, it is the productivity and holiness of good living that remains the focus of all of the commandments and values that constitute traditional Jewish life. We all recognize that death is inevitable and therefore must always be reckoned with, but it certainly is not something desirable – not a goal to be pursued and treasured.

The fascination of Jewish life is with living. This emphasis is present in all of the books of the Bible and is the core value in Jewish tradition. From this stems the Jewish attitude towards family, procreation, and generations. Though we are well aware of the past and, in fact, are bidden to study it and know it, our fascination is always with the future. The Talmud puts it succinctly and positively: "Tomorrow the Temple will be built." We are fascinated by how that will occur and when that will occur, but it is this fascination with life in progress, with redemption and hope that drives Jewish society in Israel and the world over to persevere, and eventually to triumph.

I have no idea how to eradicate this cult of death that seems to permeate so many of our enemies. It is caused by incitement against anyone who does not believe as they believe and justifies the most brutal and heinous acts of murder of innocents. The fact that it is malevolently intertwined with distorted religious beliefs only makes the problem greater. If, as is clear from terrorist events, that the murderers are themselves not afraid of death – and, in fact, are fascinated and accepting of it in almost joyful belief – our weapons to defeat them are truly impotent.

It is difficult to defeat an enemy whose young people are willing to sacrifice their lives because of an idea that death is nobler than life, and that murder is a solution to the world's problems. The fact that almost no moderate voices are heard in the Muslim world today opposing this type of mindset is very disturbing and frightening.

Only when human beings actually get down to the task of making something of their lives, of living for goals and purposes with a vision of generations yet unborn, can we hope that this fascination with death will be transformed into one of life. Only then can there be peaceful accommodation of the realities that will lead to life for all mankind.

O! Jerusalem

This past week we were witness to yet another fulfillment of a biblical prophecy: that a day will come when all of the nations – or at least a sizable portion of them – will attack Jerusalem and attempt to dislodge the Jewish people from its capital city and its holy environs. We saw 128 nations vote for a UN General Assembly resolution denying the right of Israel and the Jewish people to claim Jerusalem as its capital. Among the nations that voted for this resolution were the usual culprits – dictators, slaveholders, warmongers, and many others of that ilk. And naturally the hypocritical democracies of Europe that have never been able to overcome their anti-Jewish bias developed over centuries also supported this nefarious resolution. There were countries, led by the United States of America, who voted against the resolution and spoke up about its bias and impracticality.

In the long view of history, nations that defended Jewish rights eventually were blessed for their wisdom and kindness. The United States of America is the world's leading democracy and, with all of its warts and faults, remains a shining beacon of fairness and opportunity for individuals all over the world. Supporting Israel's claim to Jerusalem is simply choosing right over wrong and realistic history over illusory plans and policies. The United States committed its error in supporting an anti-Israel resolution last year under the Obama administration, but made good on its long-standing policy to protect Israel from continued efforts by the United Nations to undermine its sovereignty and territorial integrity.

There is no use arguing this matter logically. It matters little to the world that for the first time in many centuries Jerusalem is free for worship to all faiths and peoples. It also matters little that as a sovereign nation Israel long ago chose Jerusalem as its capital and has all of its government offices located in Jerusalem. It is not so much that the world wants Jerusalem – after all, it was a wasteland and backwater location for many centuries, whether under Christian or Muslim rule – it is simply that the world does not want the Jews to have it. There is absolutely no logical explanation for this position, but there it is anyway.

The terrible virus of anti-Semitism is broad regarding the State of Israel, and particularly Jerusalem. I certainly recognize that there are religious difficulties for both the Christian and Muslim worlds accepting the status of Jerusalem as a Jewish city and the capital of the State of Israel. However, just as portions of the Christian clergy and Muslim nations have learned to live with the reality of the existence of Israel itself – despite difficulties embedded in their theologies – so too, I am confident that they will be able to adjust to the fact that Jerusalem is the capital of the Jewish state. Reality eventually affects beliefs and previously held opinions, even those that were once considered sacred and immutable.

The city of Jerusalem is thriving as perhaps never before in its long and turbulent history. The population is at an all-time high, and every neighborhood in the city is experiencing new construction and refurbishment. The light rail system has proven to be a success, and the good old Egged buses are still plying their routes more or less on schedule. The city has enjoyed an economic upturn. Its government has improved many of the services here, and done so quietly, without boastful fanfare. The Arab citizens of Jerusalem – they are a little more than 30 percent of the population – enjoy a standard of living and of opportunity unmatched anywhere else in the Middle East.

Yet all of this means nothing to much of the world. Fortunately, the shameful United Nations resolution is nonbinding and nonenforceable. It is another one of the paper propaganda victories in which the Palestinian Authority revels, though bringing it no closer to a state of its own; something, most of us now suspect, they really don't want. Jerusalem was supposed to be a bargaining chip to extract greater concessions from Israel on any final agreement. Somehow that chip may now be lost and is no longer in play.

Revolutions and Mindsets

The revolution in Egypt that removed the Moslem Brotherhood from power reflects the ongoing instability and crosscurrents that dominate the Arab world. As usual, the Western world was surprised and overwhelmed by the event, and completely impotent in influencing the outcome of events. The mindset of the West, proven over and over in its dealings with the Middle East, is that the tiger really means no harm, poses no danger, and if fed properly will become tame and docile. Thus terrorists are only militants; hate speech is only a campaign tactic; and there are always magical solutions to centuries-old struggles and hatreds.

This Western rose-colored mindset is impervious to the realities of the situation. It is backed by long-standing prejudices (especially against Jews and the Jewish state, but paradoxically against the Arab world as well) and fueled by a leftist-oriented idealism that discounts all facts and realities. Its advocates are convinced that since Morsi was democratically elected he must be a good person who wished to rule wisely and benignly. They conveniently forget that Hitler also came to power in Germany in the 1930s through the manipulation of the democratic electoral process, and that he enjoyed the approval of the vast majority of the German people as he led them and much of the rest of the world to utter annihilation and murderous destruction. President of Syria Assad claims to have the support of most of his countrymen (this, after killing four hundred thousand of them). The ayatollahs of Iran regularly are able to get their puppets elected to office. The wild leaders of Turkey came to power through open elections. Hamas terrorists won the elections in Gaza and have only brought despair and war to their constituents, and murder to many innocents. The shambles of democratic procedures currently litter the landscape of the Middle East, just as they did of much of Europe in the previous century.

All of the above is not to be interpreted as a rejection of democracy in favor of autocratic and dictatorial rule. But it is meant to point out that democracy can only be effective in countries and societies where the populace possesses a nonviolent, tolerant, and open mindset. In countries where the mindset is rigidly narrowed by religious beliefs of exclusivity, superiority, chauvinism, fanaticism, and deeply held prejudices against "others," democracy as a governmental system is usually ineffective. It eventually gives rise to dictatorship, violence, and opposing forms of fanaticism.

Democracy entails the ability to discard ideals and philosophies, no matter how long and lovingly cherished they may have been, when those policies have now visibly failed and brought forth more harm than good to the society and nation. It requires a healthy and open mindset, a willingness to acknowledge the realities, as well as the courage to admit wrong and change course. Enshrining tactics and policies that have proven to be failures is a certain recipe for continued failures. A strongly open mindset can adopt tactics that will truly fit the situation at hand.

Israeli society is undergoing a rethinking of its mindset. Though polls may show that the majority of Israelis hope for and support a two-state solution with the Arabs, the reality that this is currently not achievable is sinking in. So the status quo, uncomfortable as it appears to be, may be the situation for many more years to come.

The mindset that unilateral Israeli concessions can achieve peace in our region is slowly but surely receding. Somehow, that changing mindset should slowly begin to seep into the mindset of European and American diplomats as well. Tilting at windmills may be a satisfying way to satisfy democratic instincts and policies, but it is ultimately a fruitless endeavor.

Within the religious community in Israel, mindsets are also slowly changing. Even though the politicians who claim to represent this section of Israeli society are as vociferous as ever in opposing the changes that are nevertheless occurring to their society, the mindset of the masses is slowly but inexorably changing. Eventually, there will be changes in the economy and the integration of that society into general Israeli life.

Abandoning long-held behavior patterns and changing direction remains a slow, arduous, and painful process. But once the mindset has begun to shift, the realities on the ground will also change, hopefully for the better of all concerned.

Feeling Uncomfortable

There is one thing that we can all agree upon: the existence and policies of the State of Israel, no matter which party is in power, makes Jews the world over feel uncomfortable. There is always some untoward incident, bad behavior, foolish governmental policy, or controversial aggressive stance that makes many Jews squirm in their seats. Because of this discomfort with Israel, there are many Jews, of all shades of religious observance, political belief, and personal inclination, who in their heart of hearts just wish that Israel would go away and not perturb them any longer.

There are those in the observant Jewish world who simply cannot come to terms with the fact that that the state was created in a seemingly rational and ordinary way. Nor can they come to terms with who the leaders of that state were and are. This is also true for the atheistic and agnostic Left – a powerful and pervasive force in Jewish society here in Israel and throughout the Jewish world – that cannot come to terms with the fact that (much to its chagrin and disappointment) in the main the Jewish state is quite Jewish in outlook, behavior, and values.

So there is plenty of room for discomfort regarding the State of Israel. And this discomfort expresses itself in many different ways, ranging from outright Israel-bashing in public forums and the media to subtleties such as the absence of wholehearted acceptance that the State of Israel is worthy of our prayers and support. In short, Israel remains a disturbing presence in world.

Lest this phenomenon remain completely mysterious and inexplicable to us, I would be bold enough to suggest that to a certain extent this was the case in Second Temple times as well. Most of the Jewish world then did not live in the Land of Israel. Major Jewish communities existed in Babylonia and Egypt, as well as in Rome and North Africa. In Alexandria, Egypt, the Jews even built their own Temple to compete with the consecrated one located in Jerusalem. The Jewish community in Rome cowered in fear and shame while their brethren in the Land of Israel struggled against their Roman oppressors. It was not easy or pleasant to be a Jew in the Roman Empire during the first century of the Common Era. One need only read the works of Josephus (and of Philo, centuries later) to sense the anguish of these Jews struggling to remain Jewish in a most alien and hostile environment.

Throughout the exile of the Jewish people, this discomfort has been experienced over and over again. It existed before there was a State of Israel. The State of Israel has only focused and intensified the problem that individual Jews always faced – how to remain loyal Jews in a world that rejects and denigrates them.

As assimilationists in the Jewish world become further and further removed from Torah knowledge and values, their animosity towards the State of Israel becomes more public and intense. Muslim terrorism against Jews and the State of Israel is almost always given a pass in the press, while pietistic handwringing over an alleged Jewish wrongdoing receives banner headlines and universal condemnation. These Jews are ashamed of being Jewish. In their tortured existence they lash out at themselves, all the while proclaiming their noble, compassionate values and unique wisdom. They are very uncomfortable with the government and people of Israel.

In his masterful book *This Is My God*, Herman Wouk describes a scene in the lobby of a magnificent Manhattan office skyscraper where a completely assimilated Jew suddenly spies a Chasidic Jew – beard, garb, and all – about to enter the elevator with him. That combination of horror, surprise, shame, guilt, and curiosity so graphically described by Wouk is a true picture of how much of the Jewish world today views the State of Israel.

The existence of a Jewish state imposes harsh choices and uncomfortable decisions upon Jews the world over. Apparently, this is what Heaven intended, discomfort and all.

I've Got Your Back

President Barack Obama has recently reassured us, proclaiming that "America has Israel's back." Given the recent controversies between the prime minister of Israel and the president of the United States, this message was meant to soothe the relationship between the two countries and to allow for a more positive progression of policies that would be in their mutual interest. The president also said that he retains the right to criticize and chastise Israel over policies that he feels are wrong, and even harmful to its own welfare. He declared that Israel somehow has departed from the founding views that almost seventy years ago created it as a state. Like many others before him and probably after him, he knows better than we do what is good for us and how moral and just we should be. By stating that "America has Israel's back," he is now free, and even compelled, to judge Israel, its policies, and government from the lofty level of the high ground that he has staked out.

There is no question that from the beginning of the State of Israel until today the United States has remained a loyal friend and a great supplier of practical and diplomatic help to the Jewish state. There is also no question that the wise course for any Israeli leader is not to be viewed as hostile or unfriendly to the persona or policies of the American president.

Yet, over the decades, America and its presidential leaders have often adopted policies that have proven to be counterproductive to the interests of Israel as well as to the United States. America is not blameless nor spotless in the creation of the terrible mess in which the Middle East finds itself today. It should therefore be somewhat wary (if not even humble) when offering advice to those who actually have to live in that region of the world.

Over our long history, the Jewish people has had many enemies, but we also have had numerous non-Jews who were good friends and appreciated the special role of the Jewish people in the story of human civilization. Nevertheless, at moments of terrible danger and crisis, when Jews were being persecuted and slaughtered, no nation – no matter how friendly its citizens may have been disposed towards Jews and Judaism – ever really had our back.

During World War II, when European Jewry was almost completely annihilated, the Allies claimed they were powerless to prevent the Holocaust from occurring. The debate among historians and scholars as to why the railroads leading to the death camps of Poland were never bombed will undoubtedly continue for years to come. But whatever the reason, and no matter how legitimate the justification for inaction may have been, the simple fact is that those trains and rails never were bombed. And the behavior of most of the Allied countries towards the survivors of the Holocaust, as well as the emerging State of Israel, was at most tepid, if not downright hostile.

So Jews can be excused for not excitedly responding to words claiming that others, no matter how well-meaning, have our back. Does anyone really believe that the United States will go to war on behalf of Israel?

The reality of truth teaches us that we alone have our back, and our front as well. We need help from the world and we certainly hope to receive it on diplomatic, political, financial, and organizational bases. We hope that the United States will continue to provide us with that type of help in the future as it has in the past. However, nations have interests and not friends, and they pursue strategic goals that are not usually affected by emotion or cozy warmth.

We would do well to accept the words of the president of the United States and be thankful for his statement. But we would be foolish if we trusted that the United States, or any other country in the world, truly has our back and will take up the cudgel of military action to defend us.

Ultimately, only God has our back. The Talmud long ago taught us that relying on humans is a futile policy and that our reliance can only be placed in the God of Israel, Who has always guided us and preserved us against all odds. It is nice to hear reassuring words of support, but let no one think that those words give anyone license to play with the future of the Jewish people and its state. With God's help, Israel survives and will prosper because of Israel itself.

Praying for Peace

The much-heralded public prayer for peace and reconciliation between Israel and the Palestinian Authority took place this week at the Vatican in Rome. The event was hosted and sponsored by Pope Francis and included the participation of religious leaders and clergy of the three main monotheistic faiths. But the main stars of the event were Shimon Peres, Mahmoud Abbas, and naturally, the pope himself. I am all in favor of prayer, and I am certainly an avid supporter of peace. But somehow I have a queasy feeling about this public relations coup to promote the Catholic Church as a diplomatic mediator in the Israeli-Palestinian dispute.

What makes this entire event somewhat questionable is the fact that neither Peres nor Abbas is well-known for participating in prayer, either public or private. As all of us are well aware, public prayer is a very delicate matter. Sometimes it is too public at the expense of meaningful prayer itself. Even though public prayer with a *minyan* is obligatory in Jewish law and tradition, we are all aware that a moment of private and truly heartfelt prayer can be most meaningful and spiritually satisfying.

In my opinion, this latest Vatican prayer session suffers from too much formality and publicity. I don't know if it was possible, but if the pope could have gotten Abbas and Peres alone in a room without media and fanfare, and their true prayers would have been offered, perhaps the entire event would have been of benefit. As it stands now, very few positive accomplishments are on the horizon from this overly advertised event.

Jews pray three times daily for peace. It is the final blessing of the *Amidah*, the central prayer of the prayer service. The reason that it is the final prayer of that service is because it encompasses all of the blessings, hopes, and longings that the preceding texts of prayer expressed. The Talmud saw peace as the proper receptacle that can carry and contain all of the other prayers, benefits, and rewards of life. Without peace and inner serenity, even the blessings of family, wealth, and physical well-being remain unfulfilled and unsatisfactory. Therefore, peace, and the prayer for peace, are viewed as the most necessary prerequisite of human attainment.

But even though we ask Heaven on a regular basis for this blessing of peace, the truth is that the fulfillment of that blessing – as perhaps of all other blessings in life – is dependent upon us. We are taught in Psalms that we are to search for peace and pursue it.

Heaven has created peace on high without the necessity for human aid or intervention. But peace is made on earth by human effort and Divine blessing. It requires Heavenly guidance and encouragement but, as in all matters here on earth, what human beings do has influence and consequence.

It is not sufficient to only pray for peace; one must search for it and pursue it in order to achieve it. And that is what makes our situation here in the Middle East one of such difficulty, since it is not at all clear that the pursuit of peace with Israel is really one of the objectives of the Palestinian Authority.

Nevertheless, I do not want to be the one to cast cold water on the pope's initiative. Many times what we initially – and even halfheartedly – pray for becomes what we actually later desire and work for. So this public media event at the Vatican can bear fruit if both parties internalize the wish for peace and pursue it.

Peace is always costly and imperfectly achieved. Many a wrenching experience must be undergone on the road to peace, whether it is on a personal level or on a national level. To a certain extent, peace involves sublimating memory and releasing one's hold on the past.

Since this effort is contrary to human nature, Divine assistance is vitally necessary. And this is why we pray thrice daily to the God of Israel that He grant us the blessing of peace and the strength to pursue it. Again, I believe that prayer without the trappings of undue publicity and media notoriety is the most effective way of invoking Heaven's blessing upon us. I hope that all of the parties involved in this week's prayer session did so in sincerity, and that they will truly pursue the search for the path to peace we need so desperately.

The Pessimists amongst Us

Purely on an anecdotal basis, I am of the opinion that the diehard secularist leftists amongst us are really pessimistic people. In a recent article written by the Israeli historian Benny Morris and published in the *Haaretz* newspaper (where else could it be published?), he posited that the Jewish state in the Land of Israel is doomed to disappear within the next half-century. He based this dire prediction on the fact that there are hundreds of millions of Muslims here in the Middle East and, at best, there will be only seven or eight million of us.

This is exactly what all of the experts said over seventy years ago when the possibility of creating a Jewish state in the Land of Israel arose. Even when the state was declared and the War of Independence was won, there were many great and knowledgeable people who stated that the state could not survive for even half a century. I feel that the reason this pessimistic outlook was present and persists is the belief that the state was founded illegitimately and without moral right.

To defend the higher moral ground that the Left always assumes, it must be that this state, which was founded "unfairly" and "unjustly," must disappear. That it must do so becomes a moral certitude for the true believers. No facts or circumstances can alter this belief or counter this completely unjustified pessimism.

Ideologues across the spectrum of beliefs and movements are by nature pessimistic people. They are not happy with the present situation, since it does not live up to their ideal expectations. And they become frustrated when events do not go their way and the utopia they seek, whether at the religious, social, or political level, is not achieved. The rabbis attributed this attitude to the basic weakness of man: he or she lacks gratitude for what is. The rabbis stated it in a pithy manner in the Talmud: "Is it not sufficient that one is alive?"

Benny Morris, and many others like him, no matter how great their scholarship or how wide their knowledge, lack spiritual perspective. They look at this world and think they understand it. They are super rational to the point of seemingly becoming irrational. And since the world does not conform to their view of it and does not really make coherent sense, they doom society to oblivion and destruction. Historians usually deal with facts and overlay those facts with their own opinions and worldview. This serves to obfuscate the facts and distort conclusions. And it creates false illusions, dire predictions, and general despondency.

The Jewish people have lived for millennia on a large diet of faith and belief. If the Jewish people as a whole would have made a rational reckoning of its situation in a hostile and inimical world, it would have disappeared long ago from the face of world civilization. However, because of faith and belief, the Jewish people weathered enormous storms and crises over its long and bitter history.

This is not to say that we should not be realistic about our future and about the problems that face us. Blind faith alone, without human action and wisdom, will not carry the day. However, Judaism is not a religion of pessimism. It casts a strong positive vote for the future. It encourages family life, children, and a long-term perspective on personal and national life.

The Jewish future always aspires to a better world without denigrating the current world. According to opinions in the Talmud and Maimonides, even the messianic era will be a time not that different from the world that we now live in. It will be our task to raise human civilization to realize that peace achieves more than war, and goodness is greater than evil.

Today, conveying this concept is a constant struggle and will remain a struggle for the future of humanity on this planet. But the struggle must be conducted in a mood of optimism and confidence that we will not only survive, we will triumph, and that all of humankind will be better because of our success and accomplishments.

Winter Blues

As I have lived in Israel for many years, the memories of winter in Monsey, New York, have faded from my memory. (That is not all that has faded from my memory, but that is a different matter which I do not intend to discuss with you.) So on a visit in midwinter to the northeastern part of the United States, I surprisingly encountered weather that was cold, very snowy, and depressing. This pattern is pretty much the reason why many millions of Americans have left that part of the country and migrated west and south to warmer climes and sunnier skies. I think that the horrid winter weather of Sweden is partially responsible for the wondrously idiotic statements of its current foreign minister about Israel. She is depressed by the Swedish winter weather and focuses her frustrations and melancholy on poor little Israel.

In fact, Israel has become the punching bag for most of the nations of the world. The United Nations Secretary-General can't do much about North

Korea, central Africa, ISIS, the Zika virus, the European migrant crisis, the Syrian civil war, or the nasty winter weather of New York City where the UN is located, so he projects his frustrations on Israel. The Jews have been the world's scapegoat for all of its self-contrived ills for millennia. Now that, unexpectedly and against all wisdom and odds, there is one Jewish state that has the temerity to exist in this world, it has taken its place in the media world to be constantly criticized and threatened. Israel is truly the seeming cause of the world's winter of discontent.

The bad weather of winter can be overcome in different ways. One need not abandon the warmth of home and hearth to venture out into the cold and snow. And if one *must* leave the house, there are coats and gloves and scarves and boots to offset the effects of the outside weather. Many of today's automobiles have the means to drive safely and gently even on snowy streets and highways. Human beings are extremely adaptable creatures, able to live and survive everywhere on this planet, from Arctic cold to equatorial and desert heat. And in our temperate zone of the globe, there is always the vision that spring is not too distant in the future. So we are able to hunker down even in the depth of winter weather and bear it stoically; and if we are young enough, even joyously.

My old Monsey winter coat is still serviceable, if no longer chic, so I was able to attend synagogue services, run errands, and waste the time of numerous doctors, friends of mine who are determined to discover the secret of my longevity. Winter can be tolerated, if not necessarily appreciated. And if properly viewed, winter becomes the harbinger of spring and of better, warmer, and sunnier times.

Well, perhaps this is true regarding the world's winter with Israel. In spite of all the criticism and unfairness directed towards it, there is always a begrudging note of admiration and wonder in the world's attitude towards the State of Israel. Firstly, Jews are not supposed to have physical prowess. We are not supposed to have a highly successful army, navy, and air force. In addition, Jews are not supposed to have independent diplomatic and military policies. In short, the situation regarding Jewry has been turned on its head after millennia of negative stereotyping. And this new reality takes quite an adjustment.

The Jewish people are better off on the whole than a century ago. We have passed through a very frigid winter; it still lingers with very little warmth towards us from the world's officialdom and media. It is still going to be a long winter, and sometimes even a freezing one. It will require patience on our part. We will have to put on our coats and gloves and bundle up against the cold. Gradually, things will change. Europe's fixation with Israel will diminish in the face of its own problems and troubles. But it will eventually adjust to the new Jewish reality, just as Jewry itself will also have to make its own adjustment to the realities that exist before us.

In spite of occasional severely cold days, the Land of Israel experiences fairly mild winters. Let us hope that this will be true metaphorically and not only weather-wise.

25 Years after Oslo

A most controversial anniversary was marked here in Israel this month. A quarter of a century ago, Israel signed the Oslo Accords establishing the Palestinian Authority and giving it control over millions of people and a large swath of territory in the Land of Israel.

I remember how hopeful and happy many Jews were when the Oslo Accords were signed and publicized. The naysayers were silenced, if not even pilloried and deplored. The agreements split the Israeli public and Israeli politics for decades. Only through a shameful public bribe of appointing a member of Knesset as a minister were the Accords ratified by the Israeli legislature with basically a one-vote majority. With perfect hindsight, I am certain that if the Oslo Accords were again to be brought for a vote by the Israeli Knesset, a substantial majority would reject the entire matter.

This anniversary was marked in almost complete silence in Israel. The hopes and optimism engendered by the Oslo Accords and the handshake between Yasser Arafat and Yitzhak Rabin have long faded and dissipated in the face of the realities of terrorism and duplicity. Israel hoped that Arafat would somehow turn into Nelson Mandela, bringing reconciliation and peace to a very troubled and frustrated society. Instead, Arafat embarked on a program of terrorism and extreme and unachievable demands, and sowed the seeds of generational hatred within Palestinian society.

The experience of a quarter-century of unremitting tension and bloodshed has certainly sobered Israeli public opinion. Israel is no longer convinced that signing pieces of paper and having ceremonies at the Rose Garden of the White House is really in its best long-term interest.

The basic fallacy of Oslo was that we listened to what Arafat said in English and willfully ignored what he was saying in Arabic. It was the classic example of whistling past the graveyard, hoping somehow that our adversaries were reciprocating our good intentions. After bitter wars in Lebanon and Gaza, and unprecedented terrorist attacks and intifadas within Israel, it has become quite clear that the vision of Oslo was at best very naïve and premature, if not even downright foolish and self-destructive.

Unfortunately, Rabin was becoming quite aware of the weakness of the Oslo Accords when he was assassinated and Israel was plunged into a terrible and bitter political divide, which persists even until today. Neither those who supported Rabin on the question of Oslo nor those who opposed him have truly forgiven the other side for their behavior. Aside from the external difficulties caused by the Oslo Accords, the internal damage to Israeli society and politics has also been enormous and most painful.

Today, most Israelis place little trust not only in the Oslo Accords but also in any new type of proposal that may be offered for peace with our Palestinian neighbors. This skepticism has created a diplomatic paralysis that undoubtedly cannot exist forever.

There are many proposals being offered to facilitate the long-term, or even short-term, arrangement between Israel and its Palestinian neighbors. The fact that the Palestinians are bitterly divided between Fatah and Hamas certainly complicates the matter. It seems obvious that even if there is any reconciliation between the two Palestinian groups it is unlikely that Palestine will be ruled as one united country. For its part, Israel seems more than satisfied to arrive at a short-term arrangement that would achieve relative security and tranquility for its immediate future. A great change of mindset must occur both in Israel and among the Palestinians in order to achieve a long-term modus vivendi between Israel and the Palestinians. It would be the challenge of the educational systems, the media, and the political leaders of both societies to help create an atmosphere that would allow for sincere negotiations and eventual accords.

As Oslo proved, the devil is always in the details. No amount of high-sounding slogans or soothing words can hide the fact that the details of the dispute between Israel and the Palestinians are many and complex. I do not think that they can be solved in one fell swoop by one grand agreement. The words of the rabbis of the Talmud – that trying to grab too much will mean that one grabs not at all – certainly apply to this situation. Let us hope that somehow progress will be made towards achieving a just and lasting agreement.

Inspiration in Everyday Experiences

My Post Office

Well, it really isn't my post office. It is only the post office that is located in my neighborhood. The postal service in Israel allegedly has been recently privatized, but to my expert eyes there are no recognizable differences from when it was government operated. For the last ten years I have been visiting the post office at least once a week. I had foolishly thought it was the job of the post office to deliver mail to my home. Yet my mail delivery person decides arbitrarily which mail is too burdensome to place in my mailbox. Instead, he or she (postpeople sightings are quite rare here in Jerusalem, so I can only guess) deposits a notice in my mailbox inviting me to come to the post office to pick up my mail. So I find myself there quite regularly. The post office also serves as a bank where one can pay utility bills, fulfill governmental obligations, and conduct other sundry monetary transactions.

All of the above guarantees that there is always – and I mean *always* – a long line of people waiting to be served. The people who service the counters are hard-working and usually courteous and helpful, but the place is seriously undermanned, and the five service counters are never in operation at the same time. So a visit to the post office invariably means a wait in line that can sometimes stretch from ten to twenty minutes, or even longer.

There are important life lessons here. The most obvious, and perhaps the most important one, is the virtue of patience. Eventually, one's turn at the counter will arrive. Nevertheless, scenes of impatience at the post office are common. And the cardinal sin there is letting someone go before you, no matter how necessary and reasonable the situation that warrants it. There are always complaints against people taking too much time at the counter from those who are still waiting in line. I've noticed that when those very same complainers reach the counter, they do not conduct their business with any greater alacrity.

Waiting in line brings out the best in people and the worst in people. It only depends on which side of one's personality one wishes to exhibit publicly. I have noticed that patience can also induce an attitude of tolerance towards others and their human foibles. So remaining calm, and even good-natured, while waiting in line is excellent training for life in general. Jews, especially here in Israel, are not particularly known for their patience. The post office is a good place to practice incorporating this virtue within ourselves.

One can meet interesting people and enjoy stimulating conversation while waiting in line. There is a Jewish expression that what intelligence and planning often cannot accomplish can be achieved through the passage of time and patience.

While standing in line at the post office, I have the opportunity to view the posters advertising the latest series of postage stamps printed by the postal authority. As a child, I was a stamp collector. Though I long ago gave up the hobby, I have never lost my fascination for stamps. I especially enjoy gazing at the holiday stamp series that always has a beautiful graphic display of traditional Jewish themes and Jewish history. Just as the street names of Jerusalem teach us a great deal about Jewish faith and history, so too, our stamps reveal our culture and our past.

I remember that as a child I was vividly impressed by my father's expression of joy at receiving a letter from then-British Mandatory Palestine because it had a stamp that bore Hebrew lettering on it. The stamp also had a picture of the Mosque of Omar, as well as English and Arabic lettering on it, but that was all irrelevant to my father, who was the quintessential believing Eastern European Jewish scholar. To him, the only thing that mattered on that stamp was its Hebrew lettering.

To such Jews, a Jewish postal service in a sovereign Jewish state in the Land of Israel is an exciting, if partial, fulfillment of biblical prophecy. Once, while waiting in line with me at the post office, he noticed my impatience at the slow progress of the line. He gently said to me: "We waited two thousand years to have a Jewish post office. We can wait another ten minutes to use its services." And so we can.

Credit Cards

One of the more fiendish banking creations of modern society is the credit card. This simple piece of plastic is the greatest source of personal convenience and freedom of opportunity. It is also the source of angst, bankruptcy, and even greater forms of tragedy to families and individuals.

For credit cards, like everything else in human existence, come at a cost. Some of it is immediate, but most of it is long term. It is not only that the monthly bill has to be paid – here in the Holy Land the money is taken out of your bank account with no prior notice – but that there are all sorts of other worries that come with a credit card: identity theft; embarrassment when the card is not accepted for some unknown, implausible, and unjustified reason; and the hassle involved if, God forbid, one loses the card.

The freedom that a credit card gives to go on a spending spree, like all other freedoms in life, can be dangerous. Many a family has been destroyed financially, and eventually domestically, because of outrageous credit card debt. And supplying a credit card to teenage children can, if not controlled and limited, be a prescription for personal and familial disaster. So, like most advances and seeming conveniences, credit cards are a two-edged sword, depending greatly on how they are wielded and sheathed. The basic rule of life that "there is no free lunch" applies here with vengeance.

In Pirkei Avot we are informed that this world is likened to a magnificent store, full of all sorts of goods that one can purchase and enjoy. Not only is the store open for business 24/7, the Storekeeper is willing to extend generous terms of credit with no immediate cash required as a down payment. But like the Israeli credit card system, payment is regularly exacted and collected, and usually without any prior notice to the debtor. Therefore we are always surprised – if not even blindsided – by the events and constant challenges confronting us. And Pirkei Avot makes this reality crystal clear to us. We are all, so to speak, living on credit card debt. And in the spiritual world, no less than in the physical and financial world, debt must eventually be paid, or at least somehow successfully negotiated and settled.

The Torah makes clear to the Jewish people the consequences of defaulting on our spiritual debt to the Almighty. All of Jewish history can be summed up as simply the story of borrowing on credit and eventually being forced to repay the debt incurred.

Much of our spiritual debt, like one's personal financial debt, has been incurred by foolish and unnecessary purchases. Our spiritual credit card, like our financial one, had limits on the amount of credit available to us. I imagine that there is much in Jewish history that we now wish to return to the store. But the Torah store has a very limited return policy; it is based solely on true repentance and further probity in using our moral and spiritual credit cards. And these terms certainly appear to limit our purchasing freedoms in this life.

One of the great problems in current Jewish society is identity theft. Our true self, our personal credit card has either been stolen or lost due to ignorance, alienation, apathy, or terrible negligence. If asked to identify ourselves successfully to our spiritual Storekeeper, many Jews are simply unable to do so. Millions of Jews have been robbed of their heritage and history, their value system, and their true mission in life and in the world. Their credit card is no longer valid, having expired over a few generations of assimilation, as well as physical and spiritual annihilation.

There are many Jews today, especially here in Israel, who are in the process of applying for a new credit card for themselves and their families. We are all aware that such applications are not easily processed, nor are they always approved. Nevertheless, the willingness of many Jews to attempt to recapture their true identity, the fact that Israel as a whole has become more traditionally Jewish in outlook (and even in behavior), is a most heartening development.

It augurs well for our future here in our land. Credit can be a blessing, but it must be used wisely.

Answering Machines

Almost all of our telephones today, whether they are landlines or cell phones, are equipped with a "leave a message" answering service. Like all of our modern technological wonders, this service has a darker side to its apparent sunny convenience. When I arrive home late at night after attending an event and I see that red light flashing on my answering machine – indicating that a caller or numerous callers have left a message – my mood darkens. I must then and there listen to those messages, for there may be an emergency situation that demands my attention and response even late at night. Most of the time, these messages can certainly wait for my response until the next day. But I must listen to them in case someone needs an immediate response.

I was born at a time when phone numbers were only four digits in length, and one spoke to a real live person called an "operator" to connect a call. Our home phone was one of four phones connected on a party line. No one thought of having an answering machine. No one had ever heard of a home answering machine. We have certainly progressed since those days, at least as far as technology is concerned. But the nostalgia that overtakes those of my age tells me that life was simply less stressful when there were no answering machines and those miraculous handheld phones were not the center point of our daily existence.

Heaven must also have an answering-machine service to receive all of our calls and requests. There is no doubt that the Lord's omniscience allows for instant awareness of all requests and entreaties. Yet we do not always receive instant responses to our calls to Heaven. Sometimes we are put on hold, and at other times our messages are recorded on the Heavenly answering machine for further attention and processing. Our calls are never ignored, for the Heavenly answering machine is always turned on and working.

According to Jewish tradition and belief, our calls can be returned, so to speak, years – and even generations – later. But once our message is recorded on that Heavenly answering machine, it remains there permanently and will be dealt with in Heaven's good time and effective manner.

The Talmud teaches us that not only our words and spoken wishes are recorded, but that even our tears, unspoken and private, are also counted and stored in the vaults of Heaven. And the gates of tears are never closed. Tears do not elicit a "leave a message" response. They are immediately assessed, counted, and considered. In a macho society, tears are sometimes considered a sign of personal weakness and soft character. In Jewish life, they are viewed as the lubricant of our souls and one of the keys to emotional holiness and psychological stability.

The call that the Jewish people placed to Heaven millennia ago regarding our restoration to national sovereignty in our ancient homeland, the Land of Israel, was on the Heavenly answering machine for a long time. Heaven never erased that original call from its answering machine, and the Jewish people never stopped making that call over and over again, certainly many millions of times, through centuries of exile and dispersion.

Unexpectedly, against all odds and rational predictions, that call has been returned by Heaven in our times. All of the tears shed over our exile and persecution have been counted and remembered and have, in fact, become the fuel for the renewal of our national energy and nation-building drive.

On a personal level too, the Heavenly answering machine records when our calls were received, but it does not indicate exactly when that call will be returned. Yet we are confident that the return call will eventually come, that our communications are never completely ignored or deemed irrelevant. The mysteries of our lives, private and national, oftentimes overwhelm and discourage us. But we should continually remember that we left a message on the Heavenly answering machine, so we certainly are not alone or forgotten in our struggles and hopes.

My Keyboard

A few days ago my computer screen showed me the dreaded words "your keyboard batteries are low." Well, even I know how to replace batteries, or so I thought. For then I discovered that one of the batteries was completely wedged into a small tube. I could not remove it no matter how hard I tried or whatever instruments of destruction I used. So I took the keyboard to my friendly Apple distributor here in Jerusalem and asked the experts there to remove the battery. They labored mightily, consulted with each other often in dire whispers, and finally told me that they would have to send the keyboard away to some mysterious laboratory that would pursue the problem, adding that they could not guarantee any results. Moreover, I would have to pay a considerable amount for the laboratory's unguaranteed attempt.

Needing my keyboard to produce my immortal prose, and seeing that a new keyboard was almost the same price as (possibly) fixing the old one, I opened my wallet and took the plunge for a new keyboard.

Arriving at home, I followed the instructions as to how to install this miraculous device so that it would pair with my computer. After a number of unsuccessful attempts to follow the instructions on the screen, some miracle happened and the keyboard began to work. Hence this brilliant article which you are now reading. Since the keyboard is a wireless one, to my technologically ignorant mind its effectiveness borders on the miraculous. I am grateful for its ability to somehow transfer my thoughts to the computer screen, and eventually onto paper and into your psyche.

It struck me that my advanced computer with all of its gadgets, programs, preferences, and connections to the entire world is fairly ineffective without a keyboard. I could not respond to my emails, nor could I work on books and articles if I did not possess a working keyboard that pairs with my computer. For the first time, I realized why this device is called a *keyboard* and not a "word board" or "letter board": because it is the key to the entire project and to all of the technology associated with it. Without the keyboard one can perhaps receive, but certainly not send, messages and responses. Without the keyboard, one cannot give written expression to one's thoughts and ideas. Without the keyboard, the computer, with all of its wondrous complexity, is pretty much a useless machine.

And this set me thinking further about how *halachah* is the keyboard to Torah and Jewish life generally. Pretty much everyone agrees to the value system and general moral ideas that the Torah represents – charity, compassion, peace, human and personal harmony, knowledge, and purposeful living. Yet that value system pretty much resembles the computer without a keyboard, for there is no detailed instruction sheet that will enable us to activate and actuate these values in our everyday lives. Without the keyboard that pairs with our moral computer, that moral system remains vacuous phrases and piously uttered platitudes.

Since I am mechanically challenged and changing a light bulb is a big deal for me, I was delighted that somehow I was able to get my new wireless keyboard paired with my computer and working. I can't really explain how I did it or how the keyboard and the computer work together to produce written words. Yet somehow it works, and pretty much to perfection.

The same is true of *halachah*, detail and ritual regarding Jewish life. The observance of the commandments, of the traditions of Israel, and of even the apparently nagging nature of minutiae in Jewish law and daily behavior connect us and pair us with the great computer of Torah values and eternal life.

All of Jewish history proves the truth of this axiom. Meaningful survival as a people and as a Jewish individual has always been connected to having a keyboard that works, pairing us with the value system and eternity of Torah. It would be wise, therefore, for all of us to recharge the batteries of our keyboard. We must make certain that they are strong and full so that we may be blessed with the greatness of Torah observance, and of a productive, valuable Jewish existence.

Seeing the Big Picture

Due to the progressive weakening of my eyesight, I have been forced to search for all types of aids to help me read and study. A few months ago I was able to purchase an excellent device that is manufactured in Holland: it is essentially a closed-circuit TV camera with great powers of magnification. By placing it over the book or item that I wish to read, it gives me the ability to magnify that text to an almost unlimited extent until it becomes legible to me. Because it operates on electricity, it is of no use to me on Shabbat and holidays. But the rest of the week it enables me to read with comparative ease, and overall it has been a great boon to my spirits.

Its power of magnification is so strong that even imperfections in the font are clearly revealed to me sometimes, even to my great annoyance.

Though no machine is perfect and there are minor difficulties with this one as well, my main problem is that because of the high magnification I am able to see only part of the page, or even just part of a sentence. There can be little flow in the continuity of thought necessary to really appreciate reading or studying texts. So it cannot give you the big picture of the page or subject that you are reading. And often, when one does not have the ability to see that big picture of the entire page, sentences and words are disassociated and hard to understand.

This is pretty much true in life as well. All of our lives we are caught up in details – often minute – and in the long run of events unnecessary and unworthy of the attention that we pay them. The big picture escapes us and we only see the magnified imperfect font of the details of our lives and society. My reading machine provides a number of backgrounds that one can choose in order to help facilitate easier reading. I have noticed that it does not work whatsoever when no background is chosen.

That is also true in life and events. Nothing in human society occurs in a vacuum. For the present to have any meaning or influence, there must first be a background to help explain it and contrast it to changing circumstances and times. Many of the major problems that beset the Jewish world today arise simply because there is no knowledge or acknowledgment of history and experience to give rise to an explanation. We are left without a rational understanding of current events, without an outline to guide us towards a better future. Without the bigger picture in mind, the current details make no sense, and often they are mere distractions of relative unimportance.

My walk to the synagogue on Shabbat entails a climb of five blocks, straight uphill. I am not embarrassed to admit that often I do not do this walk in one fell swoop; I stop to gather myself for the rest of the journey. When I do so, I invariably turn around and see how far I have already come, and I note the steepness of the road that I have already climbed. Psychologically, if not physically, this gives me a great lift, and the remaining journey no longer appears as daunting as it did at the outset of my walk. If you know how far you have come, it is easier to imagine that you will yet successfully achieve your goal and destination.

I feel that this is very true regarding the story of the Jewish people and of the State of Israel over the last century of travail, tragedy, and constant tension. Having come this far against such great odds and triumphed in such an unlikely fashion, it becomes much easier for one to feel that the rest of the journey will be as successful as the beginning. By seeing the whole picture, even the disturbing details, we become aware of milestones in the great progress of the history of the Jewish people and of Israel.

On Changing Light Bulbs

My mechanical ineptitude is legendary. I have never been any sort of handyman around the house, and from time immemorial dealing with burned out light bulbs has been a dreaded challenge. This was true regarding those good, old-fashioned screw-in light bulbs, and the arrival of halogen lighting fixtures has vastly compounded the problem. Those spindly little legs of the halogen bulbs never seem to fit correctly into the microscopically small sockets where they are intended to go, and the formidable warning not to touch the halogen bulb – God forbid! – with one's bare fingers has seriously impeded my hope of being able to replace any burned-out bulb.

Since I am, thank God, at a stage of life where I am simply spending my grandchildren's inheritance, I now wait until a significant number of light bulbs have burned out throughout our home, and then I call my beloved and trusted electrician to change all of them. There was a time when I was actually embarrassed to admit doing this. But today I am brazenly proud of my behavior and, needless to say, my electrician is also quite delighted with the arrangement. So every few months when the house turns dark enough, I purchase the necessary bulbs, the electrician arrives, and within a short time our home is again bathed in the artificial light of our technologically advanced world.

A few days ago one of the bulbs in a halogen bedside lamp burned out. In a fit of foolish bravado, I decided that this time I would change the bulb myself. It suddenly became a test of my manhood, and I was determined to accomplish it. I walked the five long blocks to the hardware store to buy the bulb. Today bulbs are available in a myriad number of watts, volts, colors, and mood tones. And the old burned-out bulb that I brought along to show the storekeeper was mysteriously illegible as to what size and color it had been originally. So the storekeeper sold me the bulb he deemed proper in his experienced judgment – the most expensive one that he had in stock – and I went home hoping for the best. I didn't know exactly what prayer the rabbis had instituted to be recited before attempting to insert a very small halogen bulb into an even smaller lamp socket, so I composed my own prayer on the spot. And lo! After only three futile attempts, I suddenly and unexpectedly succeeded in inserting the bulb into its proper socket. I then tested the lamp and it actually lit. I was overjoyed at my very small triumph. My day was made!

It is amazing how the small things in life really do matter to humans. The prophet Jonah, who was instrumental in saving the lives of hundreds of thousands of people in the great ancient city of Nineveh, rejoices not in that monumental accomplishment and in the revelation to him of God's patience and mercy towards humans. Rather, he revels in the appearance of a gourd that shades him from the sun. And when that gourd dries out and disappears, Jonah is frustrated and angry, rebellious and unappreciative of the miraculous salvation of Nineveh that he helped bring about. The Lord, so to speak, is forced to remind him of the difference between major and minor, of the central issues of life and the peripheral, temporary pleasures and inconveniences.

Though it is a long jump from Jonah and Nineveh, I am reminded of star hockey player Wayne Gretzky. He is often quoted as saying that his success was due to the fact that he never lost sight of where the puck was going. Presumably, other players were distracted by team movements and other peripheral considerations. Gretzky understood priorities.

Burned-out light bulbs and replacing them is part of our daily lives. But they are not what our lives are about. Service to God and other humans, Torah knowledge, and good character traits – those remain the central core of Jewish existence. And there is no electrician who can be relied upon to change those bulbs for us if they burn out. We are the only ones who can successfully reignite the lamp of our own souls. And the only way to do this is to keep our eye on the puck and not fall prey to the distractions that visit all of us regularly.

The Broadcaster (2016)

Those of you who regularly read my writings, few and beloved as you are, know that I like to look at baseball as a metaphor for life. The simplicity, beauty, quirky unexpectedness, and uncertainties of the game accurately mirror the events in our personal and national lives. So when I recently read an article about a revered baseball broadcaster, Vin Scully, I felt impelled to share some of my thoughts regarding him with you.

Scully is a broadcaster for the games of the Los Angeles Dodgers. He is currently eighty-eight years old. He began his career with the Dodgers in 1950, when the team was still located in Brooklyn. He is retiring at the end of this season, approximately one month from now.

Scully has no peer or imitators in the field of baseball broadcasting. He has an altogether unique voice, style, and approach to the game. In fact, over the years many an American has listened to the Dodgers' games, not so much for the result and excitement of the game itself but rather for the experience of hearing Vin Scully converse with them for a few relaxing hours. Scully has a dry but wicked sense of humor, a keen eye for human foibles and accomplishments, a dispassionate view of the world and its vagaries, and a loyalty to his team tempered by the realities of available talent and the competitiveness of others. So his comments while broadcasting the game are wide ranging and astute, and they provide the necessary backdrop to what is otherwise a mere recording of details taking place before his eyes. At this, he is the acknowledged master of his field. He is revered by all, even by those who are not particularly interested in baseball or in the Los Angeles Dodgers.

So what does all of this have to do with Jewish life? Well, I think that what our Jewish society today needs are a few good broadcasters who will be able to put current events into perspective, to be dispassionate about issues that we face, to view things realistically and not purely emotionally and judgmentally, and who are loyal to the game, but not afraid to point out errors made on the field.

Part of the craft and success of Vin Scully is the meticulous research that he does before every game, and even before describing any player in the game. He never resorts to off-the-cuff reactions or to pat slogans. Over the past sixty years of broadcasting, he recognizes how the game has changed and how the situation of the players today is far different from what it was. He is able to take all of this into consideration, so he is as timely now as he ever was.

Much of our Jewish world is still dealing with the situations and disputes that existed in Eastern Europe or other areas of the Diaspora a century ago. The realization as to how the world has changed, and especially how the Jewish world has changed, is oftentimes not reflected in the statements and positions of our leaders who command our allegiance.

The rules of baseball have never been basically altered. Yet the game today differs greatly from what it was a century ago. The same thing can be said about the Jewish world. The rules that govern us, the Torah that we study and observe, its laws and commandments, have certainly not changed. However, the Jewish world today is far different from what it was even a few decades ago, and we need observers who are able to advise us, grant us perspective, and inject realism into our lives and policies.

All of the current issues that face the Jewish religious world – the role of women in religious and secular life, the necessity for education and skills, the grinding poverty which is almost self-inflicted in large sections of the religious Jewish world, the problems of marriage and children, the attitude towards a Jewish state now practically seventy years old – all need to be looked at, reviewed, thought about, and then clearly addressed.

And they should be dealt with in a compassionate and dispassionate manner. We need good broadcasters to frame the game and the players for us. In today's world, both Jewish and general, there are few broadcasters who are able to do so. Everyone wants to root for the home team and no one is willing to look at the welfare of the entire game itself. It was this ability that made Vin Scully unique amongst all broadcasters. I regret that he is retiring at such a young age.

My Orchid Plant

I very much enjoy flowers and plants: I see in them some of the bountiful goodness of the pleasures that the Lord has arranged for humans in this world. But among my many failings is the fact that I do not have a green thumb. Plants and I do not agree; I often feel that the plants that I have in my home are just downright hostile to me. The care of the plants and the reason that they have survived so long has always been due to the distaff side of my home.

So today I persist in the watering and caring for the plants in my house in spite of my bumbling efforts to keep them sprightly, or at least alive. The only exception to this seemingly endless tale of frustration is the orchid plant. Orchids require very little care, and that is what they receive. Their flowers are absolutely magnificent and their presence has a soothing effect on rabbinic nerves that sometimes become jangled.

In My Opinion …

And the greatest thing about orchid plants is the fact that after they shed their flowers after a month or two, they do not die but rather remain dormant, sometimes for more than a year; and then they suddenly revive and begin to produce the bulbs that will produce their beautiful flowers.

I love to watch this process, for it gives me a sense of revival and resilience. There is a great human lesson to be learned from the orchid plant and I am grateful for it. The Torah indicates that humans have much to learn from nature – both the animal and plant kingdoms – and that only a fool would ignore these lessons built into God's creation.

In my home I have an orchid plant that has been dormant for well over a year. The person who helps clean my house and keep it orderly proposed about a month ago that I dispose of that plant, since it obviously was no longer going to revive itself and produce flowers. I told her that this plant has done so a number of times previously, and that I would hang onto it for a while, if for no other reasons than sentimental. The plant must've heard the warning that it was on a very short leash. Two weeks ago, it began to wake up. It now has suddenly begun to sprout bulbs, and just before Shabbat it gave birth to the first beautiful orchid flower. I was deeply touched by the event, for it highlighted to me the continuity of life, which is one of the basic values of Judaism and our Torah.

We all pass through difficult and sad times. We all, in the words of Proverbs, "fall seven times." But we are commanded to rise again to continue, for the challenges and difficulties of life are inescapable; but the strength and resilience that the Lord built into human beings must be exploited to continue doing acts of kindness, mercy, and justice. Watching my orchid plant bloom again brought home to me this attitude and duty; this mere flower served as a great comfort to me.

I realize that even orchid plants do not bloom forever. All things in this world are finite, and that applies to plants as it does to humans and other creatures. This realization, however, does not dampen my enthusiasm at seeing my orchid plant once again blossom and give forth flowers. The plant does not seem to be overly concerned about its ultimate future and demise. Meanwhile, it does what it is supposed to do – produce beautiful flowers so that human beings can enjoy the sight.

And that is also a great lesson to humans who are haunted by our sense of mortality and finiteness. Looking at Proverbs once again, we see King Solomon stating that the great woman of valor "is able to laugh even to the last day." We do not see anything humorous about the last day. But the deeper meaning is that while we have not yet arrived at our last day, we have to pursue our mission and task in life with enthusiasm and joy, and not with a sense of doom and foreboding. The gift of life and resilience that the Lord has planted within us is what makes life magical and gives it a whiff of eternity. I am very grateful to my orchid plant for having taught me so many important lessons.

Spanning Generations

My two-month-old great-grandson came to visit me last Saturday night. Naturally, he brought his parents along for the visit, but he was the honored guest, the center of all attention. He will not remember the visit, for memory kicks in later than does birth; and unfortunately, in many instances, kicks out early before death. For great-grandparents a visit from a member of the fourth generation is an occasion of note and moment. Having grown up at a time when very few of my peers ever saw or knew a grandparent, it is truly miraculous to me that I have seen and know many of my great-grandchildren.

Life spans have lengthened considerably over the past decades of progress in medicine and health care, allowing multi-generational family ties undreamt of in the generation of my parents. Because of this increased longevity, our view of life now spans many decades, even centuries.

This development is certainly valuable and important in terms of the Jewish people, for the validation of Judaism has always been dependent on family tradition and continuity. Knowing one's family, its history and traditions, its accomplishments and failures – warts and all – make up the stuff of Jewish life and is one of the secrets of Jewish survival. The dissolution and diminishing of family and generational ties caused by late marriage or no marriage at all, a very low birthrate, and the rootlessness and mobility of the young have all played a role in the erosion of non-Orthodox Jewish society in the Diaspora (and to a lesser extent, here in Israel as well).

The older generations are, and deservedly so, the memory bank for the coming generations. Though they may recall events and individuals through the haze of nostalgia and personal subjective view, they do serve as a vital and irreplaceable reservoir of direction, knowledge, and inspiration for the young who are just beginning their life's adventures.

The Torah emphasizes the connection between generations in terms of Jewish tradition and, perhaps even more importantly, in terms of Jewish destiny. "Know from where you came" has a broader meaning in Jewish life than the specific one outlined in Pirkei Avot. It is, so to speak, the call to arms of Judaism. The merit of previous generations is the bank account upon which later generations can draw sustenance and strength. But that presupposes that one knows the name of the bank and the account number where that treasure is being held. And that can only be known through the personal bond between generations in a family.

Self-identity and self-worth, the necessary ingredients for a healthy Torah personality, can only be achieved by the input of generations, knowledge of the past, and the dream of the future. Thus, the old generation and the new budding generation are interlocked in an eternal symbiotic relationship.

A few of my American great-grandchildren used the *afikoman* money they received from me towards the purchase of their first tricycles or bicycles. I am assured by their parents that when they ascend those vehicles they remember me in their newfound mobility. As they grow older and wiser, perhaps they will also read my books and listen to my recorded lectures. One can always hope, can't one?

In any event, life should not be the only connection between generations. Even though I was barely ten years old when my grandfather passed away, he has remained a constant inspiration and role model for me all of my life.

The ability to span generations is a necessary Jewish trait of survival. And it is more than the power of memory that is involved in this feat. It is also a desire to know of the past and of one's own heritage and lineage. The Torah emphasizes lineage in many areas of discussion and *halachah*. The past can neither shape nor guarantee the future, but it certainly is of influence in the development of unfolding events. So the influence of generations – the positive influence of love and attention – creates the Jewish future and is the greatest gift that the older generation can bestow upon its young emerging generation. To my mind, seeing one's generations and interacting with them is one of life's grandest triumphs.

A Sad, Sad World

There is a well-known anecdote that circulates in yeshiva circles about a young student who left the yeshiva environment to find his fortune in far distant fields. When he left the yeshiva, he had a beard and dressed modestly, as was his Jewish tradition. A decade later, he was met by chance by the head of his former yeshiva. The former student now was completely clean-shaven and dressed in the most modern and fashionable garb of the time. Nevertheless, the old mentor recognized his former student and "innocently" asked him: "Since I am not a man of the world and you obviously are, would you please answer a few questions that I have about the outside society? Are most people happy or depressed? Are most people satisfied with their wealth, or do they consider themselves poor? Are most people psychologically well-adjusted or are they anxious? And finally, are most people physically healthy, or are they afflicted with disease, discomfort, or some sort of illness?"

The student was taken aback by this line of questioning, but he dutifully replied: "Master, I must admit the truth to you. Most people are not happy; they do not consider themselves wealthy, no matter how much money they have; many psychologists and therapists are doing a thriving business because a great deal of the world is dysfunctional and even somewhat crazy; and those who are ill, in pain, and in anxiety, far outnumber those who consider themselves completely healthy, normal, and well-adjusted." To which the mentor commented: "So for such a sad, depressed, sick, poor world, you removed your beard?"

In our daily prayers we ask that "we should not toil for emptiness and nothingness, nor should we have been born to be confused and depressed." Judaism does not negate the outside world. It is a practical religion that deals with life as it is and does not make unrealistic demands upon its adherents. So even though the outside world may be one of poverty, mental strain, physical pain, suffering, and constant frustrations, it is the world we live in. We are not to shut ourselves in lonely solitude and become hermits.

But, as I have often pointed out, Judaism is always a religion of balance. And the balance here is not to allow us to remove our beard, so to speak, because of the pressures of the outside world and our desire to conform to its current standards and political correctness.

Like hundreds of millions – if not even billions of others – I own a cell phone. I rarely use it, and most of the time it is turned off. I do so purposely because I still value human conversation face-to-face. My grandchildren all text – they cannot spell correctly, and often they are flustered if they have to actually communicate with another human being personally. The outside world tells me that I am a Neanderthal, a relic of a long past era. Maybe so, but I am not willing to shave my beard on this issue. To me, it represents a very advanced technological world that is innately sad, poor, disconnected, and in many cases quite dysfunctional.

Ukraine, Syria, Lebanon, Egypt, Libya, Iraq, Afghanistan, Pakistan, Congo, Zimbabwe, Bosnia, North Korea, and a host of other countries on the globe currently are not pleasant places to be. In fact, a large part of the world and its billions of people are enveloped in sadness, violence, injustice, and impending death. If one does not have principles and beliefs that transcend current events and the present situation of the outside world, one is doomed to a constant feeling of tension, enormous frustration, and depression.

The Torah gives us a set of principles and beliefs by which one is able to live in such an uncomfortable world and yet have a feeling of satisfaction and accomplishment. The Torah promises us eternal life and unending memory. The Torah deals with the myriad details of daily life and weaves them together into a tapestry of meaningful and satisfying values. Through Torah, the sadness of the outside world can be somewhat ameliorated by a sense of serenity and accomplishment in our inner world. Prayer, study, charity, good thoughts, and good behavior are all part of building our inner world, allowing us to successfully deal with that most difficult and sad outer world. This is a daily lesson that should never be ignored.

Background Noise

In the highly charged urban setting where most of us live, there is always background noise. Traffic, honking horns, noisy pedestrians, exuberant children, strange and (mostly unintelligible) public announcements blaring from public address automobiles are omnipresent.

There was time here in Israel when we were a much smaller country. Jerusalem rolled up its streets at about 9:30 PM and quiet reigned supreme until dawn. Not so anymore. Though we are not quite the city that never sleeps – that is the self-description of other major cities throughout the world (a most dubious honor, in my opinion) – Jerusalem is anything but a quiet place for most of the night, and certainly for all of the daylight hours. Since the rarified air of Jerusalem conducts sound ably, the boisterous noise of far-distant weddings often finds its way into my bedroom as I am attempting to fall asleep.

In truth, I have become adjusted to living with constant background noise in my life. This was one of the adjustments that I had to make in moving to the urban environment of Jerusalem from the pastoral and semi-rural environment of Monsey, New York. But even in quiet Monsey, I always operated with background noise, mostly of my own volition and choice. I always listened to classical music while writing my articles and books of deathless prose. I still do so today. In fact, as I am writing this article I am listening to a flute concerto composed by Georg Philipp Telemann. Background sound has become such an integral part of my life that I find it difficult to function well in complete silence. We humans are strange creatures.

During my years of Talmud study at the yeshiva in Chicago, the major part of the learning day was spent in the study hall, where over a hundred young men studied, debated, and argued with each other at high volume and loud frequency. On the other hand, the library room of the yeshiva was an island of tranquility, and absolute silence was enforced by a most capable librarian. Yet try as I did on many occasions, I was unable to study well in the quiet library room, while I acquitted myself quite well in the noisy study hall. I think it was this experience that influenced my penchant for background noise whenever I write or prepare for a public presentation, even today.

As far as I am concerned, a reasonable amount and volume of background noise sharpens the senses and helps focus one's mind and thoughts. At least it does so for me, hence the background flute concerto wafting through the confines of my room as I write. The music is probably much more timeless than is this article, but no matter.

The Talmud also refers to the presence of constant background sounds in our lives as Jews. Every day there are recurrent echoes from Mount Sinai that goad us to improve and honor Torah and Jewish tradition. The customs and simple acts that constitute the Jewish way of life – thrice-daily prayer, charitable acts of kindness, consideration towards others, regular Torah study, etc. – are all the factors that compose the background sounds of our lives.

In one of the films produced by Destiny Foundation, I pointed out the importance of background music in a film. Without the background themes, the film is dull and uninspiring. Even in the days of silent films at the beginning of the last century, all of the movie houses engaged a pianist to provide a musical backdrop for the film.

The Torah also requires a background to make it meaningful and memorable in our individual lives. The Torah calls itself a song, a melody, and not only a set of laws and disciplines. Without hearing this background music, the Torah also becomes dull and lacks its natural verve and vibrancy. That is why the rabbis insisted that Jews feel the freshness and renewal of excitement and novelty regarding Torah every day of their lives. The Torah must be today and not merely yesterday. It requires a strong and insistent background melody to carry it into the hearts, minds, and actions of Jews at all times and places. And that makes background sounds a matter of holiness and eternity, and not just noise.

My Teacher

My beloved teacher who taught me Talmud before I was bar mitzvah age, Rabbi Dovid Silver, passed away last week. He lived a long and productive life, and in his later years was a well-known and respected neighbor in the Jerusalem neighborhood of Bayit V'Gan.

One often gives credit to the great teachers that one was privileged to have in high school or college. I was fortunate to have many great teachers in the eleven years that I spent in yeshiva. They taught me about Jews and Judaism (the two are not synonymous), about Torah and Talmud, and about life and its vicissitudes. I am eternally indebted to them for their guidance and efforts on my behalf.

But often we neglect the appreciation we owe to those who taught us in our childhood. I loved Rabbi Silver because he loved me. He taught me *hatchalat gemara* – the beginnings of Talmud study, the simple ABC's of how to navigate through the sea of the Talmud (though nothing about Talmud is really simple). But he did it with so much care and love and concern for my welfare that until today, well over half a century later, I cannot open a volume of the Talmud without feeling his warm presence and concern for me hovering over the book.

Other rabbis in the yeshiva took the limelight and were well known in the Jewish world. He was a great scholar, but a self-effacing personality. He was a master teacher, and many of the fine Torah scholars of our generation were fortunate enough to pass through his class. All of the hundreds of students whom he taught how to embark upon Talmudic studies owe him a great debt of appreciation and gratitude. Unfortunately, not all of us realize we should do so during the person's lifetime.

It is said that the great Rabbi Chaim Soloveitchik of Brisk, one of the most creative teachers of Torah and Talmud over the past few centuries, would rise to honor the teacher who taught him *aleph bet*. He stated that though he had many great teachers later in his student days, his *aleph bet* teacher taught him pure truth – an *aleph* has always remained an *aleph* and a *bet* has always remained a *bet* – while he came to realize that much that he was taught later in intricate interpretations of the Talmud was not always true and was subject to revision and modification.

I came to realize after many years of study that Rabbi Silver taught me truth. The rules and ideas of the Talmud that he explained so nobly and succinctly, the complicated issues that he so deftly and effortlessly guided me through, all of this has retained its simple truth for me until today. Only later in life did I realize the exactitude of his teachings and the depth of his explanations that appeared to me as a child to be so simple and direct.

Rabbi Silver was a warm human being. He had an infectious smile that was always there. The difference between a teacher who smiles and one who scowls is enormous, especially to students in their young and formative years. And Rabbi Silver remained a friend, a trusted confidant and advisor to his students when they matured and left the yeshiva to pursue their life careers. I knew that he was always there for me in all of my various positions in Jewish life.

He was an outstanding *baal koreh* – a public reader of the Torah. It was not only his powerful voice and his exactitude in reading the words and notes of the Torah that made him so. It was the sweetness of Torah that flowed from him as he read from the scroll. I remember that I almost looked forward to the fast days that we commemorated in the yeshiva, for on those days Rabbi Silver would be the Torah reader. When King Solomon stated that "honey and myrrh are on your tongue," he certainly could have had Rabbi Silver's Torah reading in mind.

As far as I can reckon, with his passing, all of the teachers of my generation in the yeshiva are gone. I am lonely in a way that I have not known before. King Solomon also said, "A generation must leave and a new generation comes." But the influence and memory of the generation that goes is unending. Rabbi Dovid Silver, of blessed memory, proves that point beyond dispute.

The Secret of a Happy Life

I often have occasion to travel between Israel and the United States. I do so on my favorite airline, El Al Israel Airlines. I enjoy being on El Al because it makes you feel at home more than any other airline in the world. On El Al everyone is eating kosher. On El Al the planes don't fly on the Sabbath. On El Al the passengers can get up and pray without interference. It feels like home, like a Jewish home.

Now El Al is not a perfect airline. In fact, I don't think a perfect airline has ever existed or will ever exist. I believe that because airlines are operated by human beings, and the tendency of human beings is to make errors in judgment and in speech. Things happen.

There was an incident a while back where a plane took off in the middle of a snowstorm in the United States and landed shortly before the Sabbath in Athens. The incident immediately caused a furor, petitions, and complaints. Now in my opinion, perfection is not to be expected. It is to be striven for, but it's not always achieved. So El Al is imperfect.

But I say it is a great little airline and it is something that the Jewish people should be proud of. Never before in our history have we had airplanes with the Star of David on their tail. We never before had the abilities and the prestige that we have today. That is what we should contemplate and note, rather than carping about the imperfections that exist and will always exist because of human nature.

The Talmud emphasizes over and over again that people have to be grateful. In fact, the basis of Judaism is gratitude: gratitude to God that we are alive, no matter what our problems are; gratitude to God for what we have, no matter what we think we are missing; gratitude to God for everyday life, difficult as it may be. Because of this principle, the Talmud's measure of a human being is the ability to be thankful for what exists. The rabbis state simply, "Why should a person complain about life? Is it not good enough that he is alive?"

People don't feel that way. If something is 90 percent good, it's no good. We want it to be 100 percent good; we are not willing to accept and treasure the 90 percent. But let me give you a greater example, an even more extreme example. If something is 90 percent bad but 10 percent good, people will say, "Well, I can't be grateful for this *at all*, because it's 90 percent bad."

Yet Judaism demands of us to be grateful for the 10 percent good, even though it's missing 90 percent, because that has to be our attitude towards life. It has to be our attitude towards the family, towards marriage, towards a job, towards anything that we do. If we only look at what we are missing, we will always – always – be tormented, frustrated, sad, and envious.

The secret of a happy life is gratitude. We should be grateful for the family we have, even though everybody has a crazy uncle; grateful for the job that we have, even though our boss is not perfect and our salary is not really what it should be; grateful for the fact that for the first time in millennia we have an independent Jewish state, imperfect as it may be; and grateful that we have a Jewish airline that in many, many respects exhibits the positive traits of Jewish tradition.

I notice that people are quick to complain about El Al service, prices, the size of the seats, and other issues. I do not minimize any of these complaints. I also wish that their flights would be cheaper, their seats wider, the planes much friendlier to the passenger and less friendly to the profit line of the company. But that is a very narrow view of the matter.

There was a time in Poland when the Polish government allowed a railroad spur to be built from Warsaw to the village of Góra Kalwaria, where the famous Gerrer Rebbe, the Imrei Emes, had his court. This eighteen-mile track was used almost exclusively by the followers of that great master. In a moment of tolerance, the Polish government allowed this one spur of the entire Polish national railway system to be manned by Jews. There were Jewish conductors who came to collect the tickets. That was seen as a noble gesture by the Polish government to the Jewish population! Jews were proud that there was a Jewish conductor who had the authority to ask you to give him your railway ticket.

Well, we've come a long way since then, but somehow we lost the pride on the way. We take it for granted that Jews can pilot planes, own airlines, serve their own meals, adhere to their own traditions, make it feel like home, even at thirty thousand feet in the air. This is not an advertisement for El Al: they have not commissioned me to write this, but it is my opinion and an attitude I want to foster. If we look at what we have and from where we have come, and how much we have achieved, and the blessings that have been bestowed upon us – even if it is only 40 or 50 percent of what we wanted – we are still obligated to be grateful. We are still obligated to say thank you. The more times in our life that we say thank you (in fact, we say it three times a day in our prayers), the better our life is, the more serene we will be. And there will certainly be less tension and frustration with everything that occurs in our mundane world.

Finding a Parking Space

One of the major drawbacks to driving to various destinations here in Jerusalem is that once you arrive (through the always treacherous traffic), there is absolutely no place to park the car. Our holy city has a surplus of many wonderful things, but parking spaces are not on that list. I once walked six blocks in a driving rainstorm to keep a speaking engagement. I could find no closer place. And with the continuing increase in numbers of cars on the Jerusalem streets, there is very little hope for an immediate improvement in the situation.

The fact that large – really large – garbage bins are also placed on the curbs of many streets, occupying a considerable number of potential parking spaces, also complicates matters and frustrates the hapless driver. Who can deny the logic that garbage trumps parking spaces for cars? Parking illegally is an art, but it is also a considerable risk to your pocket and emotional stability. Yet I have observed that there are many Jerusalemites who do so with abandon. I always wonder if they know something that I don't. But my determination to remain a law-abiding citizen prevents me from pursuing this solution to my continual parking problems. I often reconnoiter the place I will be driving to in advance in order to determine the parking possibilities there.

In my opinion, there is a great Jewish moral lesson involved in this difficulty. The Mishnah in Avot asks us to consider "from where you have come, and to where are you going." It also points out that when we get to where we are going – the ultimate destination of all living people – we will be obligated "to park our car," to give a reckoning and accounting of our deeds and actions. The parking space will explain how we got to where we were going, so to speak. I don't think that any illegal parking will be allowed there, no matter how daring, carefree, and intrepid a driver may have been. We may even be forced to park far away from our intended destination.

All of life has to be lived with the goal in mind of where one will be parked in the afterlife, so to speak. It is part of the defensive driving mode that Judaism demands of us. It is the logical conclusion to a long journey of curves, vicissitudes, and dangerous, often reckless, other drivers. Where to park is a paramount question in Jewish thought.

There is terrible additional frustration to the regular problem of parking one's car: often a parking space is available, but you are unable to fit the car into that space. I have been faced with that problem here in Israel, where smaller cars are the norm and my car is a lumbering American "giant." Short of dropping the car in from the air, I am unable to maneuver it so that it will fit into the treasured parking space that I so doggedly discovered. I think of that in moral terms as well. Even if I find my eventual parking space – my accounting and reckoning of my life – will I fit into the space assigned to me?

Rabbi Moshe Chaim Luzatto makes this point abundantly clear in his masterpiece work, *Messilat Yesharim*. He states that even in the World to Come one may feel deprived of what one believed to be proper recognition and honor; one may even feel envious of the parking places assigned to others. So aside from all of the altruistic and idealistic reasons that may motivate us to find a good ultimate parking space, there are also basic human drives and needs that dictate this desire and goal. One should never lose sight of this, for often this is truly the main reason that drives behavior and eternal aspirations.

No one wishes to feel shamed or embarrassed in eternity. A great Talmudic sage asked not to be buried in the white clothing of the truly pious nor in black shrouds of the less pious, lest he be out of place in his eternal resting place. The parking space has to fit the car, otherwise it cannot be used correctly and neatly.

I hope that I have given you some ideas to ponder the next time you are looking for parking.

Lost Keys

A short time ago I was attempting to lock the gates that provide entry into my apartment from the elevator. In my current usual fumbling self, the keys – precious as they are – fell from my hand. There is a very small opening between the edge of the elevator and the floor of my apartment, so small that one hardly takes notice of it. Yet somehow my keys found that aperture, and with a dull thud came to rest at the bottom of the elevator shaft, which is completely inaccessible to me. Now, if I would have tried to throw my keys towards this space hundreds of times I would not have been able to hit that spot between the elevator door and my apartment. Naturally, I had to call the elevator company and have them send someone out to retrieve them. I still do not know how that serviceman was able to do it, but I can happily report that I am again in possession of all of my keys.

This misadventure set me thinking about keys and locks generally, and in a Jewish context specifically. Like everything else in life, one does not realize the importance of keys until one has lost them.

In a physical sense, keys allow us to progress, to go where we wish, to leave or to enter spaces which otherwise are barred to us. All human progress is based on unlocking previously closed doors of science, technology, politics, and the realm of imagination. The "skeleton" key that allows us entry into these areas is the gift of human creativity, the ability to dream and to imagine what is previously unknown and not present in our current life.

The gift of prophecy, which was given to the Jewish people for millennia, is what has allowed the Jewish people to believe – and in our time, to realize – that the forced exile of the Jewish people would end, and that there would be an independent and sovereign Jewish state established once again in the Land of Israel. Without that key of prophetic promise, the locked doors of the exile never could have been opened for us and for our generations. Hope, optimism, and keeping faith with the prophecies were, and are, the keys to our Jewish future.

Despair and a feeling of hopelessness always mark the road of ruin for individuals, societies, and nations. Since our problems often can be overwhelming in scope and in intensity, it is quite understandable that the keys that could help unlock those issues are temporarily lost at the bottom of the elevator shaft of life. Human greatness – as well as the national will and strength of the Jewish people – are based on retrieving those keys and progressing onwards with hope and fortitude.

The Torah identifies these keys for us. Belief in God (and love of God), appropriately compassionate behavior towards other human beings, observance of meaningful ritual, and an optimistic, forward-looking frame of mind adorn the keychain of Judaism and Jewish life. These keys are too precious to be abandoned or lost.

The rabbis have taught us in the Talmud that the questions that a person faces in the afterlife are threefold: 1) Have you dealt honestly and kindly with your fellow human beings? 2) Have you made Torah study, knowledge, and observance a regular part of your routine in life? 3) Have you continued to hope optimistically for redemption and a better world? These are the keys to Jewish life and continuity throughout the ages. We should make every effort not to lose these keys; and even if somehow they drop down the elevator shaft, we have to make every effort to retrieve them.

Unfortunately, much of the Jewish world today is without these keys, and is thrashing about trying to find a way into our past and our future. We should be comforted that, though it may require dedicated search, and even technical and educational help, lost keys eventually do turn up.

A Sore Back

As the luggage spilled onto the moving carousel, I looked intently to find the one suitcase that was still missing from our treasured baggage. Suddenly, I spied the missing bag making its way along the carousel. It was wedged between two enormous suitcases that blocked easy access. Foolishly living in my more robust past, I wrestled with the three bags, attempting to jerk mine from the moving mess. I stretched out fully and attempted to pull my bag off of the carousel, but I was unsuccessful.

A kind, young, strong person who noticed my efforts pursued my bag and freed it from its two imposing neighbors and dragged it off of the carousel. I thanked him profusely for his help, but as I was wheeling my luggage cart out to my waiting taxi I felt a growing twinge in my back. Over the next few days it developed into a more painful ache: it slowed down my motions and impinged on my usual cheerfulness and serenity. There is an old Yiddish aphorism: no matter what position a sick person assumes in bed, he remains uncomfortable. Undoubtedly, this expression refers to backaches and stretched muscles.

Now you will correctly ask, what does this tale of personal woe have to do with Judaism and the Jewish story? Hang on and read the rest of this brilliant piece.

Judaism is a religion of moderation and good sense. The great rule of Maimonides is to avoid extremes in life and behavior. It is the clear rule of law and behavior in Jewish life. (The two exceptions to this rule are that extreme humility and the lack of anger are desirable.) Basically, it teaches us not to overreach, not to exert ourselves in a manner that is beyond our capabilities to achieve. One has to have a realistic picture of oneself, physically, emotionally, and spiritually. Overreaching can create problems and pain.

The Talmud teaches that King Saul overreached himself in his compassion towards Agag, the king of Amalek. Mercy and compassion are enormously necessary and positive attributes. But applied wrongly and emotionally in a situation where the greater long-term good demands a stricter attitude and behavior, self-righteous compassion turns into pain and tragedy, both personal and national. The Talmud also speaks against impatience. Hasty decisions, unrealistic actions, almost always result in aches and pains. Be patient in judgment, the rabbis in Avot advise us.

Letting my bag spin around the carousel until the two larger bags compressing it would be removed would have been a wise, reasoned, and correct policy. But impatience – especially at a luggage carousel after a long flight – is contagious. Attempting to overreach myself in my impatience produced back pains for which the only real cure is time and patience. Ironic how these things work out, eh?

Impatience is what leads to many of the problems that plague our little country. We want things to develop quickly, to have peace now, and to settle all matters quickly. This attitude is really an attempt to badly overreach our abilities and it misjudges our true situation. So we suffer nationally from a very sore back. Perhaps we should let our bag go around the luggage carousel a few more times, until the other heavy bags are somehow removed and it will then be much easier for us to retrieve our own rightful suitcase.

In the religious world we also suffer from overreaching. We expect the highest standard of religious observance and behavior from our secular and converted brethren immediately. We are not interested in the natural gradual process that brings people closer to their faith and tradition. Maximalism rules our street, and the competition to constantly raise the bar is the watchword on the religious street. But this leads to less, and not to more, to exclusivity and isolation, to a counterproductive attitude and its result.

The rabbis teach us in the Talmud, "Attempting to grab too much, too soon, means that one will eventually grab nothing." Grabbing less, wisely, with patience, and a long view of things always is a better policy. Haste and impatience, overreaching and unrealistic assessments of the situation, always lead, at the very least, to painful backaches. Our bodies and physical vicissitudes have much to teach us about life in general and how we should conduct ourselves in all of the challenges that constantly face us.

A Jew in Today's World

Eras

I have often been asked by friends what comparable era in Jewish history we are now living through. That really is much more of a question for a prophet than for someone who is an interested bystander to Jewish history; I feel that it would be most presumptuous for me to give any definitive answer. But since I have been asked so often, I admit that I have given it thought and consideration. So with a strong caveat that I am not certain about any of this being an accurate assessment of our times, I am venturing to share my opinions with you.

I think that our time closely resembles the period of the Shoftim – the Judges and leaders of Israel after the death of Joshua and before the rising of the strong monarchies of Saul and David. The Tanach describes that time as one of disunity in the Jewish nation. A large portion of the people had strayed from Torah observances, beliefs, and values and had aped the culture of surrounding nations. Everyone saw fit to do whatever he thought valid behavior in his own eyes, ignoring tradition and the warnings that the Torah had issued against such deviances from the Jewish mission and way of life. The Judges themselves were harshly criticized, even ridiculed, by the people, and false prophets abounded with their clarion seductive call to "be like all of the other nations." Leadership was weak; the external and internal enemies were numerous and powerful; the Jews were quarrelling (and even fighting) with one another. Dangers to the existence of the Jewish presence in the Land of Israel were ominous.

Sounds pretty familiar, doesn't it? Is this not the daily fare of our newspapers and media? Yes, I think the era of the Shoftim/Judges is repeating itself in general terms right now.

The similarities of that era to our current Jewish society here in Israel are striking. There is a determined group here that despises religion and Torah and demonizes their fellow Jews who do not subscribe to their agenda and "progressive" world outlook. In their eyes, Charedim are "parasites" and "vermin" (in the words of a noted media reporter here) and Religious Zionists are "settlers" – a term of vilification and derision. The extremists on the Left are "heroic" and "peace loving," while all others are only "undermining Israeli security." And there are no moral strictures or social inhibitions to any sort of behavior. Having children and living a traditional family life is derided, while promiscuity and unlimited experimentation with body and soul is exalted. Truly, everyone can do whatever he wishes, and there are no limits placed on behavior, speech, and debate.

Our coalition governments, by their very nature, are weak; and the politicians in the country are not held in high regard, especially in the wake of the sordid scandals that have dogged so many of them. The value systems taught in Israeli schools have little, if any, Jewish content. There is great emphasis on facts – *bagrut* – and little on spirit or loyalty.

But despite all of its gloom, the Book of Shoftim/Judges provides flashes of optimism and hope. There are military victories – Gideon, Deborah and Barak, Samson, etc. – and there are also relative periods of peace and calm in the country, decades long. And there is an obvious longing within the people to somehow return to a status of Torah observance and at least a minimum level of piety, social justice, and comportment. And there are great people waiting in the wings that will reverse all of the negative trends: the prophet Samuel and the kings Saul and David are about to appear on the scene and fight the battles of Israel, both spiritual and physical. They will triumph and ensure the continuity of the Jews and the Land of Israel.

The true test of Israel is its ability to pass through such a period of crisis and despair. Over the ages, and through all trials, the power of belief and resilience has been the greatest asset of the Jewish people. The Book of Judges is but a prelude to the book of Samuel and its story of Jewish greatness in the Land of Israel thousands of years ago. I have no doubt that, somehow, our time of Judges will also lead to an eventual strengthening of Torah wisdom and unity among us.

Departures (2011)

It seems to me that the month after the holidays of Tishrei is always marked sadly by the deaths of notable people. This past month saw how the yeshiva world was struck by the deaths of Rabbi Nosson Zvi Finkel, the head of the Mir Yeshiva in Jerusalem, and Rabbi Dov Schwartzman, a leading Torah scholar and head of the Lakewood East educational institution. There were other losses that also occurred both here in Israel and in the Diaspora. King Solomon's wry comment that "a generation comes and a generation leaves, and the world remains eternally" is significantly true.

The older generation of Torah leadership and scholarship is certainly passing from us. Who the new leaders will be is certainly not yet clear. But there is no doubt, as time inexorably marches forward, that many of the aged current leaders (may they continue to live and be well) will pass from the scene. A new generation is coming, and what shape that generation will take and who will be its acknowledged leaders is hidden from current wisdom and predictions.

Though every generation claims to be the continuation of the one that preceded it – and to a certain extent this is naturally true – the reality is that every generation and its leadership must forge its own tools and methods to meet challenges that newly arise and were not present in previous times. Even though human nature rarely changes and the problems of desire, violence, and dishonesty are constants in the human story of all generations, the circumstances of life and living do change because of new technology, political upheaval, economic dislocation, and new "isms." What was once thought to be a correct response to the challenges of the 1850s cannot be helpful or successful 150 years later.

The Jewish world loves to hold on to ancient disputes and relive battles that were fought and decided long ago. The wars between the Zionists and anti-Zionists, between the proponents of Chassidut and its opponents, between the Bundists and the other leftists, all seem to have been settled by events that have occurred over the past century. Yet the ideological wars continue as though they have true relevance to our situation.

- Now that there are six million Jews living in the State of Israel, the debate – practical, theological, or historical – as to whether that state should have come into existence originally is certainly moot and contributes nothing to guaranteeing the safety of those six million Jews.

- Since the majority of Orthodox Jewry consists of Chassidim and those who are descended from Chassidic stock, it is useless and self-defeating to continue that war. It has been settled demographically over the past number of generations.

- The Left, especially the radical Left, has been responsible for disaster after disaster – economic (look at Europe, the Soviet Union, Mao's China, etc.), social (the Gulag and the defeat of Communism) and diplomatic (The UN and all of the sham issues, conferences, and resolutions that it has fostered). Yet it persists, here in Israel and all over the world, with its pie-in-the-sky demands and proposals, apparently having learned nothing from past failures and mistakes.

It is so hard to let go of ideologies firmly held by previous generations in spite of the fact that they have proven to be wrong headed, unsuccessful, and impractical. The old generation has passed, but the old ideas somehow still hold sway.

It is imperative that the new generation bring with it new ideas. It must formulate practical plans for a better and wider system of Torah education, for stronger family life, and realistic recognition of the human and physical problems involved in marriage and child raising. There must be a confluence of practical steps to strengthen Torah knowledge and observance in Israel and the Diaspora, as well as to create realistic relations with all types of Jews and Jewish organizations.

All of these are challenges that will face the coming generation. Hopefully, that generation will prove wiser and more successful in dealing with them than its predecessors. The "world remains eternally" promises us that there never will be any easy escape from new challenges and difficulties. Every generation is judged by its responses to its specific and diverse problems. The departure of the old, sad and sorrowful as it is, creates the opportunities for those who come after them. Such is the way of the world as ordained by the Master of all of us.

Rabbis' Business (2010)

A recent rabbinic ruling by the chief rabbis of Efrat regarding the sale of cigarettes in their community has, as can always be expected, provoked criticism and discussion. There may be opinions pro and con regarding this specific issue (though I, for one, cannot imagine that smoking tobacco can be beneficial to anyone except the tobacco companies). But what is notable is the underlying tone of this discussion: "Rabbis, mind your own business!"

The argument is not about tobacco sales; it is about rabbis expressing an opinion on matters of public health and concern – a field that rabbis are not "supposed to" deal with in any way. Stick to your books and leave us – the wise men, politicians, and professors – to run everything. Keep your opinions to yourselves and concentrate on the matters given to your authority – kashrut, marriage, divorce, and other matters of ritual. But do not have the effrontery to discuss publicly any matters outside of your particular areas of religious expertise. At least that is the way the situation appears to this old battle-scarred rabbi.

Maybe it is only paranoia on my part, but as I see it, rabbis are a persecuted species who are responsible for everything, but should never attempt to express a public opinion about anything.

The Talmud states that "all matters that pertain to the general welfare of the community are the responsibility of the rabbi." Over the centuries, this injunction has been honored more in the breach than in actuality. Nevertheless, there can be no dispute that respected rabbis influence the policies of the religious parties that sit in our Knesset. We may not always agree with their opinions and advice, but in the religious world one would hope that no one would gainsay their right to express those opinions and advice publicly. Such figures as Rabbi Ovadia Yosef, the late Rabbi Elazar Shach, and the late Rebbe of Chabad have had great influence on particular segments of Israeli and Jewish society, on the general Israeli public, and on world Jewry as well.

Yet there is always controversy not only about what they said but over whether they even had a right to say it publicly and forcefully. When Rav Shach expressed himself regarding a possible settlement with the Palestinians and the dangers of isolation from the non-Jewish world, he was roundly criticized for expressing his views. "Leave our foreign and defense policies up to the experts and don't mix in to what is none of your business" was the media reaction to his words. Well, I don't see why his opinion is less valuable to our current debate on policy than the opinion of all of the so-called "experts" who are always interviewed by our media and have yet to come up with a successful formula for solving these problems.

Rabbis have a legitimate right to express their opinions on matters of public concern. Why shouldn't the rabbis of Efrat tell their community about the dangers of smoking and attempt to persuade the merchants there to discontinue selling death?

In Israel, rabbis have regularly been accused of "incitement" when expressing their opinions on public matters. Left-wing professors in Israeli universities who advocate boycotts of Israel are never accused of "incitement." Rather, they have the sacred privilege of academic freedom and freedom of speech. Apparently they can say anything they wish without being told to mind their own academic business. Are the rabbis any less academic and accomplished than the professors? Present company excluded, I think that they are not.

What lies at the bottom of this self-righteous censorship attempt is the fear that people may actually listen to the opinion of the rabbis, opinions which often contrast to current political correctness and modern lifestyle. Rabbis speak with thousands of years of tradition, Jewish experience, and personal practice behind their words.

One has the choice to hearken to their advice or ignore it. But I believe that *nobody* has the right to challenge their right to express those opinions publicly.

Beliefs and Realities

In matters of faith and religion there is always a struggle between the actualities of life that we physically see and experience and the beliefs that are mostly unable to be seen or proven empirically. To further complicate this matter, one generation's miracle often turns out to be the next generation's science. (See Mark Twain's devastating satire of a book *A Connecticut Yankee in King Arthur's Court* for an example of this.) Yet religion is basically founded on the unseen.

Matters of faith and belief must always overweigh the "real world" with its rationalities and order. Yet a sense of balance and proportion is central to Jewish thinking and a traditional way of living. Historically, overreliance on extreme beliefs that simply have no real basis in Jewish thought and experience has always led to personal tragedy and national disaster. It is not for naught that Maimonides cautioned us against messianic speculations and false messiahs. To the true believer, nothing can shake one's belief, no matter how far-fetched and unsupported by facts and tradition it may be.

Today in the Jewish world there are fringe groups who, in their perfect and unshakable faith, harm us while believing that they are helping us. A little common sense would stand us in good stead.

A smartly dressed, handsome young man came into our synagogue last week, and after the *Maariv* prayers shouted out his messianic beliefs. This naturally brought about a reaction from some of the congregants and a great deal of noisy shouting ensued. I wonder how shouting about one's messianic beliefs in an unfamiliar and definitely non-messianic-centered synagogue can in any way hasten the coming of the messianic era. That thought apparently never crossed the mind of the true believer who initiated this incident. For reality plays no role in the mindset of the misguided few who make so much noise and trouble everyone else.

There is a great brouhaha currently about the erection of a crucifix by local residents of Uman on the site where Jews have come to pray for a number of years on the High Holy Days. To me, why Jews should think that they are welcome in Jewish-blood-soaked, Roman Catholic, anti-Semitic Ukraine is completely incomprehensible. To desert the Land of Israel and leave wives to fend for themselves over the holidays in order to boost the tourist economy of a very hostile society puzzles me in the extreme. In pre-World War II Ukraine, the overwhelming number of Eastern European Jews, Chassidic and otherwise, never wished to visit Uman and never did. But a new custom, deified by the commercial ventures that it has inspired and created, now stands as a core matter of belief – though it clearly flies in the face of all past and present Jewish realities.

There is an ironic Yiddish joke about a rural synagogue from whose precincts a Cossack stole a shofar on Rosh Hashanah. He stood outside the synagogue and attempted to sound it. The Jews in the synagogue were horrified at the thought of a Cossack sounding the shofar on Rosh

Hashanah. Someone attempted to calm them by reminding them that their *Rebbe* had assured them that a Cossack is *incapable* of extracting sound from a shofar. The congregants thought it over for a moment and said: "The *Rebbe* is undoubtedly correct. But what if the Cossack actually does sound the shofar?!"

A prevailing mindset in the fringe groupings of the Charedi community and the extreme Jewish Left is that the State of Israel should never have been *capable* of arising and coming into being. Since it could not have happened, yet did, it is best to ignore it or to fight against it. The reality of its existence over many decades and the fact that over six million Jews populate it today is immaterial to the true believer. It should not have happened according to these belief systems, and therefore it did not happen, all empiric evidence to the contrary notwithstanding.

Reality should not be the enemy of faith. Rather, it should serve as the basis for a stronger and more encompassing faith in the Torah and the One Who guards Israel.

Better Times

One of the more memorable opening lines in English literature is: "It was the best of times, it was the worst of times …"[1] This view of life and current society is a variant on the theme of the half-empty/half-full glass conundrum. In effect, there are always opposing views as to the state of humanity, society, and the Jewish people world over at any given generation.

In the aftermath of the cataclysmic events of the past century, there are two distinctively different narratives regarding our time, Jewishly speaking. One narrative sees our time as far inferior to previous times. This is especially true in the yeshiva-oriented and Chassidic sections of the community. They view life, especially religious life in pre-war Eastern

---

1 Charles Dickens, *A Tale of Two Cities*

Europe, as having been idyllic, holy, and serene. With that model in their minds, they subconsciously view much of what is occurring currently in our society as insufficient and hollow. Whatever we have now is not good enough, imperfect, and politicized, while in the good old days, back there in Europe, all was suffused with piety, holiness, and solidarity. Of course, this view is a fantasy of what was, and it creates an overly pessimistic view of what actually is today. It turns all of the assets of our current times – our teachers, institutions, state, and national independence – into problematic liabilities when contrasted with our imagined fictional past. So the best of times can easily be seen as the worst of times.

The truth is that there is probably far more study of Torah, at least quantitatively, than there was in Eastern Europe before World War II. The Daf Hayomi and other such regular Torah study programs have achieved numbers and popularity previously undreamt of. The numbers of students attending yeshivot and women's seminaries dwarf any such numbers that existed in pre-World War II Jewish society. There are many more Torah journals and books being published than ever before in Jewish history.

Much of the Jewish world was poverty stricken in Europe. Our communities in the Land of Israel and the United States are now much more affluent, comfortable, healthy, and long-lived than one would have ever imagined possible a half-century ago. And despite the resurrection of anti-Semitism the world over, the existence, influence, and stability of the State of Israel gives Jews a rallying point and a potent response to those who wish us ill. In 1900 there were 6,000 Jews in the Land of Israel. In 1920 there were 60,000 Jews there. In 1948, there were 600,000 Jew there. Currently there are more than 6,300,000 Jews living in the Jewish state.

So on many fronts, it seems to any rational observer that the Jewish world is stronger than it was seventy years ago. There is widespread assimilation and alienation present in the Jewish world, but there is no longer the flight from Judaism that characterized Eastern European Jewry in past generations. Atheistic Communism, as represented by the Soviet Union, has disappeared in the main; and today's defection from religion and observance is a product of hedonism and not one of ideology and worldview.

There is a strong Jewish tradition that there is a decline in the spiritual qualities of the Jewish world the greater the time distance from the Revelation at Sinai. This principle may explain the tendency to view the past as superior *in every way* to current conditions. But it is obvious that this idea is limited to individual Torah greatness: if the sages of the past were as angels, then we are humans; but if they were humans, we are but donkeys, and not even the donkey of Pinchas ben Yair (who was able to distinguish between fodder that was tithed and that which was not tithed). It is true that in regard to individual Torah greatness, our generations do not include a Rashi, a Maimonides, or a Gaon of Vilna. There are no equals in our time to the great spiritual scholars and savants of the past.

But there is no question that the *overall* situation of the Jewish people is better now than it was in eleventh century France or eighteenth century Lithuania – far better. And that is an important concept to remember and consider.

Rabbinic Responsibility

As a young rabbi, I prided myself on the fact that for about the first twenty years of my rabbinic career no couple for whom I had performed a marriage ceremony divorced. I began to believe that I had some sort of Heavenly magical power and that simply my performance at a wedding ceremony was a guarantee of a couple living together happily ever after.

This arrogant and unfounded belief has come crashing down upon me over the past number of decades as, unfortunately, a number of couples – who were undoubtedly in love with each other and planned to live together for the rest of their lives – divorced, sometimes in bitterness and acrimony. I have often questioned myself as to whether I bear some responsibility in these later marriage breakups. My rational self exonerates me completely. I am not a prophet, and I did my duty faithfully according to *halachah* and Jewish tradition. The fact that the couple years later decided to end the marriage is not my fault and in no way invalidates the marriage ceremony that I performed.

Untrue as it may be, the myth of rabbinic infallibility has become so entrenched and exaggerated that rabbis are sometimes held responsible for dire consequences. I wish to extrapolate this idea to the current controversy regarding conversions to Judaism performed in good faith and according to the letter of *halachah*. If, decades later, after the actual conversion ceremony (or even a relatively short time later), the convert for whatever reasons is not strictly observant of Jewish law or custom, does that invalidate the previous conversion ceremony itself? It seems self-evident that it could not and should not invalidate that conversion, nor should the rabbinical court that performed the conversion be held accountable for the later lapses in observance of that convert.

The rabbinical court that performs a conversion can only go by what it sees at the moment of the conversion. If it is convinced that the potential convert will lead a Jewish life and observe Torah, it has fulfilled its obligation. It cannot peer into the future and know with certainty how the convert will behave in later life. It can only judge – and this is always subject to the errors that accompany every human judgment – the sincerity and commitment of the potential convert who stands before it at that time.

Overwhelmingly, most converts remains sincere and committed Jews. But there will always be exceptional cases when it becomes obvious that the convert has changed his mind, or at least his mode of behavior. It is a far stretch to try and invalidate the halachically valid conversion process because of the later behavior of the convert.

Retroactive cancellation of conversions was rarely allowed in Jewish tradition and only under dire circumstances. To resort to it today because of dubious reasons is very questionable, and an unfortunate reminder to us of the weakness of rabbinic leadership in our time.

Attributing prophetic and psychic powers to religious leaders often results in great tragedy. Jewish tradition tells us that there are no prophets amongst us, as prophecy disappeared from the scene millennia ago. Those who hold themselves out to be all-knowing run the risk of being responsible for the later behavior of their students, congregants, and the general public that they influence. We were cautioned long ago that "wise men should be careful in their words," and certainly in their deeds. There is no rabbi in the world who has not, at one time or another, made a mistake in judgment, in speech, or in performing religious services.

The fallibility of human beings – even of the greatest human beings – is a well-established principle, with numerous examples recorded for us in the Bible and in the Talmud. We are all responsible for the consequences of our errors; however, the Talmud explicitly teaches us "a judge can only decide upon what he sees at the given moment when he renders his decision."

Heaven eventually may correct all errors, but only Heaven can foretell the future.

Spirituality

One of the more popular buzzwords in current Jewish society is "spirituality." People wish to feel spiritual. Since "spiritual" is a very difficult thing to define, the entire quest for spirituality remains mysterious and vague. My son-in-law and I had a discussion regarding this concept. He pointed out that Jewish tradition concentrates on observance of commandments, study of Torah, acts of kindness, and goodness to others, and words for "spirituality" are lacking. However, there is a strong emphasis, especially in the mystical writings of Kabbalah and the Chassidic movement, on *dveikut* – an "attachment" to the Creator directly, so to speak.

This idea truly represents the concept of spirituality in Jewish life and tradition. Attachment is achieved through prayer, study, and meditation. However, it is most directly achieved through the intellectual realization that an attachment to God can be achieved by the most mundane of acts, if one but frames all the activities and events of life in the concept of serving and connecting one's soul to Him. As such, everyone is capable of achieving spirituality, but each person will achieve it in his/her own way and life experiences. The idea that one can cleave to the Ineffable through one's own human powers and thoughts, and needs no intermediary to connect with God, is a powerful Jewish idea. Ironically enough, this idea is repeated often in the works of the great Chassidic masters; and many of their followers believe them to be their intermediaries to Heaven.

The road to this type of spirituality has been implemented over later generations by the introduction of song and music into the prayer services. Spirituality has also been enhanced by dress codes that help create a feeling of community and solidarity within certain Jewish groups, giving them a sense of stability and connection. This, in turn, can create a feeling of spiritual growth and connection to God.

As the mundane world of reality becomes more and more complex and stressful due to the rapid innovations of technology and the ever-changing variety of social ideas and norms, it is natural for human beings to try and find within themselves some space of serenity and escape. Modern life is so fast-paced, so physically and emotionally stressful, that many people approach a breaking point, even if they are well-off financially. There is a constant nagging feeling within us that, no matter how comfortable our physical lives are, there must be something more than this – there must be a greater meaning to life and to the purpose of our being. This inner drive persists within all of us, driving the search for spirituality.

There are many rabbinic thinkers who are of the opinion that the goal of the search can never be achieved, but the effort itself uplifts us and gives the soul comfort instead of angst. The search can be conducted by many different means, each one fitted to the individual person or group seeking connection to the Creator. Hence the many different groupings and sects within the general Jewish world, and particularly in Chassidic society.

There is a constant demand for renewal of spirituality within the Jewish world and it takes many different forms. Unfortunately, some of them are merely detours that lead nowhere. But there can be no denial that the search for spirituality is an obvious component of modern Jewish life, encompassing the wide spectrum of opinions and beliefs that characterize Jewish people in our time. And there are certainly legitimate pathways to this Godly connection through prayer and activities that emulate His love and caring for every individual. The task for each of us is to develop the awareness that leads to genuine connection.

The educational systems that currently are in place in much of the religious Jewish world place a great emphasis on knowledge, text, and intense study. There is no easy way to become an informed and sophisticated Jew without possessing a great deal of Jewish textual information. There is little discussion of spirituality in the curriculum of our school systems. Even in those institutions that study ethics and mystical thought, Kabbalah and the works of the Chassidic masters of the past, it still remains more of an intellectual pursuit than one of emotion and of the soul.

So in a practical sense, we are left to our own devices in the search for spirituality. Because of this lack of guidance it is understandable that there is a great deal of confusion about the definition of spirituality and certainly about the ways to achieve it.

Much of the strife and division, political and religious, marking our current religious world and the Jewish world generally (and perhaps even the non-Jewish world as well) is the longing for spirituality and connection to something greater than ordinary life itself. It is the emptiness within us that causes us to be so vicious and prickly towards others. Our inner frustration is directed outwards, and we tend to blame others – political opponents, government, other groups and nations, etc. – for our own feelings of frustration and unworthiness.

One should never lose sight of the goal of attachment to Heaven and immortality. And again, it is not only the goal that is important; it is the search and the effort to reach it.

Victimhood

One of the most treasured psychological disorders that people love to retain is victimhood. Feeling that one is a victim, whether one really is or isn't, gives a person a sense of comfort. It is no longer his fault, no matter what he does and no matter what the results of his actions are. He finds comfort in thinking, "Everyone is against me and I'm a victim; therefore I am entitled to feel victimized."

The Jewish people have been victimized regularly over thousands of years. There's no question that terrible things have been done to us unjustly. Yet for centuries one of the greatest attributes of the Jewish people has been that even though we have been victimized, we have never allowed ourselves to feel that we are victims. Because of that resilient attitude, we have been productive. We have looked forward and not backward. We have pushed and strengthened whatever good we could do, and always looked optimistically toward the future.

The Holocaust changed that focus. To a great extent, it has institutionalized victimhood within the Jewish people. Look at all of the Holocaust museums, memorials, and remembrances. It makes us feel again and again that we have been the victims and therefore, so to speak, nothing is our fault; and we don't have to do anything more – just keep reminding the world that we are victims. This is not the attitude of the Torah and it is not the attitude of Jewish tradition. Yes, we have always memorialized sad and tragic events that occurred to our people as a whole. But we have always continued on, and we have risen to create new greatness and rebuild ourselves.

I knew many, many Jews who were survivors of the Holocaust. Some of them were great rabbis, others were simpler people, tradesmen and businesspeople. One of the outstanding features of the survivors of the Holocaust across the board, I think, is the fact that they were resilient. They pushed ahead. They built new families for themselves. They acquired wealth and they rebuilt the Jewish world in the State of Israel and throughout the Diaspora. They did not feel themselves to be victims. They felt that they had been granted life and that they had to exploit that gift and move onward.

The great Rabbi Yosef Kahaneman told me numerous times that he felt that he was saved so that he could rebuild the world of the Lithuania yeshiva in the Land of Israel. He never spoke to me about what happened to him and his family and to his yeshiva in Lithuania. He only spoke to me about what was now happening in Israel, what his plans were, how he intended to push ahead. He said that he was not a victim: he was a survivor, and there is a great difference between those two words and those two concepts. As long as we realize that we are survivors, then what has happened to us can be placed into perspective. If we feel ourselves to be purely victims, that victimhood will haunt us for all of our lives – and even for later generations as well.

The same thing is true on a personal level. All of us suffer reverses in life, tragedies, disappointments, and unexpected negative reactions. The question arises, how do we treat these events? Do we give up because life is unfair, because we have these problems? Because people are often cruel and unjust to us? Or do we push on? Somehow, we must shake off the troubles and forge ahead with our hopes and plans, utilizing our abilities to build better lives for ourselves and our families and for the Jewish people as a whole.

What is gone is gone. What has happened has happened. But what will happen and what will occur is up to us. And we have the ability, the creativity, the talent, and even the material means to construct a stronger Jewish people and, in fact, even a better world. This idea should be emphasized over and over again in our schools and synagogues, in our conversations and in our thoughts.

We should never allow ourselves to become victims of victimhood. That would be the ultimate posthumous triumph that we would give to our enemies, to those who sought to destroy us. And because of that, we have to renew ourselves daily in this idea and in the pursuit of goodness and greatness, which is part of our tradition.

Charitable Giving

One of the hallmarks of Jewish life is charitable giving. The Torah emphasizes this *mitzvah* numerous times; and according to the Talmud, it is one of the identifying features of Jews.

In our time, charitable giving has become more organized, especially in the Diaspora. Most donors never face the indigent person that their money is meant to help. So to a great extent, charitable giving has become impersonal, unemotional, and eventually boring. It may very well be that in our modern society, organizational giving is the efficient and most practical way to go. But its facelessness and blandness deprives both the giver and the recipient of the connection to each other that was part of the Torah's intent in commanding us to participate constantly in giving to others.

In my synagogue there are "collectors" who appear daily at the prayer services to collect charity. Some of these people are clearly collecting money for themselves and their families. Others may be collecting for charity funds that they distribute to the needy. Usually the amount given to these people is a small coin – a half-shekel or a full shekel. But the personal interaction between the giver and the taker makes for a meaningful experience, at least to me. Giving a greater amount to an institution certainly is a significant *mitzvah*, but no matter how worthy and no matter how large the check is, it remains an impersonal experience, often leaving the donor with a feeling of incompleteness.

Having been a fundraiser all of my professional life – for, after all, this is always part of the duties of a communal rabbi – I long ago learned that people give money more readily to other people. Mailings, drives, phone calls (usually annoying ones at odd times of the day) and the other usual methods of fundraising all have a place in our current world of fundraising. But they are never as successful or meaningful as personal visits and contacts.

The Talmud records that Rabbi Akiva was "the hand of the poor." He stretched his hand forward to receive funds to distribute to the needy. People gave to Rabbi Akiva, to his hand, knowing that he represented the poor, but also knowing that they had the privilege to give to a great person – Rabbi Akiva. The most successful fundraisers I have known are people who really and truly care about the donor and his or her welfare as much as they do about the cause or recipient that will eventually benefit from the donation. It is the personal relationship that seals the deal.

I knew a great man who was the executive vice president and leading fundraiser for one of the great institutions of Torah learning in the United States for many decades. He later moved to Israel and became a fundraiser for an Israeli educational institution. When he made his annual fundraising trip to the United States, he visited all of his old clients. Everyone gave their usual donation to his new cause, not because they were particularly enamored with this institution but rather because they were giving *him* their donation. He was their friend, and their giving was motivated by that personal relationship between them.

Basically, we live in a world that is becoming more and more impersonal in many ways. Email and texting have become the favored methods of communication between people. There is nothing more impersonal than this type of communication. And the more impersonal communication is between people, the less likely charitable giving will increase relative to the improving economy and standards of living.

Charitable giving has to be made a value in our society. Education and home practices can advance it. So can personal connections and empathy between all classes in our society. We are taught that "charity can save one from death" – and that applies to both the giver and the taker.

Telling the Truth

The rabbis of the Talmud called this world "a world of falsehood." This fact is so ingrained within us that we suspect that our leaders, political and otherwise, are never telling us the truth. Our political campaigns are based on slogans and promises that we all know to be false – but since these are apparently the rules of the game, we accept them. No politician runs on the truth that taxes have to be raised, deficits have to be closed, and that no one can guarantee an easy life to anyone else. Instead, we are surrounded by promises of rose gardens, unending prosperity, and a chicken in every pot.

Watch what happens when one of our government leaders steps out of line and actually tells us the truth: the reaction from his or her colleagues, the media, and all the professional experts is one of shock and horror. Apologies must be made for telling the truth so that we can continue to flow along the river of falsehoods, even if they eventually will endanger our survival and success. In the "world of falsehood," we really cannot expect a different result in such situations.

Recently a government official here in Israel dared to say that the emperor known as American Jewry has no clothes. There can be no denying the fact that for the vast majority of American Jews, Judaism, Israel, and traditional observance of the Jewish way of life no longer exist. The birth rate of American Jewry, if one factors out the Orthodox population, is insufficient to maintain its weak numbers. The intermarriage rate, again factoring out the Orthodox, encompasses two-thirds to three-quarters of American Jewish youth. The alienation of most Jewish youth in the United States towards any Jewish causes – philanthropic, religious, or communal – is a true and tragic fact. So, when an Israeli government minister noted this situation publicly and warned about the deterioration of Jewish values, and especially the erosion of support for the State of Israel financially and politically, she was immediately castigated by the powers-that-be for having spoken the truth. She had not been politically correct, and she was forced to apologize and restore the fake picture of American Jewry that our leadership continues to assert, even though in their heart of hearts they know that it is false.

The crisis of faith and identity that has beset American Jewry is, in my opinion, the greatest challenge and potential tragedy of our time. American Jews in the main may know that somehow they are the "people of the Book," but they don't know which book. There is little hope for their eventual survival as a vital part of the Jewish people. It is good that someone had the nerve to say so. It is tragic that, instead of supporting that message of truth, all of the sycophants deny it and force unnecessary and very false apologies.

This crisis is very telling regarding the Conservative and Reform movements here in Israel and in the United States. They are witness to their decline in numbers and in Jewish loyalty. Many of their congregations are no longer populated by Jews, no matter what standard of conversion may be applied to them. They have been unable to inspire generations of Jewish children to remain loyal to the Jewish people, no matter what type of rules or observance they espouse. There are very few great-grandchildren, or even grandchildren, within these groups; and their struggle here in Israel against the traditions of the Jewish people that most Israelis, secular or observant, hold dear is really one of the shameful chapters in our current story.

Instead of fighting about location at the Western Wall, should not the battle be against intermarriage, against remaining single, against a declining birthrate, against an abandonment of all moral tenets in the face of popular political correctness?

Admitting the truth is a painful experience, both for the teller and for the listener. For many of us – individually and communally – life is wrapped up in avoiding painful truths. But, at least once in a while, the truth should be publicly stated so that we will realize the true problems that face us and in what direction we should turn.

Defining One's Self

Individuals, societies, and nations are always pursuing the elusive goal of self-definition. God's question to Adam, "Where are you?" can easily be interpreted as "Who are you?" The search for our true inner self is the single most complicated and psychologically difficult pursuit of the human soul.

Many people unfortunately define themselves only in terms of others. They feel that only in differentiating themselves from others or in slavishly imitating the mores and behavior of others can they come to a definition of themselves. The great Rebbe of Kotzk, Rabbi Menachem Mendel Morgenstern (Halperin) pointed out the fallacy of such thinking in his pithy statement: "If I am I and you are you, then I am I and you are you. However, if I am you and you are me, then I am not I and you are not you."

The problems of egocentricity and exaggerated self-esteem are serious personality defects. But low self-esteem and feelings of persecution and paranoia, mental depression, and poor self-worth are even more serious personality problems. The history of the Jewish people has been characterized by the ability of a small, persecuted, and seemingly powerless people to remain proud, steadfast, and resilient in its self-worth and loyal to the truth of its faith and traditions. Individual Jews throughout the ages have fallen off of the wagon and become "others," but the Jewish people as a whole never wavered in understanding its special self-definition. And that has been the true source of Jewish survival over the long and mostly bitter exile of millennia.

The main obstacle, as I view it, in the decades-long struggle with our Arab neighbors is that they define themselves almost exclusively in terms of the "other" – namely, the Jews and the State of Israel. There is no real drive within them to create a state of their own. They only want to destroy and inherit our state. Their educational system is based almost exclusively on incitement and hatred towards Jews. There is no drive to initiate a productive culture of their own, or an economy independent of UN and

European Union largesse and handouts. Destruction of the "other" is not a basis for positive self-identity or nation building. No resolution passed by the United Nations General Assembly can in any way contribute to any form of self-definition.

As the words themselves indicate, self-definition, self-worth, must arise from one's own self. Many revolutions, while initially successful, descend into chaos, anarchy, and violence, ending up as tyrannies simply because there is no basis for further development of self-worth after the "other" has been eliminated. That was the reason for the failure of any Arab state to arise next to Israel over the past decades; and that continues to be the reason that prospects for any sort of resolution of the Israeli-Arab dispute in the near future remains very unlikely. It is not only that we don't have a partner to deal with. It is that our proposed partner does not know what its goals are except for the destruction of the State of Israel. It is well-nigh impossible to conduct meaningful negotiations under such circumstances.

To be a Jew requires a clear sense of self-identity that can be achieved only through a basic knowledge of Judaism and tradition. Knowing the story of our people can contribute to this necessary sense of self-identity that guarantees the Jewish future. Unfortunately, many in the Jewish world define themselves currently in terms of vague, high-sounding humanistic values, which do not relate to the practicalities of the world that we live in – certainly not to the position of the Jewish people and state in that world. Such Jews again define themselves in terms of the "other," and the result is that they eventually become that "other" and are lost to the Jewish fold.

More sadly, those who become the "other" have a terrible tendency to criticize and incite hatred, eventually destroying not only the object of their hatred but the haters themselves. Jewish history is littered with the debris of those who lost their self-definition and forgot that "I am supposed to be I, and you are supposed to be you" – the arrangement that guarantees mental and social health for both the "I" and the "you."

Stepping Out

One of the great dilemmas that plague any individual is his or her relationship to the surrounding community. What if the standards of culture and behavior of that general community do not match those of the individual concerned? Is one entitled to withdraw from the community because of this divergence of views and beliefs? What is one's responsibility to a community that does not meet one's standards and expectations?

These are important issues especially relevant to everyday Jewish life in Israel. A large section of Israeli society, principally – though not exclusively – Arab and Charedi, has no connection to the society at large or to the national agenda. In Jewish life in the Diaspora, this situation has occurred before, and no unanimously satisfactory solution was found there. I think that it will be no less difficult to find some sort of solution in our Jewish national state.

The inclination to step out of the general society is very strong in the Jewish psyche and collective memory. Though this attitude exists in all sections of Jewry, it is manifested especially in the society of religious Jewry, where the splitting into small individual groupings has become the norm. Large synagogues are no longer the usual house of prayer. Instead, there are hundreds of small prayer groupings, each one contributing little sense of unity or community support to larger Jewish society. This is the situation all over the Jewish world today – here in Israel and in the Diaspora as well.

In the nineteenth century, the Reform movement swept German Jewry into its agenda. At that time, many thousands of Jews chose to advance in German society by converting to Christianity. Reform ironically saw itself as a force against such a wave of conversions. Leadership and control of the *kehillot* – the Jewish communities – of Germany, which were part of the mandatory governmental organization of those communities, passed into the hands of Reform. The general membership as well as the majority of the members of the *kehillah* was

Reform. The leaders of the *kehillot* were willing to meet the communal needs of the remaining Orthodox minority, but the general agenda of the community was clearly in line with the programs of German Reform Jewry of the time. The question that faced German Orthodox Jews was whether to remain part of the general *kehillah* system or not.

In Frankfurt-am-Main, Rabbi Samson Raphael Hirsch established his famous *austritt* community. *Austritt* literally means "to step out." Rabbi Hirsch's community left the Reform-led Jewish *kehillah* of Frankfurt and established its own independent *kehillah* in place of it. However, great rabbis disagreed with Rabbi Hirsch's approach, foremost among them Rav Yitzchak Dov Bamberger and Rav Azriel Hildesheimer. The majority of Frankfurt's Orthodox Jews did not follow Rabbi Hirsch's *austritt* community, but remained part of the government-recognized community, even though its agenda and leadership were not in accord with their traditional beliefs and lifestyle. In Eastern Europe, Rabbi Naftali Zvi Yehuda Berlin warned against following Rabbi Hirsch's lead in the Lithuanian communities that were beginning to be dominated by secularists. He wrote strongly against separating from the general community, saying that this type of division among Jews led to the destruction of the Second Temple.

So here we have the two divergent views on how to deal with the problem of belonging to a society or national government that runs counter to our sensitivities, goals, and lifestyle. It seems that the view of Rabbi Hirsch has triumphed in our time. There are undoubtedly various reasons as to why this view has prevailed. The bitter seeds of centuries of secular-religious strife have developed poisoned fruit. The example of the successful "stepping out" of the Chassidic movement in the eighteenth century has undoubtedly strengthened the tendency to step out.

The bitter struggle over Zionism which consumed the Jewish world in pre-war Europe and America, as well as in the Land of Israel, has unfortunately not ended with the emergence of the State of Israel. One would have hoped for greater wisdom and harmony among all concerned at this point. One would have thought that by now we would all realize that we are all together in the same boat: in the middle of a voyage there is no option of "stepping out."

I hope that with new opportunities and challenges, a greater sense of tolerance and togetherness will govern in our society, leading to meaningful accomplishment and progress.

Loose Change

One of the most clichéd words that mark election campaigns is "change." Because it is a basic human drive to seek change for the better in one's personal life and in the national life of one's country, the promise of change is a potent political and psychological weapon. It is always exploited by those aspiring to power.

There is a basic feeling of dissatisfaction with the present situation that fuels our desire for change. We long for the good old days, even though they may not really have been so good. We instinctively resort to nostalgic, and often fanciful, memories of the past. So to some people change means reverting to those imagined glory years. At the same time, we dream great dreams about an idyllic future where all current problems will be resolved with a magic solution. This vision also drives our desire for change, and even eventually justifies wickedness, slander, violence, and lawlessness in the attempt to facilitate that hoped-for change. Both Jewish and general history are replete with examples of these types of behavior – all in the name of bringing about the desired positive change.

Yet King Solomon in Kohelet taught us that change is very difficult to achieve. He stated that "what was is what will be," in that human nature is pretty much unchangeable; and therefore complete change is an ephemeral and almost unattainable goal. The desire for change – any change at any cost – is a potent example of human arrogance and hubris. We are all convinced that we can change the world and refashion it in our image and according to our values and aspirations.

History mocks us in this belief. The problems that face the world generally, and the Jewish people particularly, are the same ones that existed thousands of years ago. Many of the proposals for change heard today are merely the recycled theories of the past dressed in new language and implemented by new technology. Change does occur, but it is a process; and processes take time, patience, and tenacity. The changes in Western society wrought by the ideas of the Enlightenment have taken almost five centuries to be fully absorbed in the Western world.

The attempt to achieve instant change, which is what our politicians always promise us, is futile simply because change requires time and deliberate patience. Historically, hasty and revolutionary change in the main has proven to be more destructive than beneficial. Societies where change is fostered from the bottom up (rather than from the top down) are able to experience the type of change that is most lasting and positive. Forced change, whether by fiat or legislation, rarely is able to survive the test of time.

Over the last century, there are a number of prime examples of how this forced change – immediate and radical – though initially successful, eventually collapsed because of the inability to change the nature of human beings. The Soviet Union enforced a radical change on the peoples of Russia and most of Eastern Europe. For seventy-five years this new way of life ruled, enforced by a police state and draconian methods. But atheism, lack of private property, state control of thought, and everything else are all contrary to basic human nature. The Soviet system collapsed of its own weight in a sudden and unexpected fashion a quarter of a century ago.

After World War I, Mustafa Kemal Ataturk ruthlessly transformed Turkey from a Muslim caliphate into a Western, completely secular, modern country. This change, laudatory as it may have looked through Western eyes, has also collapsed in our time. Instead, we see Turkey again as an aggressively Muslim country with caliphate ambitions that it barely hides.

So when we contemplate change in our society we should bear in mind that it is a process that takes time and deep public acceptance. Otherwise, every attempt to change, no matter how seemingly positive and necessary it may appear to be, rarely will be of lasting consequence or value. It must be deeply personal and societal in its origin for it to take hold.

The old joke – "How many psychiatrists does it take to change a light bulb? One, but the bulb must want to be changed" – is a true comment on personal and national life.

Our Miracle Minyan

The main *Shacharit* service in our congregation is at 6:45 AM. This early time proved very inconvenient to me and to a few others, so the synagogue graciously allowed for a second service later in the morning to accommodate us. It is now close to ten months since we initiated the second service, which begins at 7:45 AM. During that time, I do not recall even one morning when we did not have the necessary ten people for the service to take place.

There were many close calls and many times I despaired of finding that tenth person to complete our core. But every time somehow ten people did eventually show up and join us for morning prayers. What to me is amazing is that, to the best of my knowledge, this *minyan* has never had the same people every day. Naturally, at times there are people who travel or are under the weather and are missing for the morning count. Nevertheless, it is amazing that we always have different people showing up to comprise our core on a regular daily basis. Some of these people I recognize from the neighborhood; they must have some particular reason that morning for attending our service instead of the synagogue where they usually pray. However, many of the people who comprise our quorum are one-timers that I do not know and perhaps will never again see in our synagogue. But they always seem to turn up just when we need them, contributing to our unbroken streak of regular morning services.

Every synagogue and every *minyan* has its own good fortune. Even in times of bad weather this winter, our *Shacharit* service never missed a beat, for someone always showed up to pray with us. Many of these wonderful people just came, prayed, and left without saying a word or identifying themselves. It was as though they dropped from Heaven to pray to Heaven and then go about their daily tasks. Sometimes I have felt that one of these strangers frequenting our services was really an incarnation of the prophet Elijah.

In Jewish tradition and legend, Elijah shows up when necessary to help individual Jews or the Jewish people at a critical moment. Elijah never looks like Elijah. He comes in various forms and shapes, sometimes appearing as a drab beggar and sometimes as a distinguished stranger from a far distant land. But as far as our morning *minyan* is concerned, he always does show up.

So, in my mind, this 7:45 AM service is a miracle *minyan*. Every morning I arrive about fifteen minutes before the service is scheduled to begin with an air of anticipation, trepidation, and a touch of mystery. Though the situation always looks bleak, I wonder who is going to show up this morning to pray with us? Is this morning going to produce the twenty or more people that we sometimes have, or will we have to sweat it out waiting for the minimum number to arrive?

I have decided that this exercise in anticipation is really a test of faith. I am convinced that there are more than enough people available for the *minyan* to be guaranteed easily without stress and worry. But that would diminish the reward for the establishment and continuation of this second *Shacharit* service, for things that come easily are not usually of great worth or appreciable longevity.

We all need a reminder that miracles do happen to us on a daily basis, even if they go unnoticed and unappreciated. Perhaps now that I have revealed that this 7:45 AM service is a miracle *minyan* more people will avail themselves of the opportunity to share in its wonder.

Unfinished Business

I have often been perplexed by the statement of the rabbis in Avot that "it is not incumbent upon you to complete the work," for there is another Talmudic statement that if one begins to do a good deed one should persevere to complete it. So what should be our attitude towards unfinished business? Should one begin a project when it may be clear that one will be unable to be complete it in one's lifetime?

And we have another statement of the Talmud about a man who was planting a tree that would take seventy years to mature and produce fruit. When he was asked why he was doing so – for in the course of human mortality he would not live long enough to benefit from the tree – he answered that his forefathers had planted such trees before him; therefore he was planting such a tree for the benefit of later generations.

Yet psychologically speaking, there is an emptiness in creating a project or pursuing a goal, spiritually or physically, which will never be realized in one's lifetime. Because of our mortal nature, we are always short-term and short-range creatures. We are determined to complete what we have begun, and if we feel that we will not be able to do so we are more than willing not to begin it all. I feel that this attitude – common, and even practical as it may seem on the surface – is inherently wrong and, in fact, not very Jewish.

I once heard from the great Rabbi of Ponevezh, Rabbi Yosef Kahaneman, that he felt that one should always be engaged in a new project, no matter what his stage of life. He said to me that if Heaven is aware that one is engaged in a new project that would benefit the Jewish people and the world at large, that effort would gain advocates in Heaven for him who would argue that he be allowed to continue to live in order to fulfill that project. He said he was always engaged in building a new yeshiva or children's home, even though he did not really have the funds for it; nor was he certain that at his age he would survive long enough to witness the completion of the project, even if somehow the funds would be available.

So unfinished business is good business in the Jewish world and in the eyes of Jewish tradition. One should always have new ideas and plans for personal growth and communal benefit. I have noticed that some of the great financiers and entrepreneurs in today's business world are people who are advanced in years. Nevertheless, they remain active in their fields and look forward to achieving even greater wealth and power. As this is true in the tawdry world of money and business, it must certainly be true in the exalted word of the spirit and noble accomplishments.

Judaism teaches that every human being is constantly "dealing" in eternity. The fact that we are mortal and limited in time only emphasizes that in actuality we are dealing with eternal values, as well as long-range goals and achievements. Those who dreamt of a Jewish state in the Land of Israel a century ago certainly did not expect to see it in their lifetime. They envisioned it for their descendants and for later generations.

Behind the scenes, often out of our consciousness, this impetus of eternity governs everything in Jewish life and makes everything that we endeavor to do meaningful; and it elevates even the most mundane of efforts and plans to be instruments of eternal value. The Talmud tells us that we should attempt to finish what we can, but we should never lose sight of the fact that we are dealing with eternity and that there is no negative side to leaving over unfinished business for other generations to complete. And to me, this is a most comforting and satisfying thought.

In the Diaspora

Ignoring Realities

By our very nature, the Jewish people are an optimistic and hopeful people. We believe that things will get better, that we can and will have a rosier future, no matter how dismal and discouraging current affairs may be. I have always regarded myself as an optimist, and since I have seen many outstanding miracles and accomplishments in my lifetime, I feel that my optimism was correct and valid.

But I was born in Chicago – and after witnessing the difficulties and vicissitudes that have always visited that city and its sports teams – I retain a streak of realism that tempers my attitude about the present or the future. I feel justified in stating that I am very concerned about the future of American Jewry. I speak not only regarding the spiritual and religious demise of over half of the American Jewish population; I am worried about its physical security as well.

Even though there currently seems to be little threat of physical violence to Jews in the United States, I nevertheless sense an undercurrent of resentment against Jews that (God forbid) under circumstances that we cannot predict or control could be fanned into the fire of hatred and discrimination against them. Anti-Semitism is alive and well, having morphed into anti-Israel and BDS movements and organizations. This is especially true on college campuses throughout the United States; and as these movements grow and intensify, the danger to the American Jewish community becomes more apparent. What is most ironic is that there are many Jews who are the leaders and supporters of these destructive forces. If, God forbid, they continue to grow and have influence, even the most secular, leftist, anti-Israel Jew will also find that he or she is still Jewish. If the Holocaust taught us anything, it is that when the demon is loosed it does not differentiate between types of Jews.

I recently attended a gathering at the home of some friends of mine. The meal was in honor of grandchildren who had recently married and were celebrating the week of their marriage. The conversation at the table turned to the future of American Jewish life – a topic that seems to consume many Americans who have immigrated to Israel but still have children or close relatives living in the United States. Many around the table expressed misgivings about the future of Jewish life in America, and even about the security of Jews, their property, influence, and participation in American life generally. There is no doubt that Jews are disproportionately represented in the Left and progressive sector of the American public. There is also no doubt in my mind that the numbers, wealth, influence, and political clout of Jews in American life is exaggerated both in the Jewish and non-Jewish communities.

I was seated next to an American young man who was Charedi in dress and outlook. He was very cordial and friendly to me, as I was to him. My dinner companion cavalierly told me that there was nothing to be worried about since there were so many yeshivot in America: such a large amount of Torah being studied guarantees the preservation of the Jewish community there.

I debated with myself as to whether or not I should respond to that rather naïve claim. My rabbinic instinct told me to be quiet, whereas my historic sense of reality demanded that he must hear a different view of the matter. I finally said to him that there were greater yeshivot in Babylonia, Spain, North Africa, Iraq, France, Germany, Poland, Romania, Lithuania, Belarus, and the Czech Republic in past times than there are in the United

States today. And yet the Jewish communities in all of those countries of our dispersion are no longer in existence or of influence in the Jewish world of today. My companion was shocked at my statement of heresy. But I saw that I had struck a nerve that he did not realize was in him.

Belief is fundamental to Jewish life and to every Jew. However, reality also must play a role in how we view personal and national decisions that life and history force upon us. We cannot afford to ignore the reality that exists within the societies in which we live. The lessons of Jewish life over the past century should never be forgotten.

Hostages and Captives

The issue of the redemption of Jewish hostages and captives from enemy hands is unfortunately a very old and painful one. The Mishnah in Gittin records that even though the commandment of redeeming captured Jews is one of top priority – demanding that even holy artifacts be sold to raise funds for such a purpose – we are forbidden to pay an exorbitant price to secure the freedom of a captive. In an age when hostages and captives were sold on the slave markets of the world, it was relatively simple to judge what was an "exorbitant" price demand.

But in our times the criterion of what is considered an "exorbitant" price for the release of a Jewish prisoner is very difficult to establish. The Israeli army and government has had to deal with this painful problem quite a number of times over the past decades. The goal has always been to return the captive home in the best condition possible. Poignant, often heated, debate accompanies this situation, and I am grateful that such terrible decisions are not mine to make. Many have said that the past prices paid were "exorbitant." Others say that the price was justified. Perhaps only Heaven can decide on such impossible Hobbesian choices.

Jewish history is replete with incidents of hostages and captives. In the thirteenth century, the great Rabbi Meir of Rothenburg was taken hostage by one of the local dukes. Rabbi Meir was one of the prominent Ashkenazic scholars of the Middle Ages. He was the mentor and teacher of Rabbi Asher ben Yechiel (Rosh), the greatest of the latter Tosafists, and one of the basic decisors of halachic law. The duke demanded a huge ransom for the release of Rabbi Meir. The Jewish communities of the area, out of their great love and respect for Rabbi Meir and their loyalty to Torah scholars, were prepared to pay this exorbitant sum. However, Rabbi Meir himself forbade the Jews from so doing, arguing, undoubtedly correctly, that payment of the ransom would only encourage the duke to repeat his evil deed, with even Rabbi Meir himself becoming the victim a second time. (Under his mentor's advice, Rabbi Asher fled the German area and took up residence in Toledo, Spain.)

The duke did not relent on his extortionist demands and in 1293, after seven years of imprisonment, Rabbi Meir passed away in the castle prison. The duke then demanded the very same ransom for the release of Rabbi Meir's body for Jewish burial, also a cardinal principle and commandment in Jewish life and law. Again, according to the wishes of Rabbi Meir as he expressed them during his last years of life, the ransom was not paid. The duke held the body for thirteen years. Eventually, a very wealthy Jew, Alexander Ben Solomon Wimpfen, came to a settlement with the duke and Rabbi Meir was buried in the ancient Jewish cemetery of Worms (Rhineland). Next to his grave lies the body of Wimpfen. These two graves in the Jewish cemetery remained a place of Jewish visitation and veneration even until our very day.

During the reign of the czars of Russia during the nineteenth century, many rabbis and Jewish public figures were arrested, almost always on trumped-up charges of disloyalty or illegal monetary transactions. Enormous efforts were made to obtain their freedom, often by exerting political and diplomatic pressure on the Russian government from other world powers. Bribing corrupt police and government ministers was also employed to secure the release of these prisoners. But again, there was a great hesitation to pay "exorbitant" prices to the czar and to his cohorts for the release of the arrested prisoners. The decisions regarding these cases were basically ad hoc, depending on the exact circumstances of each case. But the problem of an "exorbitant" price always remained with us till our day.

Judaism abhors simplistic answers to very complicated problems and issues. There has never been a simple answer to the question of ransoming Jewish prisoners or hostages. Obviously, there is no simple answer to this issue today. If and when these challenges arise (God forbid), we can only pray for wisdom, patience, balanced behavior, and Godly inspiration to help us arrive at the correct decisions.

Uber

During a recent visit to the United States, I employed the services of Uber for the first time. I had previously used a local taxi company to drive me around the New York area. Its cars were old, sometimes even decrepit, but I found it to be somehow comfortable, and it worked. Maybe that's because I am also old and somewhat decrepit.

On my previous visit to the United States, however, this taxi company sent me a driver who was a fanatical Christian missionary. He insisted on playing missionary propaganda – at considerable volume – depicting heaven and hell and their inhabitants, for the entire time that I was in the car. He had recognized me as being Jewish, and he obviously wanted to bait me into a conversation with him. I remained silent the entire trip, leaving him frustrated and tip-less. Because of this experience, I decided not to risk using that taxi company again. So on this trip, I took the plunge to use Uber. My office set up an account for me, and I entered into the modern era.

Uber has a genius business plan going for it. It provides fast and efficient service and decent automobiles, and there is no necessity for cash or immediate payment to the drivers. Uber takes payment out of the passenger's credit card. Tipping is optional, though the company ostensibly has a "no tipping" policy. In the New York area, my experience was that Uber drivers were courteous, clean, and skilled drivers. It also seemed that they were all first-generation immigrants from Asia, Africa, or South America. Almost none of them spoke understandable English. This made for a quiet and relaxing drive, since there could be only minimal communication between us. They all use their cell phone apps and GPS to get to the destination, so they need not ask any questions. When one books with Uber, the destination is automatically inserted into the driver's phone, and off we go.

There was a period of time when a New York Yellow Cab medallion was worth well over a million dollars. That was because the number of such medallions issued was kept artificially low, and taxi service, especially in Manhattan, is almost a necessity of life. In fact, investing in Yellow Cab medallions was an accepted form of long-term investment, with a guaranteed retirement pot at the end of the rainbow. Uber has upended this arrangement, and the value of a Yellow Cab medallion in New York has declined by about 70 percent. Naturally, this turnabout has caused great anguish among the medallion owners, but such is the nature of capitalism: it drives previously successful and wealthy companies into bankruptcy when those companies are rendered obsolete by advancing technologies and creative new ideas.

Interestingly enough, again in my own personal experience, the rates and cost of using Uber are lower than they were for my previous taxi company or any car service. And the best part of it is that now I never worry about whether I have sufficient cash in my pocket to pay for the trip at its conclusion.

Uber has become an international company because its method of doing business is easily transferable to different countries and societies. It has an Israeli counterpart, which is not named Uber but operates under the same principle of smartphones, credit cards, and a cashless business. In Israel, the relationship between taxi drivers and their clients is much more personal than it is in the United States – again, this is only a personal assessment – and therefore I continue to use my friendly taxi driver of the last twenty years whenever I can. Somehow, he has become a member of my family, far more than a means of transportation to me. I do not know whether this is true generally of Israeli society, but I do not envision the old taxi business, based on such personal relationships, becoming obsolete as quickly here as it did in the United States.

This pattern may only be generational, though, for I do notice that my grandchildren here in Israel use the Uber counterpart regularly and almost exclusively. So I expect that eventually the Uber concept will come to dominate Israel as well.

My father was born before the Wright brothers flew an airplane, and he lived to see human beings on the moon. And in my lifetime, the changes that I have witnessed are so enormous that I often feel that I have lived through three or four different centuries. As a child growing up in Chicago at the end of the Great Depression, I still remember milk being delivered to the front stoop by horse and wagon. I have also seen science fiction turn real, and old established firms disappear in the face of the brash, new, technologically connected world.

Uber is simply symbolic of these profound changes in civilized society. Would that we would be able to change human beings and their behavior as easily and speedily as we are doing in commercial and technological fields.

A Tale of Two Seats

I recently flew to the United States from Israel. For various undoubtedly good and sundry reasons, of which I was unaware – though many of my fellow passengers who "know" everything about everything had various conflicting stories as to the cause – El Al was flying a Portuguese airplane and crew on this flight. So the airplane was not the one I was familiar with on my other El Al flights, and my seat, though business class (no longer a luxury for me at my age) felt less comfortable than I was accustomed to. Undoubtedly, it was me and my mood that made for my feelings of discontent rather than the dimensions of the seat itself. It was probably the same business class seat as on El Al.

Beginning a twelve-hour flight in an unpleasant position is not a harbinger of joy about the forthcoming flight. But I convinced myself that I should stop kvetching about nonsensical matters and just get on with it. As I finally adjusted myself, my hat, my jacket, and my carry-on to my situation on the plane, a young man, a former student of mine in my yeshiva in Monsey (now the head of a very successful "American" yeshiva in Jerusalem), appeared before my eyes. We exchanged warm greetings and he informed me that he had a seat in the first class section of the airplane due to his many frequent flyer miles. He insisted that I exchange seats with him. I at first demurred – it is not my nature to occupy a seat that I have not paid for – but he was persistent. He pointed out that he was younger, thinner, and more agile than I am currently; and so I ended up in a much more comfortable seat in the first class section of the airplane.

There are a number of important life lessons that I have learned from this seemingly innocuous and mundane incident.

1. First class is distinctly better than business class. Whether it is worth the extra price is debatable for every individual's wallet and travel tastes; but when offered a free upgrade to first class seating, one should take advantage of it. I imagine that there is a first class seating section in the immortal world as well. We should all try to earn that upgrade.

2. I was reminded how careful and positive one should be with one's students, especially in the formative high school years. I don't know how many of his family and peers would have predicted when he was in ninth grade that someday he would head a yeshiva in Jerusalem, or that he would help his old teacher with a gesture of generosity that surpasses any material gift. Because of my ex-student, I spent a long and otherwise very boring flight in pleasant reminiscences and with a feeling of accomplishment that is so rarely present in our lives.

3. One has to feel that one really belongs in first class to truly enjoy being seated there. The stewardess had to get special permission from the purser to serve me the first class meal instead of the business class meal ordered for me. She did so in a loud-enough voice that the other passengers in the first class section all realized that I was an interloper, sitting where I really did not belong. I was comforted with the realization that some of them, too, were there only because of upgrades, and not because they actually paid the outrageous fare for the seat. Nevertheless, I have never in my life been a social climber nor attempted to project myself onto a stage where I was not invited and did not belong. So my joy at being seated in first class was certainly tempered by my realization of how I had gotten to sit there.

Anyway, I will be happy when El Al stops flying Portuguese airplanes on its routes.

Jewish Education in the Age of a Godless Culture

Judaism, and hence any form of Jewish education, has always had to swim upstream against the currents of the surrounding cultures where Jews resided. Even though these cultures in the main were very hostile to us, Jews were able to navigate that river of ideas and norms successfully, in part because the surrounding culture in almost all instances was based upon the idea that there was a God – or at least other supernatural powers or gods – that influence and often determine the conditions of human life. In a world where the idea of God was prevalent, it was possible for Jewish education to focus on the uniqueness of Judaism, of Torah values and observances, and the essential "chosen" character of the Jewish people for its special mission in the world.

But now, in this twenty-first century of Western civilization, we are living in a godless society. The ascendant Left controls much of the thought and educational systems in Western society. God is not mentioned, even forbidden to be mentioned, in most of the public educational systems. So it should be no surprise that atheist attitudes and culture have written God out of all the classrooms and schoolbooks.

And this trend has had a devastating effect upon Jewish education as well, even in the most allegedly God-fearing communities and schools. Lip service is paid to prayer, but to our very great detriment God is not found readily in the hearts and minds of our students.

Please forgive an old man for nostalgia and reverence for the past. When I attended yeshiva high school long ago in Chicago, God was an ever-present participant in all of our classes, whether in Talmud or chemistry or physics. Even the non-Jewish teachers who taught us secular studies were people to whom God was a reality: they always spoke of the wonderment and exactitude of nature as indication of the presence of God in the world. I will admit that the study of Jewish history then was pretty dry, boring, and uninspiring. But if one stuck it out the entire four years of classes, as I did, the sheer irrationality of the story of the Jewish people began to resonate as the guiding hand of Heaven shepherding, challenging, and disciplining a special people on a special mission.

The books of the holy prophets of Israel were always taught with reverence and relevance. Our teachers, all Eastern European Jews and few of them blessed with academic credentials, were able to communicate to us that these prophecies and ideas were not just ancient moral mantras, but that they were meant for us. Even sections of Rashi's commentary that were purely grammatical were taught to us from the perspective of learning the holiness and precision of the Hebrew language. And when we studied Talmud, we did not skip over the sections of Aggadah. In fact, we came to realize early on that Aggadah was a primary tool for introducing God into the classroom, making the Divine presence real in our studies and eventually in our lives.

In our godless time, neither the words of the prophets of Israel, nor Rashi's grammatical probings, and certainly not the aggadic digressions in the Talmud are given adequate time nor place of honor. We are wholly devoted to demonstrable knowledge, facts, exams, and scholastic marks. The inner spirit and beauty of Judaism is lost.

In the nineteenth century, both the Chassidic and Mussar movements injected life and spirit into Jewish schools as well as into the Jewish street. Movements today are more institutionalized, frozen in time, and have much less influence than they once had. I think it fair to say, though, that the presence of God is emphasized to a greater extent in the Chassidic classrooms than elsewhere.

Our schools and homes are the last bastions of defense against the overwhelming culture of godlessness and hedonism that now dominates the Western culture. This form of destruction has already consumed millions of Jews the world over.

Defeating the enemy first requires identifying it, and this is, in my opinion, the vital role that our Jewish schools can perform. It is a critical step to ensure the survival of the eternal people with its core beliefs and value systems. From there, we can work to bring God back to the hearts and minds of our children, and ourselves.

Modern Orthodoxy

In a thought-provoking article appearing in the *Jerusalem Post* (May 2004), Samuel C. Heilman, a noted sociologist who specializes in studying the Orthodox Jewish world in the United States, described the changing attitude of "modern Orthodox" Jews. As he wrote there, "increasingly they were influenced by their haredi co-religionists and began leaning back toward the right wing." Heilman posits four main causes for this shift in attitude towards a more intense, isolated, and closed Orthodox community. The causes he cited are, in my opinion, absolutely correct.

- The precipitous decline of general American moral behavior and culture, especially in dress, speech, and entertainment;
- the influence of Charedi teachers in all Jewish Orthodox schools, and the influence of those schools on the children of the "modern Orthodox" – mainly due to the abandonment of parental influence on education to the schools and yeshivot;
- the decline in the number of talented "modern Orthodox" rabbis and educators in the field; and
- the experience of many "modern Orthodox" teens in their year or two of study in Israel, which strengthens them in religious practice and exposes them to a more rigid view of Orthodoxy and its values.

However, I believe that there are other, more subtle, causes as well. These may help explain, and even justify, this turn to the right within the ranks of the modern Orthodox.

The yeshiva and Chassidic societies in North America have successfully co-opted much of modern Orthodoxy's agenda and promised achievements. Just as Rabbi Samson Raphael Hirsch undermined the claims and achievements of nineteenth century Reform Judaism by achieving those same goals for his constituents without sacrificing their loyalty to Judaism and Torah observance, so too has the Orthodox right brought the benefits of American life to its constituency without risking undue exposure to the undermining lifestyle and value system of that society.

Instead of risking their youth in coed college dormitories and exposure to all of the "alternates" that abound in the academic world today, the right has developed its own system of granting bachelor's degrees to its men and women in its own Orthodox institutions, and then allowing its students to continue in recognized graduate and professional schools where the risks to Jewish spirit and soul are much less than in undergraduate colleges. Thus the right-wing Orthodox world has many professionals in its ranks, and no yeshiva or seminary student feels precluded if he or she desires to obtain a professional career in almost any field. All this, without their feeling that they have to make any major compromises in their value system, daily Torah studies, or personal lifestyle – compromises which unfortunately have plagued many of their modern Orthodox brothers and sisters.

Another cause for the shift to the right is that the right has proven to be much more dynamic and creative in addressing the true needs of Orthodox Jews in particular, and the Jewish community in general, than has the modern Orthodox community. Hatzolah, OHEL, Mishkan, Chai Lifeline, ArtScroll, *Yated Ne'eman, Hamodia*, Ohr Somayach, Aish Hatorah, Hineni, Gateways, Torah Umesorah, Partners in Torah, JEP, JLE, medical referral organizations, Shabbat homes near hospitals, daily *Minchah* services in major workplaces, convenient Jewish bus and transportation companies, and numerous other services, organizations, and institutions are all creations of the right, which now serve all Jews.

The modern Orthodox community, which uses all of these services, is daily influenced by the right, and often imitates and admires these achievements. In this way, the modern Orthodox and the right have come closer to each other in America, with each group taking the best of the achievements of the other group and adjusting them for use in its own particular community.

This is less likely to happen here in Israel between the modern Orthodox and the Charedi community because of the insidious effect of politics, patronage, and government monies distribution. But even here there has been a definite turn to the right in the modern Orthodox community.

There is modern Orthodox ideology, and then there is the reality of Jewish life. The ideology has not adjusted to the realities of the causes described by Heilman in his article. America of 2004 is not the America of 1904 when the Young Israel movement was founded and proved an effective, if small-scale, answer to the assimilation of its time. America in

2004 allows a Shabbat observer to be a candidate for vice president of the United States, former yeshiva students to rise to positions of importance in major American companies, Chassidic Jews to be successful entrepreneurs and professionals without changing their garb or lifestyle. On a practical level, these changes have allowed the Orthodox right to challenge the basic ideological premise of modern Orthodoxy: that success in America requires acculturation. The claims of modern Orthodox ideologues that such acculturation is a good thing in itself for Torah and its community no longer resonates well, even amongst the modern Orthodox.

The attitude towards the State of Israel no longer defines the right or modern Orthodoxy as it once may have. Right-wing Orthodox Jews are supportive of Israel, as are the modern Orthodox. They send as many of their children to study here as do the moderns, invest and help build the country with their wealth and talents with great fervor; and their rate of aliyah to Israel is as great as any other group in Jewish America. So the ideological and theological arguments over how and whether to commemorate Yom Ha'atzma'ut (and other such ideological issues) are really sterile and, in practice, irrelevant.

In short, both modern Orthodoxy and the right have much to contribute to the success and vitality of Jewish life. There is no harm in their coming closer to one another. The struggle for the heart of modern Orthodoxy that Heilman portrays is, to me, a positive sign of the eternity of Torah, its values, and the Jewish people.

College Campuses

The appalling anti-Semitism on many American college campuses is no secret. American Jewish youth attend colleges and universities in greater proportion to the general population than any other segment of the American public. These Jewish students are more subject to hate speech and abuse than any other segment of the American student population.

This fact comes as a distinct shock to American Jewry, which always believed that institutionalized anti-Semitism in American education was a thing of the past. There are no longer quotas on Jewish enrollment in American higher education institutions, and active discrimination against Jewish students by faculty, administration, or other students was deemed a fast-disappearing relic of the darker past.

This rosy picture of Jewish attainment and acceptance is no longer true. From the upper echelons of the Ivy League schools to the lowliest, almost unknown community college, the ugly truth is that anti-Semitism on campus is not only present but is also accepted, and sometimes even glorified. The disease of anti-Semitism defies any known cure or palliative. It is unreasoning and unreasonable, destructive of all civilized norms, and eventually leads to terrible political and social consequences.

Any reasoned view of the history of anti-Jewish speech and behavior will reveal the dire consequences that soon engulfed the entire society that tolerated such hatred and bigotry. One would expect that the intellectual bastions of society – the colleges and universities – would be the places least likely for anti-Semitism to flourish. Sadly, that is not the case at all.

There are numerous reasons advanced to explain why this troubling and dangerous phenomenon exists today. Some say that it is fueled by the Israel-Arab confrontation and the natural sympathy of intellectuals to side with the poor underdog, no matter how brazenly wicked that underdog may be. Others have pointed out that there is a strong undercurrent of jealousy, especially among other minority groups, of the success, wealth, achievement, and influence that the Jewish community has today. Envy is a very strong emotion that often leads to hatred and violence. And college campuses traditionally are hotbeds of envy – intellectually, professorially, and otherwise – creating an environment where the age-old scourge of anti-Semitism can thrive and grow.

Another factor often mentioned is that universities attract people with utopian ideas. Since not one of those utopias has ever been realized in practice, there is always an active search for the scapegoats who prevent the utopia from arriving. It is what the Soviet Union infamously referred to as "wreckers" and "saboteurs." The Gulag was filled with millions of these hapless victims of the failure of Marxism in bringing forth the brave, new world that it had promised. In the eyes of many intellectuals today, for some unknown reason the Jews remain the obstacle to world peace, as well as to the eradication of poverty and misery. It is the Jews' fault that the glimmering, idyllic world of the future has not materialized. Moreover, it is the State of Israel, not North Korea, Iran, Venezuela, or any other nation, that is the reason why the world does not yet live in peace and harmony. Unfortunately, on most college campuses, this nonsense is expressed, taught, validated, and accepted. Is there any wonder why anti-Semitism is so strong and virulent on those campuses?

The American Jewish community and segments of American society are awakening to the depths of this problem. They are beginning to realize that anti-Semitism hiding behind the right of free expression is an existential threat to American Jews and indirectly to American society itself.

Student campuses today are unruly places with all sorts of fringe organizations and wacky causes. True, over the years Jews have obtained legal rights undreamt of by previous generations. Yet uncertainty and insecurity for Jews on American college campuses is palpable. Young Jews have the right to wear a *kippah* in college classrooms, but today many feel that they do so at their peril.

They have hunkered down and assumed a low profile, attempting to avoid confrontations with the militant organizations that promote anti-Semitism. Whether or not this tactic is the correct one and will prove successful in the long run remains to be seen.

More Soulful

The organizations that claim to represent American Jewry meet annually at a general assembly gathering. Once every five years, this meeting takes place in Jerusalem, rotating around American cities the other four years of the cycle. After surveying the wreckage of American Jewish society, there is now a call for a "more soulful" approach to Judaism and Jewish life in order to help reverse the current trends in demographic and social realities.

For decades, official American Jewry has been trapped by its own public relations sloganeering. No one can be against a more soulful Jewish public. But what exactly does the word *soulful* mean? In what context is it to be translated into deed? In short, what and where is the key to reaching and opening the shriveled soul of American Jewish society?

Truth be said, it does not appear to be in the existing structure of organized Jewish life in America. Organizational meetings, banquets and dinners, conferences and meetings are all important events, but none of them create a soulful atmosphere. The scruffy business of fundraising, organizational turf protection, and expansion all get in the way of soulfulness, and by their very nature cannot be avoided. But it is a reality that should be recognized. It is apparent that it is outside of the realm of official organized Jewish leadership to create and pursue soulfulness. Organizational life, no matter how efficiently structured and well-intentioned, can only achieve practical results in the physical world. It is too sterile an enterprise to affect the soul.

In Jewish tradition, the house of worship, the sanctuary of prayer, was meant to be a soulful place. It was not meant to be a place of entertainment or mere fulfillment of a religious obligation. It was and is governed by physical rules and set texts in order to help the one praying achieve the goal of inner and lofty communication with himself and with God. But the rabbis characterized it as a place of *kavanah* – a Hebrew word that almost defies translation because of its exquisite sense of nuance. The word is loosely translated as direction, intent, or concentrated fervor, but in terms of prayer it really signifies connection with one's own soul, and thereby with its Creator. I have experienced such a place a few times in my lifetime.

The first was as a child in my father's large synagogue in Chicago on Rosh Hashanah and Yom Kippur: the synagogue was filled with Eastern European Jews and their prayer rose as a storm sweeping all before it. Their roar of anguish and awe was a soulful experience. Later in life, I read about the experience of the renowned Jewish philosopher Franz Rosenzweig serving with the German army in Poland in World War I. A completely assimilated German Jew, engaged to marry a non-Jew, he wandered into a small, nondescript synagogue in a Polish village on Yom Kippur night – and the soulful experience of that prayer service transformed him forever. Our synagogues and prayer services are certainly sterile and cold in comparison.

The house of study was also meant to be a place of soulful inspiration. I remember the moment when, at fifteen, the study of Talmud was transformed within me from an assigned chore into a joy and a spiritual experience. I had teachers who enabled me to feel that way and allowed me to draw inspiration from the white spaces, and not only from the black letters, on the page. Torah study was meant not only to provide necessary knowledge, it was just as importantly meant to create a conduit to one's own soul and being. That is why the rabbis stated that there are seventy facets to every word and idea of Torah. Every individual finds an attachment to a different facet of spirituality.

There is no one-size-fits-all method when it comes to matters of the soul. But the ignorant and unlettered – tragically, most of American Jewry – are almost automatically precluded from such an attachment, and for them the Torah remains an unexplored and forbidding dark continent.

It is within the synagogue and the study hall that soulfulness in Jewish life can be regained and fostered. It will require new ideas, tactics, and much determination along with human and capital investment to achieve this. But the Jewish soul is not dead within us. It needs nurturing. If organized Jewry is serious about pursuing soulfulness, maybe it will cease to continue floundering in slogans and the wilds of organizational life. Maybe there is still time for it to devote its talents and resources toward this desperately needed goal.

"It Could Never Happen Here..." (2018)

The tragic killing of eleven Jews in Pittsburgh while they were at a worship service brings home the stark reality of the Jewish past and present. After the Holocaust, the Jewish world felt that violent anti-Semitism at last had exhausted its potential. Jews really believed that "Never Again" meant never again.

But hatred is a persistent and irrational emotion. Anti-Semitism has morphed and mutated once again into a deadly virus for which no antidote has yet been discovered. The shooting in Pittsburgh was the single bloodiest event in American Jewish history. As such, it has left American Jews in shock, disbelief, and confusion.

Trying to make sense of what is essentially a senseless phenomenon, a parade of theories have been advanced from all sectors of the American Jewish world. There are those who claim the right to read God's mind: they construed the massacre as a punishment for that particular group of people, and through them for the American Jewish community because it has largely forsaken the traditional values of Judaism. There are others who are less arrogant, but just as mistaken, who place the whole blame for this slaughter on President Trump. Still others claim that it is the behavior of the American Jewish community – political, financial, and social – that brings this type of hatred upon us.

In my humble opinion, all of this is sheer nonsense. Attempting to explain anti-Semitism rationally and logically, or even spiritually, is really beyond the ken of human wisdom. The Talmud long ago stated that Esau irrationally hates Jacob; therefore, there is not too much that can be done to change that situation.

But there is a difference between anti-Semitism and anti-Semitic violence. It is one thing to be discriminated against in country club memberships and medical school admissions. This type of anti-Semitism has always existed in general American culture and has unfortunately made its way deep into the minds of many of American minorities. Many of these people have never met a Jew and have no concept of what Judaism or the Jewish people stand for.

It is another thing to treat Jews violently, threaten them physically, and kill innocent people simply because they are Jewish. That has ratcheted anti-Semitism up to a degree that the American Jewish community never felt it would witness. And it is this raising of the bar that truly troubles and endangers American Jewish life today. Deep down in the hearts of the Jewish leaders as well the Jew on the street there is a frightening realization that there is not much that they can do about this situation. They thought it could never happen in America. Pittsburgh has proved them wrong.

One of the underlying roots of current anti-Semitism is the unrelenting criticism and demonization of the State of Israel, especially in universities and social media. As Lord Jonathan Sacks stated so eloquently in the House of Lords, commenting on the anti-Semitic and virulently anti-Israel statements of Jeremy Corbyn and others in the British Labour Party: "In the Middle Ages they hated us because of our religion. In the eighteenth and nineteenth centuries, and extending into the twentieth century, they hated us because of our race. Today they hate us because of our nation state."

But whether the excuse is religion, race, or the State of Israel, it is all anti-Semitism, an ancient moral disease that has affected human civilization for millennia. The State of Israel, like all other nation states in the world, is not perfect, nor is it utopia. But it certainly is not worthy of being singled out for delegitimization by hordes of so-called intellectuals in the Western world. This continued demonization of Israel creates a fertile climate in which anti-Semitism flourishes, leading to violent actions against Jews. We are all aware that there are many places in Europe where Jews are afraid to exhibit their Judaism publicly. All of the pious statements of the governments of the European Union and the United Kingdom have had no effect on the behavior of the man in the street. And now this situation is reaching the United States as well.

It is ironic in the extreme that many of the Israel-bashers and haters somehow profess themselves to be Jewish. They have learned nothing from Jewish history. When the genie of anti-Semitism is loosed from the bottle it will reach all Jews, no matter how politically correct and progressive they profess to be.

Jewish solidarity is not easily achieved. But in our time, and in the circumstances the Jewish world faces in today's increasingly hostile world, it should be a goal of all segments of Jewish society, no matter what the differences in political belief or religious practice may be. This effort will require education and constant mental and spiritual reinforcement. Perhaps this renewal of Jewish unity will be one of the few positive legacies of what happened in Pittsburgh.

Unity and Disunity

During a recent trip to the United States, I had the honor of addressing the student bodies of a number of different Orthodox educational institutions. These schools were of different streams of Orthodoxy, so to speak. Some called themselves modern Orthodox, while others claimed to be more traditional and less open to the culture of the modern world. Some student bodies were dressed slightly differently

– and I emphasize the word *slightly* – than the students in other schools. Yet I found that if I closed my eyes and did not see who was wearing colored shirts or white shirts, or what type of head covering adorned their heads, I could not tell much of a difference. In fact, I gave pretty much the same speech at all of these different institions.

In all due modesty, I think that the words that I said had impact and were well accepted, mirroring the true goals of these yeshivot and of their students. In all of these institutions, the avowed aims are Torah knowledge, maintenance of tradition, and understanding the unique role that the Jewish people and the Land of Israel play in the scheme of world events, especially in our time. I felt very heartened because I saw that the differences among all of these groups were not only superficial, but also exaggerated. The basic core issues of Torah study, observance of Jewish tradition, the building of family and community, and the understanding this generation's special time in history were unifying factors.

I know that we love to emphasize our differences because somehow that gives self-justification for our particular brand of behavior or politics. But we must remember that the Jewish people began as twelve distinct tribes, each different from the other, but that these combined twelve tribes created and established the Jewish people and the first Jewish state in the Land of Israel in ancient times and now.

The ideas reflected in the Talmud regarding the Jewish people, both individually and as a nation, are universal to all Jews. I daresay they apply also to Jews who are not that observant, or who even identify as secular. There are basic values that lie deep within the soul of the Jewish people, and it is these basic values that unite us and give us vision for the future.

Though there are many disputes in the Jewish world – many of them, in my opinion, carryovers from the nineteenth and twentieth centuries – they cannot stand the test of time because circumstances and events always govern human reactions. Current events are of most consequence and will decide what goals we should set for our children and grandchildren.

There is no doubt that the emphasis on differences – a phenomenon on which Orthodoxy unfortunately thrives – is divisive, harmful, and eventually counterproductive. Such is the nature of human beings; and I do not feel that anyone has the power to change the nature of human beings substantially. Nevertheless, leaders and educators should look more deeply at the underlying common foundations of Jewish society and not always be caught up in the external contrasts and political divisions that exist, have always existed, and probably will always exist.

I find that delivering the same message to Jews of all kinds is most satisfying to me. I am not a member of any particular group, but I am a member of the Jewish people and what they have stood for over all of the centuries. In my time, when I was a yeshiva student, differences were minimized simply because Orthodoxy was small in numbers, weak in power and influence, and lacked self-confidence. We could not afford the luxury of arguing with ourselves. In old Chicago where I grew up, anyone who was a Sabbath observer was a member of our immediate society, no matter what political affiliation. Zionist, non-Zionist, learned, or not so learned – it all made very little difference because we were so few in number. We could not dissect ourselves into different groupings, excluding others from the periphery of our vision and care.

Because of the unbelievable growth of Orthodoxy over the past decades, and because of the position of strength that it occupies both in American and in Israeli society, we now have that luxury of emphasizing differences instead of searching for similarities and common ground. This is the blessing of riches, but as we know, all riches contain a double-edged sword that can turn out to be a curse as well as a blessing.

On my recent trip, though, I was again encouraged by the fact that these differences are not as material as one would have thought, and that there is hope for a stronger and a more unified Orthodoxy in the future. The Jewish people needs a sturdy Orthodoxy, a robust unified group that has a moral compass and a grand vision for our future. I hope that this dream of mine will be realized and come into actuality soon.

An Uncertain Future

The outer veneer of confidence of the American Jewish community masks the inner insecurity that Jews almost instinctively feel based upon centuries-long hatreds, discrimination, and violence. Ironically, American Jews today feel that they are no longer a minority in society. African-Americans, Hispanics, and Asians – though far larger in numbers than the Jewish community in America – still claim the right to be a minority and have special privileges extended to them both privately and publicly. The Jewish community has long ago discarded any of these claims, since it does not consider itself to be a minority. In fact, the Jewish community feels itself to be part of the mainstream of white, Christian, traditional American society.

In the main, it looks upon itself as part of a progressive trend in American government and society. Jews appear in prominent roles throughout government, industry, finance, academia, sports, entertainment, and the media. As has always been the case in Jewish history, Jewish prominence and participation in these areas is vastly disproportionate to its actual numbers and size. Jews often give the impression to the non-Jewish world that there must be at least fifty million Jews living in the United States, while the reality is that there are probably only about five million actual Jews residing in America.

This attitude cuts both ways. To the anti-Semite, Jews are much too powerful and numerous. After the violent killings in Pittsburgh, the Jews themselves realized that its attainments and security are precarious, and perhaps even unsustainable. Though heartened by the response of official and private America to the synagogue murders, it was still a stark wake-up call to the overt anti-Semitism that lurks within portions of American society.

Of course, Israel-bashing is the rhetoric that fuels current anti-Semitism. By now it is obvious to all that the Left is less concerned with the plight of the Palestinians and simply looking for a large stick to bash Israel, and through Israel the Jewish people as a whole. What is so tragic about this is that many Jews, especially younger Jews on college campuses, have succumbed to this lie and feel it is justified, in reality destroying themselves. Make no mistake, to the anti-Semite, every Jew is Zionist, an Israeli, an occupier, a settler, and an oppressor. World history painfully records that, in spite of all efforts to the contrary, we are all Jews.

The inner Jewish world in the United States is also suffering from a nearly fatal illness. Assimilation and intermarriage continues to decrease our numbers and influence. The Conservative and Reform movements are rapidly losing membership and relevance. According to all surveys, Jews in the United States are the least religious of all groups in American society. All of Jewish history testifies to the fact that this is a situation of suicidal self-destruction. The secular leadership of the American Jewish community exists only on paper, but not in reality. Becoming more and more leftist and drifting farther and farther away from Torah values and Jewish tradition, the American Jewish community continues to propel itself to the brink of the waterfall. A shrinking American Jewish community will sooner or later affect a weakening of Jewish political and economic influence, thereby enabling the underlying currents of anti-Semitism to grow bolder and ever more violent. The Jewish birth rate, outside of the Orthodox society, is insufficient to maintain the present numbers of Jews in the country. American Jewry – in spite of its wealth, success, and prosperity – truly faces an uncertain future.

The Orthodox community also faces great challenges. Over the past several decades it has achieved unprecedented growth and strength. Written off seventy years ago as a dead limb on the Jewish tree, it is now the only root that exhibits growth and dynamism. Nevertheless, great sections of that community see themselves as separate from the entire Jewish community and exhibit little concern over what is happening to the majority of American Jews. It lives in its gilded enclaves, and to a great extent whistles past the graveyard. It is American to the core, but somehow deludes itself into feeling that it is not part of America. It is conflicted in its attitudes towards Jewish education, modernity, the State of Israel, and the social challenges that swirl about it.

Please understand that I do not feel as pessimistic about the future of American Jewry as perhaps this article suggests. I am an old man who grew up in a different America, and I sometimes find it hard to adjust to what passes for normalcy today. I also grew up in America when anti-Semitism was much more blatant than today but, ironically, much less violent. You could not wear a *kippah* on the street, but you were not afraid that someone would enter your synagogue and shoot it up.

How individual Jews, and the Jewish community as a whole, will cope with current American challenges are the main issues that face this last bastion of the Jewish exile. I pray for the welfare of my grandchildren and great-grandchildren and the American Jewish world that they will have to inhabit.

Jewish Humor

Jewish humor is not easily defined. In Eastern Europe, it depended heavily upon the earthiness and myriad nuances of Yiddish, the lingua franca of the Jewish population. There was a popular book written a number of decades ago by Leo Rosten called *The Joys of Yiddish*. It ended up being a collection of jokes, some hilarious, some indecent, and many head-scratching. The dire circumstances of Eastern European Jewry over centuries almost forced a type of humor upon that society: self-deprecating, always mildly sarcastic, and totally ironic.

It was meant to amuse and not to hurt. It never targeted individuals per se, but nevertheless it served as astute social commentary on Jewish society and circumstances. It always had a dark side to it, but it was not depressing nor too bitter. It acknowledged human foibles, even of great people, and held them up to laughter – but not to ridicule. Probably the greatest example of Eastern European Jewish humor is found in the works of Shalom Aleichem, who lived at the turn of the twentieth century. It is said that upon meeting him, Mark Twain remarked, "They say that I am the American Shalom Aleichem," to which Shalom Aleichem responded, "They tell me that I'm the Jewish Mark Twain." In reality, there was a great deal of similarity in their works, for they both had a sharp eye for the mannerisms, trials, and hard life of the common man, and they emphasized situational humor rather than out-and-out guffaw-producing jokes.

In American vaudeville, and later on the famous Borscht Belt circuit of resorts (in New York's Catskill Mountains), Jewish comedians flourished. Jack Benny, Eddie Cantor, Milton Berle, Henny Youngman, the Marx Brothers, among others, went on to national fame and fortune employing the situational comedy that was common in Eastern European Jewish life. They were the natural heirs of the *badchan* – the jokester who performed publicly at Jewish weddings in Eastern Europe, and the Purim Rav who was a fixture at all Purim festivities. The *badchan* mocked the bride and groom, the institution of marriage itself, the in-laws, and the foibles of family life. The Purim Rav pricked the balloon of pomposity of the religious leadership. They and their American imitators portrayed themselves as a slightly daft character and somewhat of a nebbish. They looked at life and its dangers, and made fun of themselves as the ultimate defense weapon against such a world.

The rise of the stand-up comic with rapid-fire jokes is really another form of the *badchan*'s craft. It is far more difficult to be successful at this form than it is to be successful at situational comedy, which relies on the development of characters.

Both types of humor were very common in the Jewish world and paved the way for the situation comedy programs (Bill Cosby, Jerry Seinfeld, and Ray Romano, for example) that for a while dominated American television. One could say that their shows were built upon the Jewish precedent, but after all, such humor is common to the human race and not restricted to any particular ethnic group. Laughter is a cure for many human ills, and it is likely instinctive. Witness how babies learn to laugh and chuckle so early in their development.

Even the Talmud records humorous incidents and ironic comments. It recommends that teachers begin their classroom studies each day by employing humor. All public speakers will readily agree that a funny story at the beginning of a talk will go a long way toward winning the attention of the audience for the rest of one's remarks.

Yiddish humor often bordered somewhat on the risqué but never crossed the red lines of obscenity and immorality. Unfortunately, the same certainly cannot be said of the type of humor that pervades our world today.

I have noticed that there is a decline in humor in the religious world. People take themselves too seriously to be self-deprecating, and self-deprecation was always the hallmark of Jewish humor. At Jewish weddings, wild dancing and ear-splitting music has replaced the *badchan*. Too bad. We could all use a good ironic look at ourselves every so often.

My Books

I have always been a lover of books. Even as a young yeshiva student many decades ago, I would read books on all sorts of different subjects. I used the meager financial resources at my disposal to purchase books. Prices were different then; for three dollars I could obtain classic books by great Talmudic scholars.

When I was a rabbi in Miami Beach, I would often find a pile of Hebrew books on my doorstep, placed there by the heirs of the previous generation. Apparently, the children and grandchildren of the deceased had no use for their books and simply disposed of them by leaving them on the doorstep of the rabbi or of the synagogue. Most of those books I had to dispose of myself. Yet there was always a certain special book, even on occasion a rare book, in the pile that caught my eye that I kept for myself.

I never had the resources nor inclination to become a true book collector, but I acquired a very large library over my years in the rabbinate.

A number of noted rabbinic scholars visited my home in Monsey to do research in a book that was no longer commonly available, but that I had in my library. Not only did I have books of Jewish scholarship, but I also had books relating to general world history and biography, as well as some much lighter reading, which gave me psychological relief from the pressures of the rabbinate.

When I moved to Israel, I left a substantial part of my library in the United States. My much smaller quarters in our apartment here in Jerusalem did not afford me the space to bring them all with me. In the US, there was a time when I knew the location of every book on its shelf. There are times now when I am writing a book or working on a lecture that I recall a fascinating insight or anecdote that is in one of the books that I once owned. I picture the book on the shelf back in Monsey and lament that it is not here with me in Jerusalem. This happens to me often, yet my level of frustration is now considerably diminished, as I no longer expect to be able to locate the book here. Sometimes I am pleasantly surprised by the fact that I do have the book, and I am even more amazed that I was able to find it somewhere in the bookshelves that line my apartment.

I no longer purchase any new books because all of my bookshelves are full to overflowing. Though there are many that I would wish to acquire, practicality dictates that I restrain my acquisitive instincts. Softening the blow that I can no longer in good conscience bring home more books is the fact that there is an enormous amount of material accessible through certain CDs that I own, as well as the plentiful availability of books on the Internet.

Jews have always had a reverence for books. There is an anecdote regarding the Jewish professor Harry Wolfson, who was one of the first Jews to acquire tenure at Harvard University. This was in the beginning of the twentieth century, when academic anti-Semitism in the United States was open and palpable. Wolfson was once confronted by one of his colleagues, who said to him: "Why do you Jews think you are so special?" Wolfson is reported to have coolly answered: "As far as I know, we are the only people who pick up a dropped book from the floor and kiss it."

This mindset is not limited only to books of holiness and Torah. Many surveys have shown that Jews constitute a large bloc of the book-purchasing public in the United States, far greater than their numbers and population would warrant. Of course, there are a lot of trashy books in circulation, many of which actually prove more popular and outsell books of greater worth and gravity. So, like everything else in life, there are positive and potentially negative consequences in acquiring and reading books. One must discern which books are worth reading. (Incidentally, history has proven that banning a book is counterproductive. Invariably, it becomes that much more valuable and sought after.)

So one must become a connoisseur in order to derive the full value of reading and collecting books. The old Hebrew adage that "books should be members of your household" still certainly applies in the Jewish world today, and it probably always will.

Rabbi Meir Zlotowitz (2017)

I am saddened beyond words by the passing of my beloved friend of many decades, Rabbi Meir Zlotowitz. He was a person of great and many talents. A Torah scholar, a creative entrepreneur, a gifted graphic artist, a superlative fundraiser, and above all a man of great vision and daring enterprise. ArtScroll and the Mesorah Heritage Foundation were his gifts to the Jewish people, creating his everlasting eternity.

We cannot imagine the Jewish world today without his enormous contributions to the study and dissemination of Torah and Jewish thought. He opened and expanded the understanding of Talmud, prayer, the Bible, Mishnah, and the other treasuries of Judaism to the broad English-speaking public. His influence in Israel and the Hebrew-speaking public was also of immense importance. His uncanny ability to realize what the Jewish public needed to connect itself to the timeless treasures of Judaism created generations of stronger, more loyal, and more knowledgeable Jews. It is no exaggeration to say that ArtScroll, in all of its projects and publications, is the recognized teacher of the Jewish people in our time. He took great risks, but he achieved great accomplishments. Together with his colleague, Rabbi Nosson Scherman, he created a genre of Torah literature which has generated many imitators, but very few equals.

Others will undoubtedly give him his due in the many articles and eulogies that will be written about him. But I want to remember him as my personal friend and as a warm, caring human being who represented in his persona and his actions the finest ideals of Judaism, as elucidated in the publications that he authored and produced.

Rabbi Zlotowitz was a keen observer of the traits and vagaries of human behavior. He was a very normal person who often found himself in very abnormal circumstances and situations. He was a realist in the finest sense of the word, never giving in to cynicism and undue disappointment in the behavior and actions of others, even of those who did not share his vision and who misunderstood his purpose and accomplishments. His sense of humor was apparent to all who conducted conversations with him. He was able to see the sometimes-ludicrous nature of human interaction, even in matters of scholarship and religious outlook.

After a visit with him, one always left in good spirits, with a feeling of pleasantness and accomplishment. Even when he rejected an idea or project that was proposed to him, he did so with grace and kindness, and even with encouragement.

And he was a great friend to those who wished to befriend him. He was a source of comfort and cheer in difficult times, leading with constant strength and encouragement those who were associated with him and with ArtScroll. He was a rare person in today's fragmented Jewish world, for he bridged many sections of it with his good humor, deep insight, and tolerant, optimistic nature. He was a very special person; and as the Talmud records, there are few of them present in any generation.

I spoke to him barely a month ago, and he was full of plans regarding an ArtScroll Shabbaton that he was planning to conduct this fall. He also spoke of books to be published and projects that were ruminating in his fertile mind. I could not imagine that I would be writing this article only a few weeks later. But such is the uncertainty of human mortality and of God's will.

The entire Jewish people mourns his passing and recognizes the void that his absence leaves. But those of us who cherish him in his human capacity as a friend and a mentor are certainly deeply and personally affected by his untimely passing. There was so much left to be done, such a future to be realized, that it is hard to imagine that somehow he will not be here to create it.

Naturally, his legacy will now be carried on by others – his family, his colleagues, and the great Mesorah Heritage Foundation that he created and headed for decades. But to a great extent, like all other human beings, especially those of note, he is irreplaceable in uniqueness and presence. The Jewish world is orphaned by his passing, and I am saddened beyond words at the loss of such a good and loyal friend. May his memory be a blessing for his family, for his publishing house, and most importantly, for all of Israel.

Contemporary Issues

Hurricanes and Political Storms

A devastating hurricane that visited the eastern part of the United States recently spawned terrible loss of life, enormous property damage, and some soul-searching as to the *real* non-weather related cause of this disaster. Judging from the emails I have received and reading the pronouncements that have appeared, especially in Jewish publications, it is apparent that many people feel themselves expert enough to know God's mind in this matter. Well, I must confess my inadequacy regarding this subject, for I have no theory to advance as to why all of this devastation occurred and was justified in Heaven's eyes. I take the Torah at its word that "no living human being will see or understand Me."

The seemingly natural disasters that befell the people and Land of Israel in biblical times – hailstorms, locusts, droughts – were explained by the prophets of the time, and their redemptive or punitive purposes were delineated. The absence of prophecy in Israel is sorely felt at occasions such as this. We have no prophets today who can enlighten us about the spiritual causes of tsunamis in Bangladesh or hurricanes on Long Island.

So I am bewildered that there are so many who insist that they know why this hurricane struck a particular area, and that it is Divine punishment for certain sins committed there.

The simple truth is that we do not know why it happened, and that is a very humbling admission for many because we are taught and raised to be know-it-alls, especially in understanding how God runs our world. We are led to believe that there are those among us who know everything. And here comes another event that proves us to be puny, ignorant, and powerless (no unfortunate pun intended). And that is why I feel almost resentful of communications being broadcast by those who claim to know the spiritual causes of the hurricane. These explanations may or not be correct, but my persistent question is, how does one *know* that is the correct explanation?

In the midst of the political campaign that is currently consuming the Israeli media (much more than it is affecting the average Israeli voter's equilibrium), we are again faced with a plethora of know-it-alls. The pundits daily tell us what will occur, who will and should be elected and who will not, what the future holds for us, and other assorted bits of smug certainty and clucking wisdom. Again, I ask the same question: how do they know? It's a fair question, especially since the track record of all of the wise men and pundits, soothsayers, and political experts here in Israel is very spotty, at best.

Since humility is hardly the trait of "experts," and the media is blaring and sensationalist in the main – always claiming objectivity while advancing its own political agenda and favorites – many of us here just ignore the whole scene until called upon to actually vote on election day. Many of us are permanently undecided voters because we feel that there is really no viable choice; we never know what will happen when someone actually assumes office. Ariel Sharon's disastrous betrayal of Gush Katif, and his remark – "What one sees from here in office is not what one saw from there while campaigning" – has certainly made the Israeli voter a wary and suspicious being when it comes to political promises and policies.

Prophecy to enlighten us as to the causes of historical events is certainly lacking. In my opinion, the major unanswered issue that still overhangs our Jewish society is the Holocaust and the destruction of European Jewry. What was the *real* cause for that unspeakable tragedy? The actual facts of the Holocaust are documented for all to see and study. What the Heavenly causes for allowing such a thing to occur is not known. Yet, inexplicably, reasons have been advanced as to its causes in both spiritual and societal veins. There are those who blame it on Zionism and those who blame it on anti-Zionism. There are those who blame it on the forces of modernism and others who claim that exactly the opposite is true.

An accurate answer may never be known to us in this world. So those who do advance explanations and the certainty of knowing Heaven's will do so only at their own peril. Silence and acceptance, rebuilding and revitalizing, staying the course, and being humble about all matters is the wisest course for believing Jews to take.

On Being Currently Relevant

The "hot-button" topics in our ever-changing society rarely have much staying power. They seem to fizzle out of their own accord, having made a lot of noise, spawning countless op-ed pontifications, but eventually leading to little substantive change or benefit in our lives.

Sixty years ago, when I first began my rabbinic career, the issue of mixed pews allowing men and women to sit together in the synagogue was dominant. It is no longer. Having mixed pews has not in any way increased synagogue attendance nor contributed in any way to Jewish family stability. The slogan then (borrowed from a trademarked Christian ad campaign) was "the family that prays together stays together." Reinterpreted by Jews with a mixed-pew agenda, it was touted to mean "the family that sits side by side during services stays together." Time has proven that to be just another irrelevant slogan. There are far more regular worshippers in synagogues that maintain separate seating than in those that have mixed pews. The damage done sixty years ago is pretty much beyond current repair. And today the issue is completely irrelevant to the future of Judaism.

The main issue facing world Jewry is its shrinking population due to the ravages of assimilation and intermarriage, declining birth rates, and the failure of the non-Orthodox in the Diaspora to hold on to their youth in any meaningful manner. Yet a cursory glance at Jewish media would lead one to believe that the greatest issue that we must contend with today is where the Women of the Wall should be allowed to light their Chanukah menorah. There is no doubt in my mind that decades from now this currently important issue will have little resonance in the Jewish world.

Countering assimilation should be paramount to Jewish communities all over the world. Accepting intermarriage carte blanche as acceptable only worsens the problem. And it is exacerbated by "the wolf guarding the henhouse," for many of the heads of the Jewish organizations who should be fighting this trend are themselves assimilated, and even intermarried. Reform should be in the forefront of this battle; instead it is one of the chief enablers of its dire results. We can all appreciate compassion towards individuals and couples, but it is difficult to reconcile that misplaced compassion with the willful destruction of the Jewish future.

More Jews perhaps have been lost to assimilation over the past seventy years than were destroyed in World War II. There will be no museums built or memorials erected to commemorate these losses. The current tyranny of overriding political correctness has rendered this most relevant issue irrelevant: it is not nice to talk about it for fear of offending others.

The keepers of the faith – mainly, but not exclusively Orthodox – are always fair game for criticism of their faults and weaknesses. But nary a word is ever heard or written about what the true cause of assimilation is, and who in the Jewish world are its main abettors. Many feel that this is not relevant to the discussion of the problem, while others claim that it is not really a problem at all.

The security and welfare of the State of Israel should be one of the most important and relevant topics in the Jewish world. But it is not the number-one political issue in the eyes of American Jewry, nor even among many who live in Israel. As we struggled so long and bitterly to achieve our independent state, to me it is unthinkable that there are those in the Jewish world who advocate giving it up in favor of pie-in-the-sky imaginary scenarios of a peaceful world. To me, all other issues pale into irrelevance in comparison with the safety of the State of Israel and of its inhabitants.

This has nothing to do with the imperfections that exist in the government, policies, and citizenry of the state. It is just elementary that the existence of the state, its security, and stability are prime relevant issues that face Jews today. Why this is not self-understood is puzzling to me, to say the least. In the long run of history, many of the current issues and countless organizations will have proven themselves to have been irrelevant to the Jewish future.

Alcohol and the Jews

The last number of decades has brought to light an increasingly difficult problem in Jewish life, both here in Israel and in the Jewish world generally. It is the rise of alcoholism and its related tragedies. There is also a considerable amount of drug use among Jewish youth, and it is not restricted to any particular groups. It would be simple to say that these problems are restricted mainly to the secular and non-observant Jewish community. But that statement would not be a true one.

There was a time not that long ago – I recall from my youth that Jews who were alcoholics, or even who regularly drank, were a rarity. Jews drank on Simchat Torah and Purim, but were sober the rest of the year. Jews prided themselves on their sobriety and scorned their Eastern European non-Jewish neighbors because many of them were always drunk. There were even Jewish folk ballads in Yiddish that highlighted this difference between Jews and non-Jews. It was not only that being a drinker was dangerous to health, family, and economic well-being that prevented Jews from indulging in alcohol. It was because it was socially unacceptable in Jewish society. A drunkard was never a hero or a role model in the Jewish world. From the biblical story of Lot and his daughters onwards, the avoidance of the evil effects of alcohol became the norm in Jewish culture. Though Jews in Eastern Europe were heavily involved in the production and sale of liquor, Jewish mores served as the social brakes on drinking; so the rate of alcoholism among Jews was extremely low, far below the average of the general society in which they found themselves living.

All of that has changed dramatically in our time. While the advertising of liquor has been severely curtailed and the harmful effects of drinking are spelled out clearly on every liquor bottle, the rise of alcoholism has not been severely affected by these warnings. This is especially true among the young who do not yet realize their own mortality. The bar, the pub, even the Shabbat *Kiddush* are all places to drink without social disapproval.

In Israel, the traditional Friday night family dinner – observed for decades even in nonobservant homes – has given way to drunkenness, melees, and stabbings at pubs and bars. Friday night and Shabbat are the most horrendous times of the week for traffic fatalities in Israel, many of them induced by alcohol.

Jews have become experts in single malt liquors bought at outrageous prices and displayed as a sort of trophy, testament to one's success in life. The goal of twelve- and thirteen-year-olds at bar and bat mitzvah parties is to drink hard liquor, and their parents indifferently acquiesce to this pending disaster. Somehow the yeshiva world has allowed Purim to morph into drunken debauchery, which also has consequences later on, and not only the next day's hangover. The rate of alcoholism in the Jewish world is now at an all-time high equal to, if not even higher, than the average in many countries. It is one of the many unseen or purposely ignored elephants in our room.

Like drugs and tobacco, alcohol is addictive. As long as it is viewed as being socially acceptable, even desirable, all of the radio ads against drunken driving and all of the warnings on the labels of the liquor bottles will be of little avail.

So alcoholism must be defeated before it takes hold. This can only be accomplished by a change in Jewish society's attitude towards drinking. Alcoholism is not only a personal problem; it is one that affects countless Jewish families and Jewish communities. At long last, some synagogues in the United States ban liquor entirely from their premises, even for catered affairs in their social halls. This drastic step was taken as a direct result of the weekly drunken behaviors of teenagers, and even pre-teenagers, in the *shuls*. At the very least, such a rule is a statement by the congregation that drinking is no longer socially acceptable behavior. Of course, the rabbi of the congregation that first initiated this action was roundly criticized for curtailing the private lives of others. However, all of Torah is based on the necessity of curtailing imagined private life freedoms.

Judaism does not advocate absolute prohibition of alcohol. Wine is an integral part of Jewish ritual. But like all matters in life, Judaism preaches good common sense, necessary restraints, discipline, and social responsibility for the general welfare of all. The use of alcohol has to fit into that pattern.

Supply and Demand

As we all have been taught in our study of elementary economics, prices and values are established by the law of supply and demand. In theory, the greater the supply, the lower the price.

This rule of commerce applies to human resources as well. And currently, in the religious Jewish world, the supply of capable young men and women who are willing to enter the field of Jewish education far outstrips the demand. For every teaching opportunity in urban Jewish communities, especially in the higher grades of elementary school and in high school, let alone in the advanced yeshiva realm, there are far more applicants than there are teaching opportunities. Consequently, salaries in Jewish education are low, and the competition to fill any teaching vacancy is fierce.

During my recent visit to the United States, quite a number of excellent young Torah scholars who are searching for teaching positions bemoaned the lack of available positions in Jewish schools. The problem is somewhat compounded by the fact that these young people are entering the job market rather late in life. Most of them already have a number of children attending school, and if one is convinced that one's child should receive a Lakewood education, for instance, it is difficult to consider taking a position that may be available in a smaller, less Orthodox-intensive community. In some areas, the lack of secular education and professional training also militates against this type of yeshiva graduate securing a meaningful position in Jewish education.

So we end up in a catch-22 situation of wasted talent. In the United States, many of these potentially gifted educators turn to other types of work in order to survive. Usually this creates a great deal of personal angst as well as spiritual and emotional frustration.

I have been witness to such situations many times in my rabbinic and educational experience. It seems that our educational system is broken and because of many different pressures – religious, social, political, and inertia – there are very few willing to accept the challenge of fixing it. In some cases, a number of hardy young educators have created their own new institutions, but this effort has done little to solve the overall problem.

Traditionally, the profession of the teacher had been viewed in Jewish life as an exalted and noble one; while at the same time those who practice that profession are viewed as nerds or otherwise unsuccessful individuals. This schizophrenic view of the educators of our children skews even more the law of supply and demand in Jewish education. Somehow, we expect our teachers to be holy, altruistic, supremely competent and heroic figures. At the same time, we harbor inner feelings that the cream of the crop of Jewish talent is in the field of hedge funds, and that those who teach our children do not really measure up to them. These conflicting views manifest themselves in myriad ways from salary structure to tenure and social respect in the Jewish world.

There are currently initiatives and programs financed by sources outside of the field of Jewish education to physically and socially improve the lot of teachers. But these programs are palliative and not structural. During the 1940s in the United States, a number of innovative leaders created the day school revolution, which saved Orthodoxy in America. They were able to inspire a generation of educators to sacrifice much in order to achieve the goal of Jewish survival – valiantly fighting for the rebirth of Torah study and observance among American youth. Such a creative revolution is necessary again to overcome the crushing pressures that the law of supply and demand has imposed upon us.

Texting

I must preface this piece of writing by stating that I am a technological dinosaur. I hardly ever use my cell phone except in emergencies and when I am visiting outside of Israel. I do not have a smartphone, nor even a kosher phone. I just have an old-fashioned cell phone that only makes and receives calls. I admit that I never text. I do not know how to, and my currently failing eyesight would not allow me to text, even if I wanted to.

But I would have to be oblivious to everything going on around me not to realize that the preferred method of human communication today is texting. Apparently, texting obviates the necessity for personal conversation, saving both time and money. But it is very impersonal, cold, and often subject to misunderstanding and misinterpretation. Nowadays, when spoken personal communication has been minimized, the young are in danger of never being able to hold an intelligent conversation with another human being for any length of time. A number of my young friends who are currently looking for the proper mate to marry tell me that it is very hard for them to actually speak to the person they are dating. They are not accustomed to speaking directly to someone else in a friendly and conversational setting. They much prefer texting one another. Whether texting is a good venue for getting to know another person – or, for that matter, building a marriage – is a serious question, at least to me.

I am told that texting in such situations saves embarrassment and discomfort. I do not understand why this should be so: I can think of no greater distress than being told by someone through an impersonal text message that there is no reason to pursue a relationship.

Texting usually spares the person from having to offer any explanation for his decision. But my experience in life is that one only learns from disappointments and from the reasons that precipitated the disappointment. Texting can be very cruel. Like all human inventions, it can be used for very positive purposes, but it also has its negative, dark side. How it is employed and used becomes the test of its overall benefit and importance.

Texting has also destroyed the necessity to know how to spell words correctly. In fact, it revels in shortcuts: using the letter *u* for the word *you*, for instance. Now it may very well be that in our new modern age there is no necessity to spell words correctly and that we will have finally arrived at the desired goal of phonetic spelling. (In my youth, certain newspapers attempted to achieve this, but could find no followers among their readerships.) I feel that it will not be long before we find phonetic spelling reintroduced as the norm in our current printed media.

The difficulty with the printed word is that it requires oral explanation as well. The book that is the most exact and nuanced in its choice of words, the Torah, certainly requires a companion oral explanation to convey the true content and meaning of its words. In fact, in its scholarly development over the millennia, Judaism is an attempt to explain the words that we all hold to be sacred and exact. And as any student can affirm, there is wide latitude granted as to what those exact words really mean and imply. Attempts were made throughout Jewish history to deal with the written word and ignore or refute the rabbinic oral explanations given to the Torah. All such attempts ended in failure, creating sects that over time disappear from Jewish life.

The Torah does not lend itself easily to texting, slang, or verbal shortcuts. Not only that, the Torah insists upon personal teachers and a tradition that must be handed down orally and by example from one generation to the next. In this, Judaism reflects eternity – not just convenience – and continuity, not merely fleeting instructions.

Too Much, Too Fast

Profligate behavior has always been a byproduct of great personal wealth, especially wealth acquired relatively quickly. Money burns a hole in one's pocket: spending becomes foolish, ostentatious, unnecessary, and sometimes even self-destructive. And in our instant communication society, where people feel impelled to tell everything about everybody and to do so instantaneously, any act of such over-the-top spending is quickly advertised.

A wealthy Jewish businessman in the United States spent a large amount of money to have a Jewish rapper (an oxymoron, if there ever were one) to perform at his daughter's bat mitzvah celebration. For some reason, this important piece of news went viral on social media; names and precise monetary payments were all publicized to the iPhones among us. This breathless piece of news was even broadcast in the national news of an American radio network to which I was unfortunately listening.

The rich cannot expect any rights of privacy in today's world; their extreme and foolish behavior will always be held up to public scrutiny, even ridicule. One would think that this reality would be taken into account before such a course of behavior is taken. But as King Solomon pointed out long ago, wealth, good sense, and wisdom do not necessarily accompany each other.

There are many courses being offered on how to manage wealth. These courses are meant to instruct the newly wealthy – sports stars, entertainment and media celebrities, start-up computer entrepreneurs, lottery winners – how to conserve and invest their newfound wealth. But to the best of my knowledge, there is no course to help one deal psychologically, emotionally, or spiritually with sudden wealth. Everyone needs an angel whispering in his or her ear: "Don't act impulsively and foolishly; don't hold yourself up to public shame!" In fortunate circumstances, that personal angel should be one's spouse and family. But in the absence of such an intimate angel, one should certainly find such a friend and angel to help navigate the rapids of sudden wealth. Just as people engage financial advisers to help them financially, so too there is a need for a wealth adviser to help us use our wealth wisely, with sense and probity.

This caution is especially necessary in a Jewish community exposed to the anti-Semitic mindset associating Jews with money and wanton luxuries. Anti-Semitic cartoons of the last century (and now) portray Jews as porcine, greedy, and purely money oriented. A family event can unwittingly become a source of unwanted shame and notoriety, bordering on desecration.

No one does these things purposely. But the wise person, in the view of the Talmud, sees the consequences of his actions and behavior before acting. This is especially true when it comes to dealing with wealth, which often confounds the wisdom of otherwise smart people. Societal life is strewn with the debris of the errors in judgment of the rich and famous.

I have often quoted the dictum of the Talmudic rabbis that Jews do much better handling poverty than they do extreme prosperity. We are bewitched by our own successes, especially with our financial achievements. We ascribe our successes to ourselves and our failures to others, unfortunate circumstances, or the inscrutable whims of Heaven.

We pray regularly for prosperity in our individual and national lives.

Yet often we are able to live more easily with what we do not have than with what we do have.

A true and honest analysis of so many of our ills and troubles, especially with wealth, would reveal that they are usually self-inflicted. A little common sense can go a long way in preventing embarrassment and insult. At that infamous bat mitzvah party, no one, except the rapper, benefited from the incident and its ramifications. One cannot help but be perplexed as to how a lavish party and a rapper performance are true markers of a young Jewish girl reaching the age of Torah commandments. Oh, how rare is common sense, restraint, and traditional respect to Jewish institutions!

Extreme prosperity is destroying our souls and our families. We should remind ourselves that in the *Amidah,* the prayer for good sense precedes the prayer for prosperity. There is good reason for that.

Floods and Arks

The Torah's presentation of the events of the great flood and Noach's ark is well known to all of us, no matter our position on the religious spectrum. In reviewing human history, it seems pretty accurate because since that event we seem to be always perched on the precipice of a cataclysmic event of horrendous consequences, whether it is man-made or of natural causes. In our time, we are faced with recurring natural disasters that have taken hundreds of thousands of lives, with economic crises that sap the vitality of societies, nations, and individuals – not to mention the ever-present threat of nuclear war and untold destruction.

There is very little optimism to go around in today's world. The messengers of hope and change are not very convincing in their words, and certainly not in their deeds. So there is an overall malaise that besets us. We see little broadcast about big dreams, bold policies, acceptances of risk, or visions of what can and should be accomplished. The great ideals and movements that marked the beginning of the twentieth century became shattered idols at the beginning of the current century. Political rhetoric has lost all credibility; the "kabbalist" soothsayers and human rights activists are, in the main, imposters. We pray for rain, but are fearful of the flood.

Enter the ark. The ark symbolizes not only the salvation of one person and his family from the ravages of catastrophe, it more importantly symbolizes the ability to rise above our fears and salvage the purpose of our lives from pessimism and nihilism. As a reinforcement of this idea, there is also the natural phenomenon of the rainbow, which represents an eternal covenant between humankind and the Creator: the flood will not recur. This rainbow is not to be misinterpreted, nor its impact exaggerated. We have no guarantees against other disasters, natural and man-made, wars and strife, but we do have a promise that somehow human life will continue.

So it is incumbent upon us to make that life productive, meaningful, and, in a true sense, eternal. The ark is the will of humankind to not only survive the omnipresent threat of extinction but also to overcome its dangers and attempt to reinforce the rainbow. We must not be distracted by false messages of unrealistic hopes on one hand, nor by the prophets of impending doom on the other.

Every generation is charged with the task of building an ark for itself anew. It is also instructed to teach the message of the rainbow to the next generation – to implant belief, tradition, values, and concern for others into the lives of those who will follow us here on earth.

As all of this is true for humankind generally, it is certainly true for the Jewish people particularly. Israel and world Jewry finds itself hemmed in by enemies and beset by complex problems. We are the only people targeted openly by others for a "great flood" to befall us. The world is unaware that the fate of all is tied inextricably to the fate of the Jews. One would have thought that the story of the twentieth century and its horrific events would have made this lesson clear. Obviously, this is not the case.

Nevertheless, we Jews have to continue building our ark. This small, seemingly flimsy ark has withstood all of the floods that time has thrown against us. We should revitalize ourselves, dream magnificent dreams again, see the big picture and not concentrate so much on the picayune details which so blind us to our accomplishments and goals.

We have to rebuild ourselves anew, but without discarding the treasures of our past. God promised the Jewish people a new heart and the ability to rise to all challenges. And above all, we must educate our generation and future generations to see the rainbow reflected in the Torah, in our teachings, and in our traditions. Jewish ignorance, hedonism, and worshipping false idols that mask themselves as the utopian wave of the future are the real flood that threatens our future existence and success.

The rainbow teaches us that our ark is waterproof. Those wise enough to enter it will surely succeed in avoiding all permanent disasters.

On Being a Skeptic

One of the troubling challenges in life is retaining belief and optimism regarding human behavior when in his heart of hearts he is a confirmed skeptic. This test is confirmed by King Solomon, considered the wisest of all humans, in his eternal monumental work, the book of Kohelet. There is a great deal of difference between realism and skepticism, on the one hand, and pessimism and depression, on the other hand. The bulk of Kohelet is skeptical, but it does not descend into depression.

Belief and faith in God, Torah, and the traditions of ages are the fundamental mainstays of Judaism. Yet the Torah warns us against believing too readily in strange gods and superstitions, following the ways of our wandering eyes and willful hearts. In Jewish life we are traditionally bidden to regard leaders with respect, but also to be skeptical of their motives and promises. Solomon himself said that a fool is someone who believes whatever he is told.

In our era of biased media reporting, fake news, and willful distortion of facts and history, skepticism is more than ever necessary for a wise assessment of current situations. The famous statement of the Mussar movement was that not everything that is thought should be expressed, not everything that is expressed should be written, not everything that is written should be published and disseminated, and that not everything that is read should be believed. There is a great deal of wisdom in that maxim.

Since the events that regularly occur in our world do not fit a pattern of logic nor have complete rationality, there's plenty of room to search for answers to problems outside of normal human consultation and advice. There is no question that the supernatural is part of our existence. And there is also no question that there are people in this world, and in the Jewish religious world, who do seem to have such powers of guidance. But the healthy skeptic remains unconvinced that all those who claim to be omniscient are really legitimate, and that all advice they advance is truly helpful.

Unfortunately, charlatans have always abounded in every community, and ours is no exception. It troubles me greatly that holiness and reputed omniscience seem to be always tied up with money. That link raises my level of skepticism and challenges my powers of belief. I have met some truly holy people in my lifetime, and some extraordinary events have occurred to me, so I do not deny in any way that such people do truly exist. Yet I have also seen how thieves and con men, dressed in holy garb and bearing false credentials, have victimized the innocent and gullible. Most of us have witnessed or heard of such demagogues. A little healthy skepticism regarding such matters is certainly in order.

Our world is a dangerous and confusing place. Without faith or belief in our Creator, the arbiter of ultimate justice in all affairs, one is likely to suffer from a paralyzing pessimism. But Judaism does not allow for such a somber assessment. Skepticism is allowed, and in fact encouraged, but depression and pessimism are to be avoided at almost all costs.

Drawing this fine line is really the challenge of human life and of our society. Skepticism is not synonymous with cynicism.

The Jewish people and the State of Israel have a perfect historical right to be skeptical about the true intentions of those who proclaim themselves to be our friends, and certainly about those who openly state that they are enemies and wish to destroy us. But we should never give up hope that better times can and will come, and that what currently seems to be beyond any solution or reasonable compromise will eventually be settled. Again, patience and realism are the necessary ingredients to create the proper balance of skepticism and belief.

Skepticism based on experience teaches us that there usually are no shortcuts on the road to personal and national achievement. Belief teaches us that there is always a better tomorrow that can be achieved, that one should never despair despite omnipresent challenges. So, to sum it all up, I imagine I can call myself a satisfied, believing skeptic.

Price Gouging

When demand far outstrips supply, or when someone obtains a monopoly over goods that the public needs or wants, or when tragedies strike and people are forced to obtain certain goods and services to survive – greed takes over and the prices for these items are suddenly overly inflated. The Talmud calls this phenomenon *hafkaat shearim* – the "removal" of ordinary fair pricing by overcharging for the critical items. Needless to say, the Talmud regards this as an unfair business practice.

A number of news reports over the past month have brought this issue to mind. In the aftermath of Hurricane Katrina, there were numerous instances of unconscionable price gouging in the US Gulf states for all imaginable items, ranging from gasoline to water. Profiting from another human being's suffering or desperate need is an ancient vice of humankind. Only a moral conscience can counteract this built-in venality that afflicts many in times of shortages.

In an article that recently appeared in the *Jerusalem Post*, a particular type of Jewish price gouging was reported. It seems that only one dealer was able to obtain *lulavim* – the palm fronds that Jews require for Succot – from Egypt this year. According to the article, having cornered the market, the dealer intends to charge up to five times the normal price for a *lulav*. I do not know whether this will actually happen, although the temptation to commit this travesty is certainly a strong one. Jews go to great lengths to fulfill the *mitzvah* of *arba minim* on Succot. Usually the *etrog*/citron is the most expensive of the four required plant species, but if the threat of the *lulav* price gouging comes to pass, the price of the usually inexpensive *lulav* would now rival the *etrog*.

Taking unfair monetary advantage of Jews who are attempting to observe a *mitzvah* was especially condemned by the rabbis of the Talmud. They likened the practice to charging usurious interest and as a violation of the Torah principle that "your brother shall be enabled to live with you on equal terms." The Torah envisions a fair, equal, and level playing field in a just society's economic functions. Price gouging is a clear violation of this basic rule of the Torah. Talmud Yerushalmi states that those who are *mafkiei shearim* – price gougers – are subject to particular Divine wrath and will be eventually "broken" by God.

The *halachah* does provide for the recovery of actual costs and a reasonable profit by the seller (usually estimated at no more than a sixth, but sometimes it can be as much as half on certain "luxury" items). If and when the seller's costs rise, he may legitimately pass that increase on to the consumer. The Torah also allows for price fluctuations due to market conditions and real shortages. But if the seller's new higher price is based on his artificially created monopoly and his control of the supply, that price charged to the consumer is considered excessive and a clear violation of Torah law. The rabbis even hesitated to proclaim extra fast days (because of drought, disease, or other dangers) because of the danger of price gouging on food items immediately after the fast. When fish mongers raised the price of fish before Shabbat or Yom Tov, the rabbis decreed that people should abstain from purchasing fish for

Shabbat and Yom Tov unless the price returned to normal levels.

The Mishnah relates that once, in Temple times, the sellers of doves necessary for certain sacrifices raised their prices inordinately. The rabbis threatened to free the people (through an ingenious halachic procedure) from having to bring doves at all for the sacrifice. The price of doves immediately returned to its normal level.

In our time, in many communities rabbis have decreed a price ceiling on what can be spent to purchase an *etrog*. In many instances, entering a "partnership" to purchase the *arba minim*, thus reducing demand, is encouraged. So I doubt that the threat of the *lulav* price gouging will actually materialize before Succot this year.

Nevertheless, the threat of price gouging, especially on items necessary for the performance of *mitzvot*, should be roundly condemned. It is a clear violation of the basic Jewish tenet regarding Torah – that "all its paths are the ways of pleasantness."

Just Let Go

Long-held ideologies and beliefs die hard. Even when they have been surpassed by events and circumstances, those who believed in them and promulgated them find it difficult, if not impossible, to adjust to the reality of the current situation.

There are many examples of this principle in today's world. There are still anarchists and Marxists in academia and in other influential positions. The events of the past century are ignored by them; they continue to hold onto the fantasy of some sort of perfect world built upon utopian Marxist philosophy. Ignoring facts is often a bad habit that affects the intelligentsia and elite.

After twenty years, a case can be made that the Oslo Accords were not such a good idea after all. A stronger case can be made that the withdrawal from Gaza was really a very bad idea. Yet the ideologues who foisted these very questionable policies upon us stubbornly refuse to admit that perhaps they were mistaken. Those who desire an illusory peace at almost any price still abound, and they gain considerable media coverage to continue promoting ideas that have long since become irrelevant. But in the world of the doctrinaire Left (and the doctrinaire Right, as well), once a believer, always a believer. Recycling past beliefs and policies that have been proven by events to have been mistaken only serves to prevent the creation of new initiatives that could be beneficial.

In the United States, we are witness to the fact that the Democratic Party simply cannot accept the fact that it was defeated in the last presidential election. Mrs. Clinton continues to blame her defeat upon everyone besides herself. Time and effort are being spent on issues that are not relevant to the welfare and future of the United States, but rather are purely political in nature and partisan in their presentations. Donald Trump was not elected by Vladimir Putin. He was elected by the disgruntled voters of Pennsylvania, Michigan, Ohio, and Florida. Recognizing this fact and internalizing these results will allow the Democrats to move forward and be a constructive force in the American political process. But the idea that Mrs. Clinton was entitled to win, *should have* won, dies very hard. Somehow, events must be wrong and reversible if they do not fit into the preconceived notions of the pundits and experts. After all, how can it be that all of the smart and beautiful people should been mistaken on such an important issue as electing a president of the United States of America? This unwillingness to let go creates enormous problems for a country that is already beset with major difficulties.

There was a rally last week in Barclay Center in Brooklyn protesting the drafting of Charedim into the IDF. The rally was sponsored by certain Orthodox Jewish extremist groups in both Israel and the United States. It costs a lot of money to lease Barclay Center for such an event. But money is no object when religious ideology is being promoted. The rally turned into an anti-Zionist forum and predictably became an anti-Israel gathering as well.

The question of Zionism in the Jewish world was perhaps a valid and understandable one a century ago. It has no validity today. Opposing the Jewish state today is tantamount to opposing the survival and welfare of the Jewish people as a whole. The mainstream of Charedi Judaism here in Israel participates in the state, in its government, and in its political and social life. It is slowly undergoing a change that will eventually bring it into the economic cycle of Israeli society as well. Accompanying this development is a small, gradual trickle of Charedi participation in the IDF. This is a very complicated and sensitive issue, and both sides are aware of the difficulties involved. Nevertheless, the issue is being addressed in different ways, and mainly under the radar of public media.

Those who cannot let go of the ideologies of a century ago and have made them "religious principles" do themselves and the Jewish people as a whole a huge disservice. They also must learn to just let go.

Murder

Judaism places human life and its preservation at the highest level of spiritual, social, and moral behavior. The commandment "you shall not murder" is the cornerstone of Jewish life. And throughout the ages of Jewish history, murder was always considered the most heinous of crimes. Even when killing was necessary and justified, such as in wars of self-defense and other extraordinary circumstances, it left a scar on the Jewish psyche. There is tradition that Moses was punished by God for his justifiable killing of the Egyptian taskmaster. He spent almost sixty years in exile from his brethren in Egypt.

King David, the most illustrious and pious of all Judean kings of Israel, was denied the privilege of building the Holy Temple in Jerusalem because he had killed people, albeit justifiably and legally. One who had spilled human blood was not ever going to be privileged to build the house of God. It is noteworthy that King Solomon, David's son and heir, who actually did construct the First Temple, never fought a war. His government did execute criminals and traitors, but Solomon was never seen by his generation or later generations as a killer.

During the long Exile of Israel, Jewish society generally knew of few, if any, cases of murder in its midst. Violent personal crime was also almost an unknown here in the Land of Israel for almost all of the last century. Unfortunately, there were political killings, ideologically motivated, such as those of de Haan, Arlazarov, and Rabin, but the general Israeli population felt itself safe from wanton murder.

Somehow, this situation changed in the opening decade of the twenty-first century. The Israeli underworld has grown wealthier, more powerful, and more violent over time. Their internal wars have grown more public and more brutal, with innocent victims dragged into the collateral damage. The police and the courts seem to be badly outflanked in dealing with the problem.

In addition to organized crime headlines, it seems there is hardly a day that passes when a murder – horrendous and shocking – by Israelis against Israelis is not featured in the media. Children against parents, neighbors against neighbors, spouses against spouses are all in the daily news. Drunken fights in pubs on Friday nights often lead to murder. Children bring knives to school, and stabbings inevitably occur. And here too, the authorities seem to be at a loss as to how to deal with this ugliness and its effect on our society. There seems to be no segment of our very diverse society that is exempted from this problem.

There are no easy or immediate solutions that anyone can propose to alter this bleak picture. Education towards civility, tolerance, and nonviolent disagreement is probably the only viable long-term solution. Every school in Israel, as well as every home and family, should teach, explain, and stress the imperative: "You shall not murder." Respect for this Torah prohibition should be constantly drilled into all segments of Jewish society. The relative absence of violent personal crime in past Jewish society was based on this type of repetitive education.

It was also based on a much more homogeneous society than is our current Israeli community. The conscious attempt by the early Zionists to create the "new Jew" produced a much more aggressive personality than the "old Jew" of the Diaspora. But with this strengthening of Jewish physical power, there also slowly arose a gradual erosion of the prohibition against violence and murder.

The absorption of immigrants, many of whom have no Jewish background whatsoever and who come from countries where violence is unfortunately all too common, has also complicated matters. The rabbis of the Talmud warned us that "the day of the ingathering of the exiles will be a most difficult one."

Prevailing versus Winning (2010)

Judaism always encourages taking a long view of matters. It is not wise to judge long-range outcomes and consequences on the basis of short-term appearances and happenings. The parable of the tortoise and the hare is one of the greatest truths of human existence. Because of our impatience, we often confuse prevailing in the short term with winning in the long term. Our world demands instantaneous results and has very little patience with what the long term will eventually hold for us.

Yet we are bitterly aware that prevailing in the short term is certainly no guarantee of what the long-term result will really be. Robert E. Lee won more victories on the battlefield than did Ulysses S. Grant. But in the end, the Confederacy was destroyed and the Federal Union was preserved. Here in Israel, hopes for peace prevailed and they led to Oslo, Wye, Hebron, Lebanon, and Gaza. Our dreams for peace prevailed, but they certainly did not win for us any of the intended results.

It is difficult to judge the future from the present. What one sees from here may not be what one sees from there; and what one sees from here is no guarantee that policies implemented so confidently, even arrogantly, will have beneficial outcomes. There is far too much emphasis on currently prevailing rather than upon ultimately winning.

Politicians, always aware of the next election, can only operate in this world of prevailing. That is why so few of them actually ever really win anything.

The contretemps regarding David Rotem's proposed Knesset bill altering the Law of Return and giving increased power to the Chief Rabbinate over conversion is a perfect example of prevailing over winning. The opponents to the bill, mainly non-Orthodox groups in the United States, have prevailed. With a specious argument about "dividing the Jewish people" (it is perfectly united currently, isn't it?), they have prevailed in forcing a six-month postponement of further consideration of the bill. Whether the bill in its present form is a perfect solution to the almost insoluble problem of non-Jewish immigration is certainly a matter of doubt and debate. But it should be clear to all by now, after decades of trying to square the circle regarding conversion procedures, that anything less than traditional, halachically acceptable courts and conversion procedures will not be recognized by a large and constantly growing community in the Jewish world.

The successful drive of the non-Orthodox groups gives them a sense of prevailing – especially with the Israeli Supreme Court on their side – but ultimately, in many cases, these "converts" suffer tragic social and familial consequences, if not immediately, certainly in the future. With more than fifty years of rabbinic experience, I can testify to the heartbreak of grandchildren who wish to marry into an observant Jewish family and find that their grandparents' conversions are deemed questionable at best, if not downright invalid. It is clear that temporary court and legislative accomplishments can mean very little a few generations down the pike.

The statistics regarding the eventual Jewishness of such converts who underwent a non-halachic conversion bear out the toll taken on the Jewish world and its future. If there is no minimal halachic observance in a house, the likelihood is abysmally low that the children raised there will have any positive attitude to Judaism or identification with Israel and the Jewish people. If nothing is demanded of the potential convert in terms of lifestyle changes, and all is left simply to words and pious declarations, there is little hope that the Jewish people – or even the convert himself or herself – will benefit from what is an essentially empty ceremony.

The Torah mentions thirty-six times – more times than any other commandment – the necessity to treat converts well, honestly, and with great respect, in recognition of the life-changing decision and action taken in becoming part of the Jewish people and its destiny. But the convert must be informed, realize, and accept the true cost of a decision to be part of the Jewish experience. And that cost is outlined by the same *halachah*, the same Torah that mandates warmth and consideration towards the convert, for his own true benefit. Confirming this halachic norm and tradition guarantees not only prevailing, but eventually winning for the entire Jewish nation as well.

Is Democracy Jewish?

Having survived the Knesset elections, perhaps it is time to take a cursory look at the democratic process of elections from the perspective of Jewish history. At first glance, Judaism does not seem to favor the electoral process for choosing its leaders. Moses was chosen by God to lead Israel, not by any sort of popular vote. The priesthood – the status of *Kohanim* – was reserved for Aaron and his descendants, also by Godly fiat. Joshua was appointed by Moses, again under God's instruction, to succeed him as the leader of the people. The Judges were self-appointed (though some of them, such as Yiftach, Gideon, Abimelech, and even Samson, were popularly confirmed because of their exploits in defending Israel against its enemies). And when the populace wanted a king appointed over them, the prophet Samuel voiced strong objections to an empowered, dynastic monarchy, criticizing the manner of demand for a king to rule over them "like all of the other nations."

It was in the field of Torah education that democratic ideals took hold. A woodchopper such as Hillel could become the *Nasi* – the head of the yeshiva and the Sanhedrin. Halachic decisions were made by majority vote. Raban Gamliel was temporarily deposed from the office of *Nasi* – impeached, if you will – because of his undemocratic behavior towards other scholars. Rabbi Elazar ben Azarya opened the study hall to all, not just the intellectually elite or the aristocrats. The heads of the main yeshivot of Babylonia during the period of the composition and editing of the Talmud were chosen by popular opinion among the scholars. The yeshivot of France during the time of Rashi were noted for their openness and tolerance of differing views. The history of the yeshivot of Eastern Europe is marked with incidents of student revolts, and the students always had the option of voting with their feet and leaving one institution to study somewhere else.

Since in the European exile there was no independent Jewish government (with the limited exception, perhaps, of the Council of the Four Lands in sixteenth, seventeenth, and part of eighteenth century Eastern Europe), Jewish leaders were chosen and recognized by popular approval and approbation. Elections, often very divisive and contentious, were held to choose rabbis of the communities. Even the lay leaders of the communities were subject to popular approval and always faced the threat of recall from office if the populace was sufficiently disgruntled with their rule. In the yeshivot, the students pretty much ruled the roost, deciding who should be the main scholars delivering the lectures and heading the institutions.

For its first century, Chassidism was fiercely meritocratic. The opponents of Chassidut mocked eighteenth-century Chassidim by saying, "If one says he is a *Rebbe*, then he is a *Rebbe*!" To a certain extent this was a backhanded compliment, for Chassidut opened the field of participation in the public arena of Judaism to millions. Only in the middle of the nineteenth century did Chassidut become overwhelmingly dynastic, though even then there was room allowed for new dynasties to be created and become popular.

In all facets of the Jewish world, popular opinion held sway, for good or for better. Many of the great religious Torah leaders did not hold major public positions; rather, they were "elected" to be followed by popular acclaim and recognition. In the twentieth century, Jewish life was governed almost completely by elections, sparring parties, and nonstop campaigning, which continues today in our State of Israel.

So Jewish life is quite democratic, one could even say too democratic, for it tends to be fractious and chaotic. As Winston Churchill said in the House of Commons in 1947 (quoting an unknown predecessor): "It has been said that democracy is the worst form of government – except for all those other forms that have been tried from time to time…"

Teachers

Education is in the forefront of the news here in Israel, what with a long strike of secondary school teachers and the somewhat disappointing ranking of Israeli children in certain subject ratings. Even though there is general consensus that money is the problem (and the solution), I feel that though money is important, the heart of the problem lies far deeper.

In the current atmosphere of secular Israeli society, basic Jewish values are almost unknown, let alone taught. In his monumental code of Jewish law, Maimonides has an entire section devoted to teaching, knowledge, and education. The basic value he emphasizes is that teachers are to be respected and given honor: one should rise before one's teacher, speak respectfully to the teacher, and treat the teacher with greater probity than even one's parent.

The Talmud pithily states that "parents bring a child into this world, but a teacher can bring a child into the World to Come" – into a world of spirit, creativity, ideas, self-worth, and ultimately immortality. Thus teaching transcends even parenting, a concept that automatically produces respect and honor for the profession.

Teaching has never been a well-paying profession in Jewish society. In monetary terms, the tribe of Simeon – who were teachers and scribes – were viewed as the poorest of all of the tribes of Israel. But in a society that does not measure success or honor only in monetary coin, the highest compliment in Israel was that one was called a teacher. In fact, the Talmud attributes to God, so to speak, the characteristic of being a teacher – "He Who teaches Torah to His people, Israel." In Judaism, even mortal teachers are viewed as being engaged in holy work.

But the teacher-student relationship is reciprocal. Maimonides teaches us that in Judaism the teacher-student relationship is really a parent-child relationship. A teacher must not only respect the students, but must *love* them. Depending on circumstances, this love sometimes can be tough love and sometimes cuddly, fuzzy warmth. But the student has to be aware that the teacher loves him or her. In an atmosphere of love, much can be accomplished, even under less than ideal physical conditions. I am perplexed why the demand of the teachers for a smaller number of students in a given class was not buttressed by the opinion of the Talmud (in Baba Batra) that class size should be restricted to twenty-five students per teacher so the teacher can provide the guidance every individual student needs. Excelling in mathematics and science may not be for everyone, but being loved and guided correctly in traditional Jewish life values is for everyone.

I suppose I should not have been surprised by this lack of traditional thinking, for the Israeli secular school system slowly has been divested of any Jewish values over the decades. Teaching our children that the Bible is a collection of currently irrelevant myths, that the long experience of millennia of Jewish life in the Exile was essentially worthless, and that the Jewish mission of being "a light unto the nations" is restricted to high-tech research is a certain recipe for poor educational results, and eventually for a dysfunctional society.

The teachers are entitled to a decent living salary and to proper physical working conditions. But again, Judaism places a high value on personal dedication and preparation in teaching. Education is the "labor of Heaven." The Talmud tells us that there is no comparison between reviewing a lesson one hundred and one times and reviewing it only one hundred times. It is always the "extra" that counts most.

The great decisors of *halachah* have always justified the right of teachers to strike for improvement in educational and financial circumstances. This is especially true in our society, where the schools themselves do not control the purse strings and an all-powerful central government decides these issues.

But ultimately the responsibility of all concerned is the proper education of the children. The bitter residue of the current dispute will not be easily dissipated, even when all of the issues have been settled. Again, the rabbis of the Talmud stated: "Who is the wise person? One who sees in advance the consequences of his actions." A little application of Talmudic wisdom and traditional Jewish values will go a long way to help raise our educational system to the desired level of excellence.

The Past and the Future

Judaism preaches a forward-looking outlook on life and a positive take on the human situation. It also encourages, and in fact commands, that even though one must concentrate on the future, one is never to forget the past. For what happened in the past to a great degree shapes our future and influences it greatly. Much of our current society is so meshed in the present that it has little memory of the past and scant vision of what the future should be like.

The present is the wink of an eye and the breath of the moment. So basically, we are left with the past and the future. Much of the frustration and tension that exists in modern society, in my opinion, stems from the fact that we are always trying to win in the present, and it consistently eludes us. There can be no purpose in life if it is only the pursuit of the present, its pleasures, and imagined joys.

One of the extraordinary accomplishments of the Jewish people over its long history has been that it never relinquished the dream of the future, while at the same time it always remembered and commemorated the past. In effect, the present was always shaped and guided by our memories of the past and our vision of the future.

And this was not only true for Jewish society as a whole. Perhaps just as importantly, it was the basis for individual attainment and Jewish family life. In a Jewish family, we always remember those who went before us and we attempt to emulate their good qualities and achievements. At the same time, we concentrate on our future, on our children. We are constantly asking ourselves two important questions:

- How do I and my family rate according to my ancestors' aspirations and judgments of life?
- What do I want my family legacy to look like in future generations?

These two questions frame our behavior in the present. We want those who come after us to be able to look back at our lives and be proud of us. That is our road to immortality and eternity.

It may be more comfortable in the present to remain unburdened with family and children and all that entails, but just a glimpse into the future will show us that this is the only way that we truly can be remembered. Moreover, the continuity of the Jewish people and Judaism itself is dependent upon the formation of families and instilling within those families timeless Torah values that they will preserve.

Remembering the past is often painful and disturbing. That is especially true of our own personal lives: we have all made mistakes, and there are many things that we are not necessarily proud to remember. Usually we are able to sublimate these thoughts into our unconscious, and this is necessary for us to continue to live and improve. There is no use in brooding over the past. The only thing that we can do is regret our mistakes, learn from them, and be careful not to repeat them. That is the basis of the Jewish concept of true repentance.

However, one is not allowed to say to oneself that because of those past errors, no matter how severe they may have been, all was lost. One of the great weapons of the Satan within us is to convince us that we have no self-worth and that no situation can be improved – that we are not worthy of being remembered in a positive way.

Yes, we have to be realistic about our past and ourselves, but our eyes should be towards the future and what can yet be accomplished. What benefit can I be to myself and to others? How can my life yet make a difference to future generations? I think that these are important ideas to keep in our thoughts.

Human Nature

Old Magazines

When I moved away from Chicago and close proximity to my parents, my mother was ever-concerned about my continued intellectual development. To ensure that I would be wise about current events, she would mail the previous month's collection of *Time* magazines to me. Invariably, when I read these magazines weeks after their time-sensitive publication, I found that they had gotten everything all wrong. Their predictions of events that would occur were woefully inaccurate, and their analyses of situations proved shallow and of little value. Yet I had to keep on reading these magazines for, after all, my mother had sent them to me, and she always asked me about them.

This experience – receiving old magazines for many years – cured me of believing in political pundits and economic experts. Unforeseen events always arose to mock their oracular predictions. I always thought of the verse in the second chapter of Psalms: "He Who sits in Heaven laughs, the Lord mocks them."

So I developed the habit of reading *only* old magazines, taking fiendish enjoyment and perverse pleasure in their now-evident false understanding of events and arrogant pontifications. I imagine that since few people read old magazines, except when sitting in a doctor's waiting room, the publishers can keep on churning out their assessments, predictions, and analyses without fear of exposure as being consistently mistaken, as they truly are.

I recently read a March 2011 issue of a popular English-language Israeli magazine. It was just gushing with articles and an editorial about the creation of a "new Middle East" due to the "Arab Spring" that deposed the rulers of Tunisia, Egypt, and Libya – and would now proceed to do so in Syria, Jordan, and the Gulf States as well. Well, the "Arab Spring" has turned out to be pretty much of a bust, with no real political or economic progress left in its wake. Hundreds of thousands of Arabs have been killed by their fellow Arabs since the "Arab Spring" sprung. The Middle East has become even more unstable and volatile than before, and those rosy predictions about the "new Middle East" are pathetic in retrospect. The usual tired rhetoric about the plight of the Palestinians and the proposed solutions to their problems advanced in that magazine now read as unrealistic and preposterous.

I am forced to wonder whether the political and diplomatic leaders of the world ever bother to read old magazines. I am confident that if they did, their policies, statements, and goals would be much more realistic than they currently are. Read the magazines of the Oslo era and weep. Events on the ground truly mock the past wisdom of journalistic experts.

The Torah bids us to remember the past in a meaningful fashion. That means not only to remember past events and personalities, but also to remember the inaccurate assessments that were regarded as infallible in the past. Remember what wise men once said was "impossible to occur," and nevertheless did occur. Remember the fallibility of all human beings, and the fact that great people often are capable of great mistakes. Remember that the race is not always to the swift or the battle to the courageous and mighty.

In the memory bank of the Jewish people we must preserve the eras of false messiahs who led us astray, and great scholars who erred in their assessment of future events that would befall the Jewish people. Remembrance of the past limits present hubris and arrogance, fanaticism, and wild innovations. There were many who said that the Holocaust could never happen, but it did. There were others from diametrically opposed poles of the Jewish world who said that a Jewish state could not be created; and if created, would collapse within fifteen years of its establishment. They have also been proven to be inaccurate in their predictions and in their understanding of God's will. That does not diminish their greatness, but it does prove their fallible humanity. If you have doubts about this, just read through some old magazines.

Oops!
(2011)

So the Goldstone Report condemning Israel for "war crimes" in the Gaza operation against Hamas got it wrong. Richard Goldstone, after whom this infamous document is named, has come out publicly and declared that the UN Human Rights Commission erred in its findings against Israel. He also recognized that body's prejudice and past animus towards Israel. While it is certainly admirable for Goldstone to come forth now (two years after its publication) and admit his error, it is undoubtedly impossible to fully correct the damage done to Israel by his initial report. Nevertheless, he is to be admired for publicly confessing error. This is a trait that is noticeably absent in public officials, who normally assert that they have never been wrong in their decisions, statements, judgments, or policies.

The damage done to Israel by Goldstone's original report is almost irreparable; and even in his retraction, Judge Goldstone offers no true apology for the report and its vicious conclusions regarding Israeli "war crimes," insinuating that Israel's noncooperation with the commission carries major responsibility for the commission's erroneous report.

Goldstone admits that it was naïve in the extreme to think that Hamas would conduct any investigations or regret the indiscriminate firing of rockets at Israeli civilian targets. And though he hints at it, it would have been naïve in the extreme for Israel to receive a fair hearing from a UN commission that is blatantly biased against it. The whole sordid process was just another stunt of delegitimizing Israel by the Muslim and European world, a process begun at the notorious UN-authorized Durban Conference of 2001, and continuing throughout the world since then.

Still, Goldstone's admission of error has a certain air of nobility to it. Shimon Peres never admitted that Oslo was an error. Tzipi Livni and Ehud Olmert never admitted that their support of the destruction of Gush Katif was badly mistaken. Ehud Barak never revisited his shameful abandonment of Lebanon, which has led to wars and the rise of Hezbollah. In our country, all of our leaders – religious, governmental, social, societal, and educational – are never wrong. There is no personal accountability for errors in judgment or policy. It is only the criminal behavior of our leadership that eventually brings them down, but even then, there is scant evidence of admission of guilt or of apology to the long-suffering public. They are all innocent, even when found to be guilty. Richard Goldstone's admission of error should serve as a reprimand to our society and its leaders.

Admitting guilt and identifying one's sins of commission and omission is a central tenet of Judaism. The Torah teaches us that no individual, great as that person may be, is truly infallible. Judaism recognizes that people in leadership roles make mistakes. Such is our human condition. But it always demands accountability and remorse from those leaders for those errors. Jewish tradition teaches us that a key difference between King Saul and King David lay in Saul's inability to admit his blunder in the war against Amalek, while David publicly acknowledged his mistakes and sins.

In Proverbs, King Solomon states that "one who admits [errors] and forsakes repeating them will be mercifully pardoned." Without personal admission of error, there can be no pardon, no forgiveness. The high priest of Israel had to confess his own personal shortcomings on Yom Kippur before he could beseech Heaven for forgiveness on behalf of all of Israel. Throughout rabbinic literature we see the willingness of great men to admit that they overlooked something, or that they erred in their judgment or logic in a previous decision. We see numerous instances in rabbinic responsa where a later response to an issue concedes that the original response was wrong and should no longer be followed.

Every author will tell you that if it were not for the insistence of his or her editor, no precious original word would have been changed or corrected. It is difficult to erase or delete in one's own masterpiece.

It is even more difficult to admit to one's self, let alone publicly, that one has made a mistake. Judge Goldstone has perhaps redeemed his name from eternal infamy in Jewish history by his statement retracting his earlier judgment regarding Israeli actions against Hamas. It is not my task to decide what action he should take to try and undo the effects of his original report. But I feel he is to be complimented for issuing this new statement on the matter and owning up to the gross inaccuracy that originally was his. Would that there were more responsible officials who would emulate his honesty.

Confusing Roles

All people are duty bound to try and help other people in need; and rabbis are especially called upon to be available to others in their times of distress. Yet it is essential for one to be able to recognize one's limitations and true role. Many a rabbi has gotten himself into deep trouble by acting as a psychologist, therapist, financial advisor, marriage counselor, or business consultant when he had no particular training or talent in that profession.

You would not consult your stockbroker regarding medical issues, just as you would not consult your physician on which stocks to purchase. But this seemingly logical and axiomatic lesson is violated daily, often with sad, even tragic, results. Especially in our highly specialized world, it should be apparent that one should not pose as an expert in a specialty for which one has no training or education.

In biblical times, Jews turned to prophets for advice and succor. But prophets disappeared from our world millennia ago. With the rise of the Chassidic movement in the eighteenth century, the figure of an almost omniscient spiritual leader was recreated. That person was consulted on all issues of life because it was felt that he had a special connection to Heaven. This concept, rooted in certain kabbalistic thought, soon spilled over into the general rabbinate.

No matter how rabbis attempted to avoid such an image and such practices, the idea of the rabbi being an expert in all fields of life, available for consultation on all matters, has taken hold in the Jewish world. It has made life very uncomfortable for the ordinary communal/congregational rabbi – if there is such an "ordinary" creature.

Of course, a rabbi must possess wisdom and compassion. But that is true of every Jew, if not of every human being. Many of the difficult situations that have occurred over the past decade involving rabbis and their congregants, as well as educators and their students, are simply products of the person confusing his role and playing the professional or prophet.

It is easy to become sucked into the morass of others' problems, and there is great temptation to be of help. But such help often turns into harm, exacerbating problems instead of solving them. It is very difficult to say no to people who ask for help. I do not mean that one should be inattentive to someone else's narrative of problems. But it does mean that one should be cautious in response and must keep in mind that, in most cases, the wrong answer is far worse than getting no answer at all.

We are warned by the rabbis of old that we must be extreme in avoiding angry outbursts, for when a person loses his temper and goes into a rage, he severs his connection to God. So there is a place in life for everything, including extremism, but only in the two instances pinpointed by our sages' wisdom.

I come from a generation where rabbis were very reticent, not readily advancing solutions to people's personal issues. The world has changed greatly since I observed the behavior of my father and his rabbinic colleagues. Nevertheless, I think that one should not expect one's rabbi, physician, financial advisor, or even good friend to become a psychological therapist. It just will not turn out well.

Confusing one's role is a sign of arrogance and is indicative of hubris. The greatest teachers of Israel, from Moses till today, were and are people who can say, "I don't know. Consult someone who perhaps does."

Extremism

Contrary to all rumors and actions, Judaism abhors extremism. The prudent rabbis and teachers of Israel have always advocated moderation and the golden mean. Talmud Yerushalmi compares human choices in life and behavior, attitudes and philosophy, to a person who has a choice between two roads. One road is sunlit, but burning hot like a desert at high noon. The other road is snow covered and bitterly cold. If the person goes on the sunlit road, he may die of heat prostration and sunstroke. If the person goes on the snow-covered road, death from frostbite and hypothermia may eventually occur. What, then, should the person do? Construct a third road, one that is warm, but not hot, moderate in temperature and condition, and not extreme.

Extremes of behavior and of religious fervor are ultimately negative and harmful. One may feel that one's extremism serves God's purposes here on earth. But the Torah teaches us that this is not true. The middle road in life and manners, character traits and lifestyle, is the preferred choice of the Torah and rabbinic tradition. Maimonides called the middle way "the golden path" in life. Extremism, in his opinion, was allowed only in order to achieve a return to the golden middle way.

Extremism negates tolerance and increases hatreds; it triggers verbal abuse and, inevitability, violence. It is counterproductive to its own goals and eventually – usually after a heavy price is extracted in human feelings, reputations, even human lives – it collapses of its own weight and misdeeds. But instead of learning this clear lesson of history, extremism on many fronts remains alive and well in our Jewish world, not to mention in general society as well.

Moderation is difficult to maintain and popularize, for it promises no certain, easy answers to the complexities of life. On the other hand, there is a great attraction to extremism. It provides certainty in a very uncertain world and provides a moral underpinning to one's hatreds, prejudices, and frustrations. So it is very popular.

Extremism in religion is especially appealing, for then one is convinced that he is accomplishing God's purposes in a superior fashion. As a byproduct, extremism in religion also breeds the rationale of exclusivity. Clearly, everyone else in the world is wrong, culpable, and doomed, except for the extremist who knows exactly God's will. Anyone who sees things differently, even slightly differently, is a condemned heretic. And as the Muslim extremists prove to us daily, such heretics are fair game to be maimed and murdered. Extremism allows for the worst crimes to be justified and exalted because it skews any sort of proportion in human life and subverts common sense, rational thought, and acceptable behavior.

In his acceptance speech of the presidential nomination at the Republican National Convention in 1964, Senator Barry Goldwater destroyed any hope of being elected when he stated that "extremism in the cause of democracy is a virtue." That statement sufficed to frighten away many a potential voter. The tragic truth is that extremism, even in defense of a just cause, often causes the use of unjust means.

This is the import of the rabbis' disapproval of *mitzvah haba'ah b'aveirah* – a positive commandment of the Torah that was fulfilled through the commission of a sin or an immoral act. The Torah teaches us that righteousness as an end goal is ultimately only achieved through righteous means. Zealots and extremists shun such Torah principles and thus poison the atmosphere for all of us. Witness the debacle of extremist Jews at the 2006 Tehran conference reinforcing Holocaust denial.

Maimonides permits extremism in two areas of life. One is humility. There is no limit to humility, for arrogance and false pride create monstrous people and terrible situations. Moses is complimented in the Torah not for his strength, intellect, or leadership abilities, but only for his humility, for being a true servant of God. And a second area where extremism is permitted is in control of anger. Words spoken and actions committed in fury are lethal to relationships, families, communities, and nations.

Certainty and Uncertainty

We have all heard the famous phrase that the only certainties in life are death and taxes. We are also well aware that humans crave certainty. We plan for our future, we attempt to provide funds and care for our later years, and for our descendants as well.

Yet even a cursory glance at history will illustrate that there is no real certainty in any facet of life – health, wealth, success, power, national stability, etc. – and that uncertainty is the norm in all human existence – personal, national, and international. But uncertainty is such an uncomfortable state of being that humans prefer to deny it. We listen to our financial planners and invest our money according to their projections of what our wealth will be twenty or thirty years hence; and yet our rational mind tells us that they don't really know the future, since no human being knows it. Yet we crave certainty so desperately that often we behave in a fashion that is truly counterproductive to our best interests.

There is no people in the world that has existed as long and as dangerously in the milieu of uncertainty as the people of Israel. Lately, I have been studying works of rabbinic responsa spanning four centuries. All of them carry the caveat that circumstances can change rapidly and that their decisions are not to be taken as prophecy, for "plague, war, expulsion, and persecution" may certainly intervene. Yet interestingly enough, there is almost never any note of pessimism or depression in their words and writings. Apparently, they all acquired the knack of living productive, meaningful, and holy lives in a world of complete uncertainty.

They did so by grasping the essence of Torah values – that good is ultimately a wiser path in life than evil; that faith in God is a necessary component in personal and national Jewish life; and that by raising generations of loyal and committed Jews, the certainty of Jewish survival will conquer the uncertainties of the circumstances ahead.

A person needs some certainty as an anchor in life. The Torah and Jewish traditions, the history and memories of the Jewish people, can provide that anchor in our turbulent tide of constant uncertainty.

Judaism recognizes that all predictions regarding the future, all analyses of the present, are inherently tenuous, if not downright false.

The Torah writes: "What is hidden belongs to the realm of the Lord our God, but what is clearly revealed is that we and our descendants are to live a Torah way of life." The Talmud teaches us: "Why are you curious to attempt to decipher what has been hidden by Heaven?"

All of the nineteenth and twentieth century "certainties" and ideological "waves of the future" have already been reduced to ashes. So now we are being fed a diet of new certainties utilizing popular words such as democracy, human rights, progressivism, and international interdependence. But even as these new certainties are being advanced and propagated, we begin to feel the sneaking suspicion that these certainties are not so certain. Could it be that they may not turn out to be the predicted panacea for all human struggles?

For what is hidden from us – future events and upheavals (and we can be certain that there will be upheavals) – belongs to Heaven. This is why Judaism prefers to deal with the present and pragmatic rather than with the unknown, mysterious future.

Probably all we can glean with assurance from the events of human life that currently surround us is that we must do our best. We must be our most noble, our kindest selves, and we must be committed to the preservation of our Torah, our people, and our state. We have it on good authority that this is our only certainty.

Difficult Decisions (2017)

One of the traditions of rabbinic jurisprudence is that courts of law should attempt – at almost all costs – to arrive at a compromise/arbitration decision rather than enforce the letter of the law. This is undoubtedly because true justice is often beyond the capabilities of ordinary humans. In all major decisions in life, there are generally winners and losers. This is certainly true when two adversarial parties are involved and decisions must be rendered that benefit one and damage the other. There is also the question of the public good, the overall impression that the decision may make upon society, and the question of precedent regarding future decisions. As Abraham Lincoln phrased it, "A poor compromise settlement is always better than a good lawsuit."

But people are rarely satisfied with compromises and settlements, especially when questions of doctrine, policy, belief, and ideology are intermixed with the specific issues. In those cases, compromises are viewed as a betrayal of values, something to be avoided.

There are a number of issues on the front burner of Israeli news today that are illustrative of this fact. Is there any possibility of a just compromise regarding the settlement of Amona and its impending forced evacuation? What are the rights of the people living there for decades? What are the rights of those who claim that the settlement was built upon their land? What about the national political and international diplomatic consequences of evacuation or retention of the settlement?

There seems to be no compromise that would be acceptable to all; and no matter what happens, the issue will simmer for years to come.

In Israeli criminal justice there is a tendency, almost an unwritten rule, that plea bargains are the way to dispose of criminal cases. This is not an Israeli invention. The same is true in the United States and perhaps in most Western countries operating under the rule of law. The plea bargain usually satisfies no one completely. The person is essentially found guilty of a serious crime, but because of the difficulties that the legal system poses in pursuing the matter, the charges are lessened and the punishment is usually radically decreased. People harmed by the crime are always outraged that the perpetrator got off so easy. Yet the paralysis of the legal systems as they exist in the Western world and here in Israel almost dictate that bargains are the necessary oil that lubricates the wheels of justice in the court system. Plea bargains are practical answers to difficult matters, but they belie any sense of true justice and rarely, if ever, provide closure for the victims. The courts are forced to make a difficult choice between the practical and the moral, the temporary and the eternal.

These factors reemphasize to us the inadequacy of human wisdom. The Talmud ruefully states that the Lord (so to speak) is busy righting the wrongs committed by well-meaning but erroneous legal decisions of human courts. So it becomes the job of Heaven to remove wealth from the fraudulent and provide for the defrauded when human courts charged with that task were unable to accomplish it correctly. Heaven apparently is a very busy place.

The Talmud teaches us that a judge can only base a decision on what the eye sees. One can use only one's best judgment to arrive at a verdict. Whether or not that ruling will ultimately prove to be the wise and correct one – a judgment that will stand the tests of time, circumstance, and later knowledge – is never known at the moment of decision.

Because of this limitation, ultimate justice is rarely to be found in human affairs. We are too narrow in our scope to achieve that noble goal. And that fact is the justification for all of the shortcuts that our legal system takes – compromises, plea bargains, etc. – in order to keep society moving, even with limited justice as a result.

Frustrations

Every day of life automatically brings a share of frustrations and disappointments. Very rarely do things turn out for us exactly as we had hoped. Some frustrations are relatively minor even in our personal scheme of things – my inability to easily change a halogen light bulb or carry a tune, for instance. Other frustrations, such as health problems and financial difficulties, take on a greater dimension in our lives.

Frustration usually leads to feelings of anger, and anger leads to bitterness of spirit, even to violence. I have seen articles by psychologists advocating expressions of anger as a positive reaction to frustrations. "Blowing off steam" is an understandable reaction to moments of extreme frustration. Yet the Torah and Jewish tradition strongly oppose such expressions of anger in almost all circumstances of life. The Talmud is replete with statements denigrating anger.

If that's the case, how is one to deal with the inevitable daily frustrations of life? Is there no antidote to the roiling emotions that boil up within us so regularly?

Yes, there is. Jewish tradition advances the idea of perspective in viewing life. When scrutinizing a painting by an impressionist or pointillist artist, we are advised to look at it from some distance and not close up. Standing near the canvas, it appears to be composed of disconnected blotches of paint that convey no message or scene. But by positioning ourselves ten feet away from the painting, the genius of the artist is revealed; instead of small smears of paint, we see a masterpiece of color and form. Likewise, if we stand too close to the mundane occurrences that are our daily lot we are very prone to frustrations and all of the negative emotions that they produce within us. Life must be viewed as a whole. Awareness of the general picture can help us deal with the particular issues that confront us.

The rabbis went so far as to teach that a living human being should not complain about life's circumstances and problems – is it not sufficient that the person is still alive? The Jew begins each day by acknowledging the fact that he or she is still alive to live another day. Taken from this standpoint, frustrations and disappointments are more easily borne and dealt with. Perspective is the key to mental health and spiritual strength.

Acceptance of one's inherent limitations also helps combat frustration. There are many things that I simply cannot do. By realizing that I do not have that necessary skill, talent, or ability, I am no longer as frustrated by my inability to accomplish that mundane goal that so baffles me. Professional athletes always proclaim that they have to "play within themselves" and "not try to do too much." Bluntly put, this means that they recognize their limitations and concentrate on what they can do. They don't fret too much over what they cannot do. This is a good lesson for everyone in all of life's circumstances.

Of course, acceptance of one's limitations requires a lowered ego. Maimonides links humility with the absence of anger. Someone who is haughty and arrogant will automatically live a life of frustration and anger. Everything that does not go right for them is perceived as a personal slight and as a blow to the ego. The illustrious men of the Lithuanian Mussar movement used reaction to life's frustrations as a litmus-paper test of spiritual status. Serenity in life and in dealing with life's challenges became the hallmark of the truly pious Torah Jew.

The prophet Isaiah taught us that "the wicked storm like the raging sea." King David blessed God for "leading him to the calm waters." Life is always replete with frustrations. How we deal with them is the true measure of our spiritual selves.

Doing Favors

Charity is built into the fabric of Jewish life and law. The *halachah* prescribes the minimum, and sometimes even the maximum, amounts to be donated to charity. In this sense, charity encompasses support of Torah institutions and scholars, donations directly to the needy, and the funding of other well-established educational, social, and health-related institutions. We are all aware of the continuing fundraising drives of such organizations and the growing needs of individuals.

However, this form of charitable giving, vital and important as it is in its own right, is not the full range of the Jewish concept of *chesed* – kindness to others. The word *chesed* itself indicates a breaking down of barriers between people, an ability to relate to another's feelings as well as his material and spiritual needs. Thus when the prophets demand that we do acts of *chesed*, they are not only speaking about charitable donations of wealth and goods, but also about a donation of time, positive attitudes, and creating a sense of empathy for one another.

Home hospitality sometimes proves that it is much more convenient to pay for someone's hotel lodging than to have that person stay over in one's house. It then becomes an act of charity – not to be minimized – but it is not yet an act of true *chesed*. For *chesed* requires and demands personal involvement with others, and oftentimes in life people find it difficult to become so involved. By nature, human beings are hesitant about breaking down such barriers. So the Torah appears to go out of its way to impress upon us the necessity of performing acts of *chesed*. Somehow it is against our inborn nature.

Part of this reluctance is that no one wishes to be seen as a naïve patsy who can easily be taken advantage of. When someone asks a favor from us, not money, but just a favor – pick up my mail or groceries, etc. – we have a natural tendency to refuse, because of our vulnerability to exploitation by others. There is a voice within us that says, "Why should I do you a favor? When have you ever done something for me?" The Torah wishes to break us of thinking in such a mode. One is not allowed to do a favor for someone else and at the same time remind that person that when the circumstances were reversed the other person refused to do the favor.

So true *chesed* becomes a very demanding goal. It requires a revamping of attitudes towards others and a reworking of our individual personalities. The Talmud sees that wishing others a good morning is an act of *chesed* that has the potential of lengthening one's life span. We do not often think of a friendly greeting in that vein, but the Talmud views this ordinary act of sociability as having cosmic importance. The Mussar movement placed such seemingly small gestures of sociability and concern for the feelings and well-being of others at the forefront of its definition of Jewish ethical values. Being a good Jew meant being able to do favors for others without a feeling of resentment or reluctance. Not an easy task.

Many schools have instituted *chesed* programs requiring the students to perform specific acts of *chesed* at appointed times to assigned people and groups. In unguarded moments, a number of students over the years have complained to me about such coerced *chesed*. Instead of training these young people to love doing *chesed*, the program had a completely opposite effect upon them. Coercion rarely breeds acceptance in the soul and mind of the coerced person. (Very few ardent Communists were created in Stalin's Gulag or Chairman Mao's retraining camps.) *Chesed* is a habit that should be learned at home and emphasized in society.

Here is Israel, where the prevailing fear is not to be considered a *freyer* – a naïve simpleton who can be exploited – *chesed* often has difficulty bursting forth. Good defensive driving and giving consideration to others on the road – even to the idiot who is trying to get back in your lane – ultimately is an act of *chesed*.

Our sages teach us that the world itself is built on the idea of *chesed*. Our father Abraham and our mother Sarah built the Jewish people on the pillar of *chesed* to others. Their example is worth emulating, especially in this rushed, impersonal domain of ours.

Hypocrisy

One of the greatest crimes in the eyes of the general public is behavior of public figures that is patently hypocritical. Based on the leaders' previous pronouncements, the public creates high, if not unreasonable, expectations of them. But people are people, with frailties and temptations, and people in high office are also people. This is not to condone any illegal or immoral activities on the part of anyone; but the fact that leaders weave such an aura of selflessness in their high-sounding utterances and public declarations leaves them very vulnerable to charges of hypocrisy.

I have always felt that part of Winston Churchill's greatness in the leadership of Great Britain in World War II lay in his refusal to make sweeping assurances or proclaim easy solutions. He told the English people, "I have nothing to offer but blood and toil, sweat and tears" and expressed the hope that eventually victory would come their way. This promise, in all of its forms, was eventually fulfilled in full. There were no pledges of settling ancient disputes in a matter of months, no brazen commitments for immediate victories, and no hiding from the evident facts of the situation. This straightforward honesty enabled him to escape from the plague of hypocrisy that has accompanied so many of our leaders on the social, military, and diplomatic fronts. The greater the promises, the more outlandish the projections, the greater the toll that exposed hypocrisy exacts from the body politic.

The fall from grace and office of political leaders in the United States because of their immoral behavior was hastened by the fact that they portrayed themselves as crusaders for family values, ethical business relationships, and honesty in all matters of public and private behavior. This promise of high standards doomed them when their own failings were revealed. The public loves to punish a hypocrite, to puncture the balloon of pompous self-righteousness and personal infallibility.

Hypocrisy is also the paramount enemy of religious leaders. Fallen clergy are the stuff of legend in popular literature and investigative media.

They are especially vulnerable because of their usual posture of moral self-righteousness and their penchant for criticizing those whom they feel are derelict in their behavior, policies, thoughts, and attitudes. When their faults are exposed, not only do they fall, they take down the faith that they represent as well.

The tendency in some religious circles to glorify its leadership to the extent that these people are regarded as irreproachable only exacerbates the vulnerability to hypocrisy. Once revealed, hypocrisy drags down the entire structures of idealism and morality that once were represented by this leader. Religious leaders have to be careful not only in their private behavior – for in our times, all private behavior eventually becomes public knowledge – but in their public statements regarding matters of morality and human behavior.

The Hasmonean king, Alexander Yannai, is recorded in the Talmud as warning his son against those "who behave as Zimri, but expect to be rewarded as though they were Pinchas." Hypocrisy was seen as a greater sin in public life than being a Sadducee.

The Talmud warned the wise men of Israel to be very circumspect in their statements and words. Overstatements lead to exposure. Creating idols out of men, no matter how worthy and holy they may be (and there are many such holy people still in our midst, thank God) is dangerous and against Torah principles. It certainly raises the specter of hypocrisy to a warning level.

To create a spirit of humility in all humans, especially in those who find themselves in influential positions, the Torah teaches that there are no perfect people. Even the righteous have failings and sins. Arrogance leads to brazen claims, overstatements, hasty judgments, and great risks. It is stated in the name of the Gaon of Vilna that he predicted that later generations would be dominated by external appearances and posturing, not by true inner beliefs and pure motives. The greater the emphasis on externals, the more likely the emergence of hypocrisy.

It is possible to recover from mistakes, errors, and foolish behavior. But it is almost impossible for the public person in any forum to recover from revealed hypocrisy.

Undoing the Past

One of the impossible tasks in human life is undoing the past. Perhaps even more tragic and unfair is judging the past by current norms and standards. Since all of us make mistakes in our lifetimes, the past is always a danger to us. In the scheme of things, we are always remembered for our past failings rather than for our later accomplishments. The Talmud warns about this human habit, for it forbids us to remind a convert to Judaism of his or her pagan origins or one who has repented of previous sins.

But the nature of people is never that generous, especially in a world of aggressive investigative reporting, Wikileaks mindset, and mostly unsubstantiated scandal-mongering. The past is always the present in current society. Sometimes the sins and indiscretions of the past, the mistakes and errors of judgment, are so important and monumental that they will never be erased.

We find in the Bible that Menasseh, the king of Judah, promoted idolatry as the state religion during the first seventeen years of his reign. The Talmud records that he even executed his own grandfather, the prophet Isaiah, in his zealousness to eradicate Judaism. Yet we are also taught that he repented of his actions and policies, and that for the last thirty-three years of his reign he observed Jewish practice and reintroduced Torah law as the basis of societal life in Judah. Nevertheless, despite scattered references in Talmud, Midrash, and prayer which attempt to rehabilitate his historical reputation, his past always resurfaces to gain him condemnation in Jewish thought and writings. Apparently, we can never truly undo the past.

If this be the case, one can legitimately ask: "Of what value is repentance?" The answer to that question is complicated, and often confusingly vague and unsatisfying. It is the subject of a significant number of philosophic writings by the profound thinkers of Judaism throughout the ages. Suffice it to say that the gist of the matter is that on a personal level, true and sincere repentance erases the sins of the past and may even be deemed as bringing merit to the individual. But the consequences – public, national, affecting the lives of others and future generations – generated by those past sins can never be completely eradicated. And therefore Menasseh's repentance on a personal level is accepted by Heaven, and he may have achieved his own redemption, but the idolatry that he initiated was of such an influential nature that it cannot be undone or ignored: the verdict of history still finds him guilty.

The murderer may truly regret his deed, but the victim remains dead. A pornographer may repent of his writings and productions, but the influence that these had upon others is never undone. It is a permanent stain on the fabric of society and cannot be completely removed. Clearly, a person's actions and influence always live on, even after passing from this life.

A professor of mine in law school once taught us that all lawyers, entrepreneurs, and professionals make at least one great mistake in their careers. He then declared: "Fortunate is the person who makes that mistake early on. Doomed is the one who makes it towards the end of an active career or public life, for that person will always be remembered unfairly not for lifetime accomplishments but rather for that late mistake and error of judgment."

There are numerous examples of this tendency in our current society. Decades of great public service are swallowed up by the current revelations of past blunders. And the past is always prejudicially judged by the current standards of behavior and probity. Generations far removed from worshipping stone and wooden idols certainly cannot understand how intelligent people in previous generations blindly did so.

So it is not only the future that is inscrutable; it is the past as well. We should always be wary of our past. It will not go away.

Privileges and Rights

The nature of human beings is to automatically transfer that which began as a privilege – an extra perk in life – into a right, something that the person is automatically entitled to have. Once attained, no one ever wants to experience the loss of that privilege. A reduction in salary, loss of the professional or commercial title, the defeats suffered in an election, all of these are painful experiences to absorb.

So we are witness to former government and legislative position holders – even when they are no longer serving in that position – called by their former titles. This practice is not necessarily arrogance on their part, but rather is an example of how something that once was a privilege is now deemed a right. A very large portion of the governmental budget in all Western societies, including the State of Israel, is euphemistically called entitlements. Social Security, healthcare programs, Workmen's Compensation, unemployment benefits, and many other types of welfare programs all began as privileges granted by the government, but today they are untouchable rights that no political party or ambitious politician would dare curtail.

The Western world is based on the belief that there are "certain inalienable rights" that exist for the benefit of all human beings equally. The American Declaration of Independence listed these rights as life, liberty, and the pursuit of happiness, among other unspecified ones. The French phrased it differently as liberty, equality, and fraternity. Whatever phrases or words are used, it is obvious that all believe that there are certain basic rights to which all human beings are entitled. Simply being alive is sufficient to acquire these entitlements.

There are precious few things left in our world that we would consider a privilege. And so, when an entitlement is diminished or removed from our lives, for whatever reason, a personal or national crisis develops. A loss of what we consider our inalienable rights leads to untold frustrations.

This attitude drives much of society today, especially our young. Growing up with a sense of entitlement often leads to immense complications in later life when those entitlements somehow disappear, or even are only diminished. Something we feel entitled to is never quite as appreciated or valued as something that is seen as a gift.

Affluence contributes to changing privileges into rights. Pesach vacations, school trips to Poland, a gap year or two of study in Israel, a college education, major support from others while continuing to study after marriage, all are examples in our current Jewish world of privileges, many of which were completely unknown to an earlier generation. Many of these things are regarded as rights, if not outright obligations. There is little gratitude expressed for receiving these gifts, for, after all, they are viewed as rights and not privileges.

The unfortunate result is a narcissistic and skewed society. The basis of the Torah is gratitude – to our parents, teachers, elders, and even to governmental authorities. This mindset is meant to ultimately translate into gratitude to our Creator for the life and sustenance that has been granted to us.

The attitude of Judaism is that *everything* is a privilege, even life itself. It is easier to deal with the challenges and disappointments in life if one views them from the vantage point of privilege rather than that of entitlement.

Optimism

It seems that our intrinsic nature is to be optimistic about the future, and about life generally. This is a very strange phenomenon, since it flies in the face of human experience. We are all aware that the rule "whatever can go wrong will eventually go wrong" has had very few exceptions in human history. When foreign policy or military preparedness is based upon unfounded optimism, it must be deemed foolhardy and dangerous. We may hope for the best, but we must always prepare for the worst.

Yet being too much of a pessimist leads one to be depressed, offering a self-fulfilling prophecy of doom and sadness. In fact, we are told that optimistic people are healthier and live longer lives than those who are depressed.

It's interesting to note that even a nation that is optimistic lives longer. One of the unique qualities of the Jewish people over the millennia is that no matter how bitter and disappointing our past experiences have been, we retain a sense of hopefulness regarding our future, and that of humankind generally.

Judaism, as a faith and way of life, encourages optimism. It always points towards a better future and provides ample means for repentance for past errors and sins. It treasures life itself as a gift that is continually bestowed upon us by our Creator. I have always felt that it is this buoyant attitude created within us by Judaism that is part of the secret of Jewish survival against all odds, despite all enemies that attempted to destroy us.

I think that any realistic observer today must realize that the greatest enemy to confidence regarding our present (or future) condition is the incessant pillorying of our society, our accomplishments, and our leaders by the media. The negativity dominating most of mainstream media, here in Israel and throughout the world, destroys any glimmer of brightness.

I do not suggest that we should be blind to our troubles and failings, or that the future of the world – and especially of the Middle East – will overnight be transformed into a bed of roses. The problems are real, the dangers are mortal, and caution must be the byword of our leaders. Yet we should not succumb to the cynicism and negativity that permeates so much of our media and rubs off on us.

Part of the joy of seeing generations in one's own family is the sense of hope that there is continuity, that later generations can redeem the errors of their forbears. We feel that perhaps future generations will be able to cope with the problems of life in a better fashion than we were able to do. And that thought generates a resilient form of optimism that can permeate all facets of our existence.

The pinnacle of optimism in world affairs, again in my opinion, has been and is the restoration of the Jewish people's sovereignty in their ancient homeland. Even in the darkest days of exile, Jews believed that someday we would be able to return home and rebuild life in the Land of Israel. The song of the Jewish partisans of World War II was not one of revenge but rather one that affirmed that this is not our last road.

The Jewish world, in spite of all of its ongoing problems and difficulties, has rebuilt itself over the last seventy-five years in a manner that defies realistic rational thought. I am astounded by the Torah world: its numbers, options, and institutions that my grandchildren participate in. They do so without giving it a second thought, since they have no personal memory of how weak and few we were just a half-century ago.

But I remember as a youth that my teachers and mentors were always optimistic about the future despite living under the shadow of the Holocaust and the difficulties facing the nascent State of Israel. They inspired their students to believe that great things were possible and that the future would create positive opportunities for the growth of Torah and the security of the Jewish people. And I have lived long enough to see that seemingly outlandish, wildly optimistic prediction come true.

Rivalries

As an only child in my parents' home, I was spared the experiences and challenges of sibling rivalries. With no competition, I was blissfully unaware of the possibility that there could be others entitled to parental love, weekly allowances, and unlimited bathroom privileges. No one ever dared to wear my clothing, play with my toys, or read my books. Naturally, in school and yeshiva there were constant rivalries, but in the main they were never really personal or long lasting.

Yet, as all of the biblical commentators point out to us, the book of Genesis is a book of sibling and familial rivalries. Cain and Abel, Abraham and Lot, Ishmael and Isaac, Jacob and Esau, Rachel and Leah, Joseph and his brothers, are all examples of the intensity of emotion and of the dire consequences of family rivalries. And the consequences of these rivalries over the span of human history have been immeasurable, often tragic, and of unending influence. The current turmoil in the Middle East of Sunni versus Shiite, Moslems versus Christians and Jews, the Arab world against Israel are basically products of ancient sibling rivalries perpetuated through the ages by familial traditions and the inherent evil nature of human beings.

When visiting the USA, I am witness to the interactions of my grandchildren and great-grandchildren, and I can conclusively report that sibling rivalry is still thriving. This reality is pretty sobering for the old patriarch of the family, who firmly believes that all of his offspring are pious, perfect, peaceful, and generous to a fault. But as the old Yiddish aphorism goes: "In a time of plague, my goat apparently is also an animal."

So what is to be done to try and ameliorate the situation? In many if not most cases, sibling rivalries are outgrown. Many situations in life are resolved simply by benign neglect: let time and life experiences work their magic. "What logic cannot heal, time will." The prophets of Israel seem to indicate that this is what will happen regarding the internal squabbles that plague the Jewish world. Unfortunately, patience, silence, and waiting are not primarily Jewish traits in our time.

But many a serious, bloody rivalry between families, countries, and even religions has dissipated over time. In spite of the stabbings, incitement, and terrorism that are currently our daily fare, I believe that it is possible for Israel to live in peace – albeit a cold one, perhaps – in our ancient homeland. If we persist in a fatalistic approach that none of our rivalries can ever be overcome, that attitude will certainly give rise to self-perpetuating prophecy. I regret that I have no recommendation to actualize my hopes. But I am willing to let time run its course.

There is an essential difference between the concepts of competitiveness and that of rivalry. Competitiveness presupposes a goal that, if reached, is beneficial to all concerned; it is not predicated on the destruction of the "other." Rivalries have less to do with achieving anything; they concentrate on depriving others of any gain, and even trying to destroy that "other."

The rabbis of the Talmud proclaimed that "competitiveness amongst Torah scholars increases wisdom [for all concerned]." Throughout the Talmud we are aware of the differing and competing opinions and personalities of the great men of Jewish tradition. Yet there are no rivalries present on its pages. In a strange way, their differences of opinion – and even of their behavior – are blended together into the partnership that created the Talmudic way of life and shaped Jewish tradition until our very day. The Talmud records the competing views of illustrious scholars without passionate rancor or personal insult.

The lessons of the damaging rivalries narrated in the Bible were apparently well-learned by the men of the Talmud. They attributed the destruction of the Second Temple to the unreasoning climate of hatred generated by the political, religious, and social rivalries of the time. In those tumultuous years before the horrific destruction of Jerusalem, it was believed that it is better to destroy one's rival than to work with him for the common good.

That belief still remains today as a sure recipe for societal sadness, social turmoil, and foolish policies. Just look around at our current world of rivalries and the dangers they yield.

Inconsistencies

One of the most damning accusations that can be hurled at an individual is that the person is a hypocrite. Yet all human beings are hypocrites in the sense that there is always an element of inconsistency in their words, statements, and actual behavior. And in the course of human events sometimes we find that the greater the person is, the greater are is or her inconsistencies.

I think the prime example of this phenomenon is Thomas Jefferson. He was the author of the American Declaration of Independence, a document that remains a ringing defense of human liberty, tolerance, and freedom from tyranny. He was also the third president of the United States; the founder of the Republican-Democrat Party that later morphed into the Democratic Party; an intellectual of astounding proportions; a Renaissance man who was a philosopher, scientist, architect, agricultural expert, author, diplomat, and a crafty politician. On his tombstone he ordered inscribed what he considered the three major achievements of his lifetime: the Declaration of Independence, the bill for religious freedom that he championed and passed in the Virginia legislature, and the founding of the University of Virginia. With such a résumé, it is no wonder that Jefferson's face is on US currency and that there is a beautiful, almost haunting, marble memorial to him in Washington, DC. But human beings are complex and inconsistent, and Thomas Jefferson was no exception to the rule.

The dark side of Jefferson – a subject which has been hotly debated for centuries among historians and political scientists – was that he was a slaveholder; and, unlike other founding fathers who were slaveholders, he never emancipated any of his slaves. George Washington freed his slaves, as did John Randolph and other notable personages from Virginia. But Jefferson, for reasons known only to himself, never did so.

Ironically, he did write a long essay about emancipation, about the evils of slavery as an institution and as a corruption of human morals and decency. Much of this essay later inspired Abraham Lincoln in his drive towards emancipating the slaves in the United States. Lincoln saw himself as a disciple of Jefferson, and the soaring cadence and poetry of Lincoln's words contain some of the majesty of Jefferson's prose a half-century earlier.

But the inconsistency of writing about the evils of slavery while owning, buying, and selling slaves is glaring. And the fact that Jefferson is such a towering figure in the story of American and human freedom only makes this inconsistency that much more troubling. Jefferson held that liberty – personal and national – was a God-given right; as he phrased it, an "inalienable right." He supported the French Revolution even though he admitted that it was gory and murderous, but he thought that "the tree of liberty has to be refreshed periodically by the blood of patriots and tyrants." And yet he remained a slaveholder to his death.

We are puzzled by other inconsistencies in his character and behavior as well. Though a gifted writer, Jefferson was a poor speaker. He had a very soft voice and often listeners were hard-pressed to make sense of what he was saying. He was prolific, yet when he died his debts were enormous. He was forced to sell his library of well over six thousand books – a mammoth collection in his time – in order to raise funds to forestall complete bankruptcy. (This original collection of Jefferson's books became the foundation of the famed US Library of Congress.) But Jefferson kept on buying and collecting books until his death, oblivious to his economic inability to do so. He also loved fine wine and imported crate after crate from France at considerable expense. He lived like a patrician, always in luxury, even though he did not have the wherewithal to support this lifestyle. How such a great person could be so financially irresponsible and unwise only illustrates how inconsistencies run through all human lives, even the most intelligent.

Eventually Jefferson's home in Charlottesville, Virginia, which he named Monticello, also had to be sold to pay off his debts. It was purchased by a Jewish family, the Levys, and there is a Jewish cemetery at the back of the garden in Monticello. In the early twentieth century a foundation repurchased and refurbished Monticello, turning it into one of the most interesting and beautiful museums in the United States.

I was deeply touched when I visited there. Strangely enough, the spirit of Thomas Jefferson and his personality still seem to hover in this house that he designed and redesigned so many times in his lifetime. Maybe one of his drives that created his inconsistencies was the fact that he was never satisfied with what was; he always strove to perfect the present, whether physically or politically.

We tend to judge others too harshly for being inconsistent. The life story of such sublime leaders as Thomas Jefferson proves that it is part of our human DNA, like it or not.

Half-Birthdays

I have long noted that when one speaks to small children and asks them their age, they will answer in terms of half-birthdays. They will say that they are four and a half, or five and a half years old. This is because when we are very young we want to become older, anxious to possess the enticing fruit of privileges granted to children as they advance in years. This idea of half-birthdays begins to wane when children come close to the age of adolescence, and by the time they become young adults it disappears completely. Yet subliminally the concept continues to lurk within us during our active years of life.

It begins to emerge once more as we reach our so-called golden years. It is then that we count time far differently than we did in our earlier decades. We are very cognizant of the importance of each and every passing day, and we realize how precious time is. So we begin once again to mark the passing of half-birthdays in our minds. King David advised us to count our days to help bring about a heart of wisdom within us. I think that he may have had the concept of half-birthdays in mind. They are gifts to us if we view them as such and treat them with the respect and contemplation that they deserve.

When we are young, our birthdays mark our view of the future. We look forward to being old enough to drive an automobile, to vote, to marry and raise a family, and to make our way in life. We want to get started, thinking in terms of years, even decades, and not in terms of days. But later in life, birthdays bring about a flood of memories. They remind us of where we have been, of our successes and shortcomings, of those we loved, and of the enormous challenges and vicissitudes that life has brought upon us. We no longer think in grandiose long-term sections of time but rather realize how fleeting and elusive time itself really is.

In the prayer services of Tishrei, we twice recite memorial prayers for those who are no longer with us. Even as we prayed for the benefits and blessings of the coming good year, we were compelled – not only by custom, but also by the emotions that dwell within us – to look back and mark what is irretrievable. We were forced to count the days that already happened, not only the days that lie ahead. The concept of half-birthdays suddenly reemerged in our consciousness. And in that sense we became young children once again.

We live in a culture that glorifies youth. All the commercial enterprises devote their advertisements to attracting a young crowd. The culture in music, drama, and media is overwhelmingly devoted to capturing the youth market. Perhaps we older people would like to have the physical stamina and abilities that we once had in our youth. But overall, I think there are very few people who would like to repeat their years of uncertainty and adolescence. The great wise men of Israel, when celebrating the drawing of the water for the Temple service on Succot, said that they were happy that their later lives and actions were able to atone for the follies of their youth. Judaism teaches that we should always look forward to a productive future, but it suggests at the very same time that we look back at the road we have traversed in life.

In order to achieve such an attitude, I believe that one must begin to count half-birthdays once more. It will give an immediacy of time and purpose to the regularity of everyday life. All of the stages of life have their own importance and messages to us. By marking our half-birthdays, it will become easier for us to give correct definition to our days. And that is a great blessing that everyone can and should appreciate.

Punctuality

We have all experienced the discomfort of arriving at a wedding called for 6:30 PM and waiting around for the ceremony to begin till after 8:00 PM or later. I have never been able to fathom what it is within us that allows us to so abuse the time and patience of others. The fact that "everyone does it," that this is a common social malady in our circles, in no way justifies this behavior. And among the guests, there are even people who purposely come late in order to make an impression. I always feel that the impression, no matter how important the person may be, is a negative one.

My father-in-law, of blessed memory, was a product of the Mussar movement of pre-war Lithuanian Jewry. He was punctilious about arriving at any rabbinic function to which he was invited before the time called for. He told me: "I never want anyone to become impatient waiting for my arrival." I have always tried to follow his example, with varying degrees of success, in my own rabbinic career.

Early in my stay in Israel, I was invited to officiate at a wedding in Jerusalem. It was called for 6:30, so I arrived at 6:10 to complete the necessary documents and prepare for the wedding ceremony. Imagine my consternation when I arrived at the hall and discovered that I was there before the bride and groom and their respective families, before the photographer, the band, and the catering staff! The wedding ceremony took place at 8:30 and I was vastly disturbed that no one thought that this was unacceptable behavior. Since then, I try to avoid being the first person to arrive at the wedding hall, though no matter how hard I try, I always seem to come too early.

I find it interesting that people who are exacting and scrupulous regarding times of prayer, reciting the Shema, and other religious obligations are yet so callous regarding other people's time. Rabbi Yisrael Lipkin of Salant said that the other person's earthly comforts that I can provide are the basis of my merits in the World to Come. It seems that few people operate on that level anymore.

The Israeli medical system creates an appointment schedule that any sensible person knows cannot be kept. Thus a great deal of time is spent impatiently waiting for appointments that are always running considerably late. This system reinforces the notion in society that the other person's time is of little value.

Intellectually, we are all aware of the precious nature of time. It is irreplaceable. People of genius may be allowed tolerance for being unaware of time, but we ordinary mortals are usually not granted such latitude. In our world, all standards of efficiency and productivity are based upon effective use of time. Almost all major sports contests are governed by the exact measurement of time. In a world that produces and sells millions of timepieces annually, destroying other people's time needlessly seems most paradoxical.

In the Jewish world, there were and are different communities that differ in their attitude toward punctuality. German Jews and certain segments of Lithuanian Jewry were famous – even notorious – for their punctuality. Other parts of world Jewry were just as renowned for their tardiness. It seems that the surrounding non-Jewish culture was of strong influence in creating these wide differences within the Jewish society in their midst.

In an age where there were no watches or accurate timepieces, there is an opinion in the Talmud that there is a one-hour leeway in judging the correct time. But that tolerance no longer applies to our age when Friday eve candle lighting is exact to the minute, as are many other measurements of time relating to the strict observance of Jewish ritual. We don't want to keep God waiting, so to speak.

Well, we should not fall into the bad habit of keeping our fellow human beings waiting either. People should expect a certain flexibility in scheduled events, but that is usually only a few minutes. Exceeding that tolerance is certainly an abuse of others. Their time is being wasted, and that is a waste of life itself. And any abuse of others in any fashion is against Torah standards and values. Seeing life through Torah values in all of its aspects, and not only in terms of strict law and ritual, is the necessary moral compass that every Jew should strive to possess.

Holidays and Special Days

Erev Shabbat

Friday afternoon is a special time here in Jerusalem. Vehicular traffic is sparse and people rush to the stores for their last-minute Shabbat needs. But there is a general mood of relaxed anticipation. The fact that Friday afternoons are already times of business closings and home preparations contribute greatly to this Erev Shabbat atmosphere.

The quality of one's Erev Shabbat plays an important role in the Shabbat mood later on. I remember my days in the United States when we poured into the synagogue for the Friday night Shabbat services, still tense and nerve-wracked from commuter traffic, and often arriving only minutes before the onset of Shabbat. It took hours to get our bodies, minds, and souls into the Shabbat mode. With his inimitable talent for saying everything in a few words, the late, great Rabbi Yaakov Kaminetzky once told me: "We have been successful in saving Shabbos in America, but not Erev Shabbos."

One of the great pluses, among many others, that I have found living in Jerusalem is Erev Shabbat. I am engaged in Shabbat preparations from early Friday morning until it finally arrives. And when Shabbat makes its holy entrance into my life, I am calm, almost serene, and able to welcome it and absorb it into my being. I am struck by the hush that precedes its entrance, even in a neighborhood such as mine, where there are traffic arteries that operate on Shabbat and fine neighbors who are not necessarily complete Shabbat observers.

The Talmud records that many of the prominent rabbis and scholars of the time were personally involved in preparing their houses, tables, and meals for Shabbat. From setting the table to curing the salted fish to sweeping the floors, all of these were considered noble and important activities in readying the home and one's self for the arrival of Shabbat.

Though I am neither prominent nor overly scholarly, in our home I am in charge of setting the table and supervising the Shabbat food cooking in our oven. The latter is done surreptitiously, since that is really my wife's domain – and exclusivity of division of labor is a wise course for a successful marriage relationship. Nevertheless, checking the oven allows me to tell guests at our Shabbat table that the food was prepared under strict rabbinical supervision. Jewish tradition also prescribes that the husband should prepare the candles that his wife will later light to welcome Shabbat to their home. I find this to be an act of affection to both my wife and to Shabbat. The custom is that the husband actually lights the candles to make certain that the wicks are in proper order and then extinguishes them. It is the small things in life and home that build meaningful relationships. Judaism does not recognize anything as a small thing – and certainly not in relation to preparing for Shabbat.

The Talmud uses the relationship of Erev Shabbat and Shabbat itself as a metaphor for life. It states: "One who toils on Erev Shabbat will eat well on Shabbat." This is not only valid in a literal sense; it reflects the Jewish attitude towards living in general. Enjoying success – "Shabbat" – or any endeavor, be it educational, commercial, or personal, is always conditioned on toiling beforehand – "Erev Shabbat."

Judaism posits no free lunch to anyone. The rabbis in Avot stated: "According to the effort and pain is the reward and payment." It is Erev Shabbat that alone creates Shabbat in all of its grandeur, simplicity, and serenity.

No matter how some Jews have attempted to create a Jewish life without a traditional, observant Shabbat, it is now abundantly clear that Shabbat remains the cornerstone of Jewish life and continuity. The famous slogan, "More than the Jews have kept the Shabbat, the Shabbat has kept and preserved the Jews," has never been more true and telling than in our time. When all of the ideologies that were supposed to redeem us from our troubles have visibly and miserably failed, Shabbat remains a beacon of hope for Israel and is a symbol of our eternal covenant with our Creator. And that is what makes Erev Shabbat so vital for all Jews.

Saturday Night

Saturday night has a special title: Motzaei Shabbat – the departure of Shabbat. Like all welcome guests, Shabbat is such a special day that it requires special courtesies upon its leave-taking. Guests should be accompanied to the door of the house, at least. This is in accordance with the tradition of our father Abraham, who never allowed his guests to leave unescorted.

So our virtual guest's departure must be accorded proper respect and ceremony. There is a custom, mentioned in the *Shulchan Aruch*, to host a special meal on Saturday night called *Melaveh Malkah* – "the accompaniment of the Shabbat Queen" – as it leaves our home. Meals are always an important component of Jewish milestones. Weddings, circumcisions, the redeeming of the firstborn, the conclusion of studying a holy book, and other religious occasions are always celebrated by a meal. So the tradition of *Melaveh Malkah* is an understandable and fitting method of taking leave of Shabbat. In a most spiritual vein, the *Melaveh Malkah* meal is seen to nurture an indestructible bone in our skeleton from which eventually the resurrection of our body will occur at the appointed time.

In the Western world, Saturday night has a connotation of entertainment, leisure, and social events. In the Jewish world, Saturday night is viewed as a night of relaxation, of a slow and serene departure from the Shabbat and a gentle reentry into the mundane world of the workweek.

Communal *Melaveh Malkah* meals, either family gatherings or fundraising events on behalf of charitable organizations, have become the norm for Motzaei Shabbat, especially during the winter months of shorter days and longer nights. These affairs combine the custom of *Melaveh Malkah* with the merit of raising funds for the support of worthwhile causes. Here in Israel, lectures and other educational events are also scheduled fairly regularly on Saturday nights.

Many Jews still wear their Shabbat clothing on Saturday night in honor of the departing Shabbat Queen. Tradition also dictates that candles are lit in honor of the *Melaveh Malkah* meal to show that the "bookends" of the holy Shabbat, its coming and going, are marked with light and serenity of soul and spirit.

Special songs, melodies, and poems are woven into the traditional *Melaveh Malkah*. Since the messiah will not come on a Shabbat day, Motzaei Shabbat becomes the proper moment to ask for his appearance. Based upon a verse in the book of the prophet Malachi, tradition teaches us that the forerunner to the messianic era will be the prophet Elijah who will announce the coming of the messiah. Thus there are a number of special poems, usually sung to hauntingly yearning melodies, regarding this loyal prophet of Israel, who is always on eternal call to attend us on the Seder night and at circumcisions, and who will inform us of the messiah's approach. Other poems deal with the transition from holiness to the mundane and the unique mission of Israel in God's world. Understandably, there are also prayers that ask for health and success during the coming workweek. We look forward to the week with anticipation, but not necessarily with dread. We pray that God will grant us and ours a good and peaceful week.

Observed with sensitivity, Motzaei Shabbat allows us to leave the past Shabbat peacefully because it also renews our anticipation. Our eyes are already focused on the Shabbat that will bless us with its presence next week.

The serious month of the Jewish calendar is upon us. All months are serious, but Elul is more so. It has no special holidays or commemorative days, but it certainly serves as the transitional month between the seasons of summer and autumn, of school vacations, trips, and camps and the solemnity of the High Holy Days of Tishrei. As such, it has always occupied a special place in Jewish tradition.

The entire month became a time of very intensive Torah study in the schools of higher Jewish education. Venerated Chassidic mentors who greeted and advised thousands during most of the year went into private seclusion, receiving no visitors in Elul. Esteemed rabbis took leave of their communal and congregational positions during Elul to refresh themselves in an atmosphere of Torah learning and piety in the yeshivot. An atmosphere of anticipation, introspection, and a search for one's better self was created.

That atmosphere of Elul contemplation eludes us in our world of 24/7 pressures of work, finance, family, and just getting to where we wish to go. (Though looking for a parking space in Tel Aviv or Jerusalem is a special form of penance imposed upon us for our misdeeds.) Yet it is unthinkable that we should approach the High Holy Days without some measure of preparation. After all, in the long view, it is who we really are that determines the value of our lives and accomplishments. So Elul should be exploited to the extent possible and not simply ignored or dissipated.

A unique aspect of Elul is that it dwells upon the future. Months that contain days of commemorations and holidays always possess a necessary emphasis on past events, on history and momentous events that have previously occurred. Because Elul has no such holidays, its thrust is forward looking. Its message to us is that the misdeeds and sad events of the past should be considered as having ended; and now we can only look forward to better times and more positive behavior in the new year that appears on the horizon. The emphasis on introspection that I previously described as part of the Elul package – and introspection always concentrates on dealing with past events and behavior – is tempered and balanced by Elul's demand to deal with the future in a hopeful and positive fashion.

Balancing the past and the future in our lives is always a difficult task. Dwelling on the past often induces unrealistic and distorted nostalgia that cripples our ability to deal with our current lives and our future. Thinking only of the future and ignoring the lessons of the past can only lead to frustrations and disappointments when our rosy predictions and seeming certainties turn out to be wrong, useless, and possibly dangerous. Elul sets the right tone, ensuring that a measure of introspection will allow one to learn from the year gone by and create a better emotional and psychological frame of mind and soul for approaching the future.

Elul is marked by the sounding of the shofar in the morning synagogue prayer services and by the recitation of *Selichot* in the Sephardic and Near Eastern Jewish communities. These customs are meant to help us internalize the opportunities that the month of Elul offers for our spiritual restoration and enhanced growth.

There are no easy or proven methods to help this process along. Every individual must find his or her way alone. Judaism generally is not a one-size-fits all faith when it comes to spiritual growth. While we are all bound to perform the commandments of the Torah in their entirety, no explicit guide to finding spirituality in one's life is granted to us.

But we have the gift of Elul – a time to search deep into one's own self for the personal road that we seek to become closer to the Creator and to leave a legacy of decency and Jewish commitment to those who will follow us. We must make the most of it.

Our Annual Report – Rosh Hashanah

The basis for Judaism and its value system can be summed up in one word: accountability. The gift of freedom of choice and action that God has granted to humans comes, as do most gifts, with a price. And that price is that all of us are completely accountable for our actions and behavior.

We each have an account sheet, so to speak, with columns for credits and debits. How our lifetime account sheet looks eventually determines our fate and our eternity. But there are temporary stock-taking times as well. The Holy Days of Rosh Hashanah and Yom Kippur are such times. We pass in review, individually and without cover or pretense, before the Heavenly court to have our account sheet examined.

The message of the Holy Days is a clear one. We are held accountable for our past deeds as well as for our budding intents. As responsible individuals, our account sheet is of vital importance in determining our true life status and future. Just as all publicly held firms must produce an annual fiscal report attested to by reputable accounting firms, so too during this season of the year we individually publish our own annual report; and it is attested to by the Heavenly court that is aware of all of our thoughts and actions.

One of the ills of our current society is its acceptance of unlimited freedom of choice and behavior coupled with its refusal to hold people answerable to the results of this uninhibited freedom. Another hallmark of our society is the inability to admit error in previous decisions, policies, and behavior. No one is held accountable for all of the colossal mistakes of the past centuries. The moral and spiritual bankruptcy of Jewish organizations and individuals who fled from Torah and tradition is evident to all by now, but many of them – those still in existence – continue along their merry way as though there were no past to reexamine and no future to contemplate. But the law of accountability allows for no exceptions; eventually it overtakes everyone.

That pattern should be apparent to anyone with even rudimentary knowledge of the story of Israel throughout the ages. The *parshiyot* of the Torah read in the synagogue during this season concern themselves almost exclusively with this idea of culpability – of reward and punishment, and the aspects of the covenant of Sinai between God and Israel. The Torah declares that this "covenant shall respond to them even till the end of days." In a covenant – a contractual agreement – each side is held to its agreed-upon terms and conditions. We are bound to our end of the covenant, and the Lord, so to speak, states that He also is bound to His commitments. Accountability is the key to the entire covenantal experience and challenge.

One should feel that one is answerable not only to God and to one's fellow human beings, but perhaps most importantly to one's own self. The primary questions addressed by Judaism are: "To what purpose is my life worth living? Why am I here? And what is asked of me in this life?" If these questions are never really addressed, or they are sloughed off and defined in purely material or monetary terms, obviously life has little meaning to it. If it has no deep meaning, no duty of accountability for our behavior can ever arise in our minds and hearts.

For life to have any sense of purpose, sincere goals must resonate within the individual person. And such resonance must inevitably lead to a realization of the imperative of accountability in our lives. This is why the prayers of the Holy Days stress not only God's greatness and man's relative puniness, but also the coming to terms of each individual with past deeds as well as future aspirations. True *teshuvah* – repentance – requires this simultaneous look both backwards and forwards.

Rigorous accountability helps us formulate a meaningful plan for our goals and aspirations in life. It allows us to age and mature gracefully, and it creates the proper backdrop for our future actions. It is the ultimate blessing in our lives.

Gifts – Yom Kippur

A precious gift is always treasured by the one who received it not only for the value of the item itself but, more importantly, for the relationship it creates or solidifies between the giver and the receiver. To view one's life as a gift from Heaven automatically gives one a connection with our Creator and with eternity. During the High Holiday season, our prayers constantly reemphasize this gift of life, for without life all other blessings are nonexistent. The constant repetition of prayers for life is meant to impress upon us the transient nature of this gift and realization that it is a gift, not something that we are automatically entitled to have.

At different times in our lives, we all yearn to wipe the slate clean, to shut down the past and its consequences, and to make a fresh start. In the physical world in which we are engaged, this revision of our lives is usually a practical impossibility. We live with our past decisions, whether they were fortuitous or ill-advised. But in spiritual matters regarding our soul we are granted this extraordinary gift of starting over. And this is not a once-in-a-lifetime opportunity; we are granted this gift annually on this holy day of Yom Kippur.

Our relations with our fellow human beings are always measured in the real and physical world in which we live. Therefore, the Yom Kippur gift of renewal cannot affect those relationships. On a human level, we can try to mend past hurts and soothe personal slights. But God's gift to us of forgiveness, erasing the awkwardness and embarrassment of past behavior, extends to our spiritual relationship with Heaven itself. Human relationships are vital and should be treasured. How much more cherished should be our relationship with our Creator. For this essential yet exalted purpose, Yom Kippur is the supreme gift, after life itself.

Children are often more interested by a gift's box and wrappings than by the gift itself. I vividly remember purchasing what I thought to be a most educational and skill-oriented toy for my two-year-old grandchild.

When I proudly and graciously delivered the toy, I noticed that the child happily played with the box rather than with the toy itself.

To a certain extent, we are all like that child. We discuss how long the services took on Yom Kippur; whether the break was sufficiently long or short; whether the cantor was on key or not; and how much rest we were able to gather during the rabbi's sermon. But none of these are the present itself – Yom Kippur – but only the box and the wrappings that come with it.

Yom Kippur should provide us with the ability to maintain a conversation with Heaven, and it should not be easily squandered or neglected. This unique and holy day has the power to erase past sins, mistakes, and transgressions, but it can do so only if we wish that those past errors truly be expunged and we are prepared to remove them from our persona and attitude. I believe that this life-saving objective can only be accomplished if we view Yom Kippur as a gift to us and not just as a day of fasting and physical abstinence.

The Eternal Struggle – Chanukah

Let us remember to keep the hell in Hellenism. The holiday of Chanukah marks the struggle between the Hellenistic view of life and traditional Jewish values.

The Hellenistic world was a superstitious world. It was a world where human beings were represented as gods. Where idols, icons, and statues were glorified and worshipped, even at the expense of human life. It was a dominant culture, and like all successful cultures, it had an attractive side to it. It was not all bad, because if it would have been all bad, no one would have followed it. Its appealing elements included music and drama, art and architecture; it had philosophy and new ideas, and a system of government that would eventually develop into what today we call democracy.

So Hellenism was able to enter all areas of human life, but with it came a plethora of negative cultural characteristics: its paganism and violence; its immorality and depravity; its wars and constant struggles for power and dominion. These mores infected the Jewish world as well. Paganism was rampant during the time of the second Holy Temple. Greek language and culture was dominant in many areas of Jewish life. Even in religious Jewish life, and in the language of the Mishnah and Talmud itself, we find many Greek words; and Greek words always bring with them Greek ideas. But the success of the rabbis in avoiding this dark side of Greek culture lay in their ability to clearly identify its ideas and values, and soundly reject them.

In the emerging world of the fourth and fifth centuries, paganism began to die out, and Hellenism waned as well. Christianity became the dominant force in the Western world, and it soon conquered all of Europe. Christianity adopted much of Hellenism: statues and icons remained, and it had a number of pagan superstitions built into its structure.

As a persecuted minority, the Jews attempted to combat this pervasive culture through denial of its basic beliefs and value systems. Judaism always represented a lonely road, but it was always the road to survival and to eternity. That itself is a message of Chanukah and of the lights of Chanukah, which – by all natural human calculations – should have been extinguished long ago. Yet they burn ever more brightly, even in our day.

Christianity has also begun to wane. It is no longer the force that it once was in the world, and a new brand of Hellenism has invaded human society. This new form of Hellenism is a combination of atheism, agnosticism, immorality, and to a certain extent the agreement that violence is not only necessary, but even somewhat acceptable in human society.

Once again, the Jewish world is challenged by these coarse ideas of Hellenism. Again it faces the same challenges that it did millennia ago. No longer can we ignore the fact that Hellenism has penetrated every corner of Jewish life and threatens us with moral, and possibly physical, destruction.

Chanukah comes to remind us that the struggle is unceasing. It goads us to remember that Hellenism leads not only to a dead end, but also to a hellish end. This lesson must be remembered and should serve as a warning to all of us. In essence, this is the message of Chanukah as reflected in the flickering lights, warming and inspiring us, and giving us a vision of a better and stronger Jewish future.

It's Never Too Late – Tu B'shvat

The week after Tu B'Shvat, I usually still have figs, dates, and other fruits in prominent display in my kitchen. Throughout the years of the Jewish exile, the day of Tu B'Shvat – the New Year of the trees in our beloved Land – served as a heartening reminder of our unbreakable connection to our Land, and eating its fruits confirmed the holiness of Israel – the people, and the Land.

I remember that as a child when the holiday came (always during the freezing Chicago winters), my parents would insist on my eating a piece of *boksar* – carob. The *boksar* was hard as a rock and tasteless as wood. Yet I noticed that my parents, Jews of an earlier generation who were born before there was a State of Israel or a time when free and open Jewish worship was allowed at the Western wall without Arab or government interference, ate their *boksar* slowly and with great affection. Only later in my life did I realize that eating that piece of *boksar* validated their hope and belief that the Land of Israel would yet flourish and grow under Jewish sovereignty, and that the vineyards and orchards of the Land promised to us by our prophets would someday become abundant reality.

Every society needs physical symbols to validate its faiths and aspirations. That is why countries have flags and seals. The fruits of the Land of Israel became the flag and seal of the Jewish people regarding its beloved homeland, even when there was little Jewish population and no Jewish sovereignty there. The fruit reminded Jews of who they were, where they came from, and most importantly, where they were heading.

In 1890 Baron Edmond de Rothschild's Carmel Wine Company produced its first bottles of wine in Rishon L'Ziyon. At that time, Rabbi Naftali Zvi Yehuda Berlin (Netziv) was the *rav* and head of the famed yeshiva in Volozhin in Lithuania. He was also the titular chairman of Chovevei Tziyon – The Lovers of Zion – an organization that encouraged Jewish immigration to the Land of Israel and helped support the nascent, but growing, population of the *yishuv hayashan* – the nineteenth century pre-Zionist settlers in the Land of Israel. His nephew, Rabbi Baruch Halevi Epstein (the author of *Torah Temimah*, a popular commentary to the Torah), lived with his uncle and aunt in their home while he was a young student at the yeshiva. He recorded in his writings that the Carmel Wine Company sent a bottle of wine from its first production to Rabbi Berlin in recognition of his efforts on behalf of the Jewish settlers in the Land of Israel. When that bottle of Israeli wine finally reached the small town of Volozhin and was delivered to the house of Rabbi Berlin, the great rabbi first went to his bedroom and changed into his Shabbat garments in honor of a bottle of wine produced by Jews from the grapes of the Holy Land and upon which all of the agricultural *mitzvot* of the Torah had been fulfilled.

I have often thought about this vignette when I hear observant Jews say they prefer wines from France, Argentina, Chile, Australia, South Africa, or California over Israeli wines. They just don't get it. The lesson of the Tu B'Shvat *boksar* apparently has not taken hold in their souls.

So Tu B'Shvat is not just a date (no pun intended) on the Jewish calendar year. It represents our undying and never-failing attachment to the Land of Israel. It connects us to the two-thousand-year-old entry in the Mishnah that names the fifteenth of Shvat the New Year for trees in the Land of Israel. The day is a slight holiday in Jewish ritual and synagogue service.

I still ate *boksar* this year and its taste has not materially improved. Yet

I enjoyed every bite, and again I saw my parents eating it with me. There were many other tastier and more delicious Israeli fruits on the table before me. But none carried with them the emotional impact in my heart of that piece of *boksar*.

So to me the message of Tu B'Shvat does not end with the passing of the day. Rather, it serves every day to strengthen our claim to this piece of holy ground and to confirm the great epoch – each person under his vine and fig tree in security and happiness – that was promised to us by our prophets.

Costumes – Purim

To mark the holiday of Purim, I am taking the liberty of commenting on costumes, past and present. Each year, I receive pictures of my blessed great-grandchildren, all of them dressed in costume. Some are airline pilots and flight attendants, while others are mail carriers and even letters. There are a number of Queen Esthers, police officers, monkeys, rabbits, and other assorted wildlife.

Of course, wearing costumes on Purim is one of the traditions of the joyous holiday. But as the Lord has blessed us with affluence beyond our imagination in earlier times, costumes have become more ornate and creative than they were in my youth in Chicago. Back then, wearing a mask over your eyes was sufficient.

The entire concept of wearing a disguise is based on the fact that the holiday is one of hidden Divine guidance, emphasizing that what appears to us may not be the reality of what truly is. The Talmud teaches that even judges can only rule upon the facts as they appear to their eyes. That is the limitation our finite human nature imposes upon us. But we are all aware that what appears before our eyes may not be true reality; we may even sense that we are being fooled by camouflage, or even by our own gullibility. That is certainly one of the more important messages that the holiday of Purim impresses upon us.

When we are young children, we delight in wearing costumes because in our imagination we can still be whatever we want to be – a fireman, a policeman, a queen, an astronaut. But as we grow older, these dreams fade before the realities of life. Our choices become much narrower and much less exotic. We shed our youthful costumes, but we replace them with other ones. We wear suits and ties, dresses and aprons, and now pretend that these garments truly represent who we are. But there is always the still small voice within us that yearns to be someone different than what our outside garb announces to the world. In turn, a sense of tension and frustration are created.

There are entire segments of the Jewish people whose clothing is imposed upon them by society, both secular and religious. But that attire may not be truly representative of the person who is inside the costume.

Most of life, therefore, is a struggle to try and be what we really are. This is very difficult to achieve, for the constraints of the societies that we live in are powerful. My only experience in escaping from a costume was when I was a very young rabbi. The officers of that synagogue wanted me to wear a robe during the Sabbath service. They said that it would lend dignity to the congregation, and to me as well. I refused to do so because I knew that was certainly not who I was. Eventually the congregation became accustomed to a rabbi who did not wear a robe. I reckon this to be one of my small triumphs in my rabbinic career.

The Torah relates that Moses had to wear a mask while addressing the Jewish people because a spiritual light emanated from within him. After communicating with Heaven, so to speak, his face shone with such a godly radiance that human beings found it difficult to be in his presence. But Moses without the mask was the true Moses. Often, circumstances force a leader to wear a "mask" in order to relate to his people and guide them in the path of goodness and righteousness. There is no matter of dishonesty or subterfuge in wearing this mask. The leader must be relevant to his generation and his people in order to be effective. But the leader must always realize that he is wearing a mask, that his true essence may be different from his public persona.

Rare are the people who are able to say that their inside and outside match perfectly. Most of us are always in costume, but we should never fool ourselves into believing that the façade is our true essence.

The Fifth Son – Pesach

Many of us are aware that there is a detailed discussion amongst the commentators to the Seder night Haggadah regarding the possibility of a fifth cup of wine as part of the Seder service. Some are of the opinion that the "Cup of Elijah" serves as this fifth cup.

Be that as it may, I wish to discuss another foursome that may have developed into five in our time. We are taught in the Haggadah that there are four categories of children in the Jewish world: the wise son; the wicked son; the naïve, simple son; and the son who knows nothing and cannot even begin to ask anything intelligently.

We are all acquainted with the wise son. He has had a thorough Jewish education and is intelligently loyal to the Torah, its value system, and the traditional way of life. Unfortunately, we also are able to clearly identify the evil child among us – the apostate, the self-hater, the one who is addicted to anti-Jewish ideologies and practices. The simple son is also known to us. He has no real animus towards God, though he may be repelled by the behavior and statements of those of us who arrogantly claim to represent Him and His Torah. He only asks: "What is this all about?" It is a legitimate, if somewhat depressing, question. After all, after three thousand, five hundred years of Jewish life and history, the son should by now have an inkling of what it is all about. Nevertheless, there is still hope for this son – life and its events, and the non-Jewish world, will eventually explain the matter to him. And finally, the son who knows nothing, not even what to ask, can also be salvaged by education, warmth, direction, role models, and proper mentoring. Even the evil son can be corrected and redeemed, but not without pain and discomfort. After all, it was Stalin who basically cured the Jewish Communists of their malignant Marxist disease and made them Jews once again.

But there is a fifth child sitting at the Seder table in our time. He has no qualms about marrying a non-Jew, he is liberally pro-Palestinian, he has never visited Israel, though he knows it to be a racist/apartheid place, he considers himself to be part of the intellectual elite, he has no real knowledge of Torah or Judaism yet considers himself an expert on both. He knows the best policy for Jews and Israel to follow, and he is so convinced of his rectitude and astuteness that he is willing, nay demanding, to use all types of force to coerce the Jewish people and its small national state to adopt his will. He is out to fix the world and is willing to sacrifice Israel, Judaism, and Jews in the process. He sits on boards of Jewish organizations; he chooses rabbis and proclaims himself to be a faithful Jew. Yet he will contribute generously to non-Jewish charities, and gives only a pittance towards Jewish educational projects. He is not an evil son, nor is he a wise one. He will deny that he is simple or naïve, and he claims to know with certainty what questions to pose.

Yet he may be the most tragic of all the sons, for though he is able to pose the questions, he is unwilling to hear the answers. In the words of the prophet Isaiah, "The heart of the people is overladen with fat and their ears are stopped up." It is this hedonistic, intelligent, but very deaf son that troubles us so deeply, for we have developed no plan or method to deal with him – either to exclude him from Jewish society completely or to somehow redeem him and bring him closer to Jewish reality and positive participation in Jewish life. It is certainly not clear to us how to accomplish this second option.

So perhaps we must rely on the inspiration represented by the fifth cup of wine – on the miraculous powers of the prophet Elijah and on his unfailing faith in the restoration of Jews and the Jewish people. Pesach teaches us never to say never. It is the holiday of rebirth and constant renewal. So will it be for all of our different children, all of whom we gather and embrace around our Pesach Seder table.

Righteous Women – Pesach

One of the well-known statements of Midrash about the Exodus of Israel from Egyptian bondage is that our ancestors were redeemed from Egypt in the merit of the righteous Jewish women of the time. We tend to judge Jewish righteousness purely in terms of ritual and observance, and though that is certainly true, it is not the entire truth. Jewish women, then and now, were a source of everyday inspiration and hope for men, who, in their hard-hearted realism, were given to despair and pessimism. Amram, Moses's father, refused to live with his wife, Yocheved, after Pharaoh's decree to cast all Jewish male infants into the crocodile-infested waters of the Nile. According to the Talmud, he was the most righteous person of his generation, completely free of sin, yet he despaired of any Jewish future. His daughter Miriam convinced him otherwise, and from his reconciliation with Yocheved, Moses, the greatest leader of Israel, was born.

The Midrash tells us that the copper used for the Laver that stood in the Tabernacle came from the mirrors that the women of Israel used to entice their husbands to create a future generation of Jews when all seemed lost and redemption from Egyptian bondage appeared to be impossible. For these actions, the women were deemed righteous. Apparently, in the eyes of Heaven, righteousness comes in many different forms. Bearing children in a world inimical to Jewish survival is perhaps the highest form of righteousness for such a time.

Bringing children into the world is a statement of faith and hope in the Jewish future. Even in our day, every Jewish child who is born represents a declaration of faith as well as hope for future well-being. Children are also a declaration that one does not live only for one's self. The entire idea of selflessness and responsibility one for another is based on children and family. Parents care for and raise their children, and children care for their parents later in life. The statement of Rabbi Akiva that the great rule of Torah to "love others as you love yourself" begins with family and children.

And it has always been the righteous women of Israel – our wives, mothers, and daughters – who have epitomized this highest of all standards of human behavior. In the crushing, dark, murderous environment of Egypt, the courageous midwives, Shifra and Puah, stood for humane behavior and Godly virtues. They helped Jewish children live and survive. It is no wonder that Jewish tradition places the credit for our freedom from Egyptian bondage at their feet.

The Torah links its imperative to "choose life" with the other imperative of "reviving, saving, and helping children live." While in the animal kingdom, offspring are abandoned by the parents after a period of time, in human culture a child always remains one's child till the end of life itself – because that child represents all of one's hopes and accomplishments in this world, and in immortality as well.

Our current society has made great strides in improving the status of women. There still is a long way to go, but there is no comparison in terms of education, professions, mobility, and opportunity for women to what was available even a few short decades ago. This is true in Jewish religious society today as well. Our great-grandmothers in Eastern Europe may have been in the main illiterate, but our daughters and granddaughters are biblical scholars, physicians, professors, and educators. What a boon this has been to Jewish life and its richness of thought and knowledge!

So the righteousness of our women is not only measured in their ritual piety – necessary as that is for Jewish continuity – but in their vast influence that has so enriched our society. From the women of Israel in Egypt to Deborah, Hulda, Esther, Doña Gracia Nasi, Sarah Schenirer, and the women in our own families, the spirit of Israel has been nurtured by the optimism and sacrifice of Jewish women. It is they who provide significant merit for our ultimate redemption and freedom. So the story of the Exodus from Egypt repeats itself in this fashion in our days as well. And so may it be.

Memorial Days — Yom Hashoah and Yom Ha'atzma'ut

Official days of national remembrance are the feeble attempts of governments to bolster and revitalize national memory. They recall difficult times and immense human sacrifice; and they always attempt to teach a lesson from previous generations to the next. The problem with these commemorative days is that they are formalized, run by committees, and usually not that meaningful to the general populace. They simply provide a well-anticipated day off from work. Much of the purpose of memorial days is lost at the barbecue and the beach.

But one should not be too cynical about the value of these days of reminiscence, because without them there would be no background to our current lives and little understanding of the issues we face. It is obvious that even after more than seventy years have passed, the events of World War II and the Holocaust still haunt us. They not only haunt the Jewish people, its primary victim, but the world generally, provoking uncertainty, fear, hatred, and controversy. The Holocaust deniers are in reality only trying to get rid of that ghost. But as the current world situation shows us, the possibility for genocide and brazen inhumanity still remains part of our lives. Memorializing the Holocaust with a memorial day of observance only intensifies the presence of that disturbing ghost that gives our generation no peace nor respite.

The day commemorating the founding of the State of Israel represents to me not so much what occurred but what it prevented from occurring. Because I lived through the last half of the 1940s, I clearly remember how desperate the worldwide situation of the Jewish people was at that time. No one was optimistic about our future. All of the wise savants and military experts predicted the conquest of Palestine by the invading armies and Arab militia. Today, there are many who say that it was a foregone conclusion that Israel would survive and win its war of independence. But often these statements are written not only in perfect hindsight but also with an intended agenda attached to them.

In May 1948, I was a student in Chicago. Our faces were drawn and our hopes very limited as to the fate of our people then fighting for their lives in the new State of Israel. To those who were not alive at that time, Israel Independence Day is a day of celebration and leisure. But to those of us who witnessed that original Israel Independence Day, it remains a day of wonder and joyful surprise. Israel became the driving force in the Jewish world, the center of Torah and Judaism, and in its own way a glimmer of "light unto the nations." Without it, I hazard to say, the Jewish world today would be far smaller, far weaker, far more secular, and in great danger of annihilation.

The road has not been easy, and the cost is been very dear. And the butcher bill still demands payment regularly throughout the Jewish world. Nevertheless, we have every cause for optimism. These days of remembrance remind us not only of the dangers through which we passed but also of the fortitude and determination of the Jewish people to survive and prosper.

I have often pointed out that throughout human history there have been no great national comebacks. Rome will never again be an empire, nor will Great Britain rule over a quarter of the globe's surface again. History's inexorable rule has been that gone is gone.

These days of remembrance remind us that the Jewish nation is an exception to this rule. We have come back in a fashion so remarkable that it truly staggers the imagination. The Holocaust haunts us, but it did not destroy us. Much of Russian Jewry escaped to better lives and better times and places. Anti-Semitism and anti-Israel rhetoric abound, but in no way does this inhibit the growth of the Jewish people and the State of Israel. These are important things to remember and contemplate during this time of national memory. These realizations will stand us in a very good stead as we continue on our future path of growth, accomplishment, and holiness.

Days of Fasting

With the passing of the fast day of the Seventeenth of Tammuz, the Jewish world sadly prepares for the fast day of the Ninth of Av, the day that marks the destruction of both Temples and commemorates other later national tragedies in Jewish history.

The most fundamental day of fasting on the Jewish calendar, of course, is Yom Kippur. However, Yom Kippur differs from the other four fast days – the Fast of Gedaliah, the Tenth of Tevet, the Seventeenth of Tammuz, and the Ninth of Av – in that it does not commemorate any tragedy. It is rather a holiday, a day of peace and forgiveness, of contemplation, repentance, and spirituality. In fact, in his legal code of *Mishneh Torah*, Maimonides describes Yom Kippur as a day of rest and not as a fast day per se. Part of our "rest" on that day is that we abstain from consuming food and drink.

So we see that there are two types of fast days in Jewish life. One is to commemorate historical national tragedies, while the other is an act of contrition and repentance, a means of spiritual self-improvement. Because of this second type of fast day, the one of repentance, there is a custom of *BeHaB – bet, hey, bet* – Monday, Thursday, and Monday – fast days that occur at the beginning of Cheshvan and Iyar. These are days of repentance to ask forgiveness for any excesses of behavior that may have occurred during the preceding holiday months of Tishrei and Nissan. There also was an additional fast day observed in Ashkenazic Jewry on the twentieth of Sivan, which first commemorated the martyrdom of the Jews in Blois, France, in 1171, and later pogroms and destruction of large Jewish communities in Eastern Europe in 1648–9. Individual Jewish communities also instituted local fast days to commemorate sad events that befell them. There was a time in Jewish life when days of fasting were common.

Over the last century, however, extra fast days have become less popular in the Jewish world. In his monumental halachic work, *Mishnah Brurah,* Rabbi Yisrael Meir Kagan, known as the Chafetz Chaim (1839–1933), noted that physical fasting was no longer possible for most of the Jewish people. He therefore proposed that instead of fasting from food and drink, one should "fast" by abstaining from speech on that day. The avoidance of silliness, pettiness, slander, and obscenity – all of which are intimately associated with the words of one's mouth – would truly make the day one of commemoration, repentance, and spiritual self-improvement.

In today's Jewish world, even *BeHaB* is no longer observed so much as days of physical fasting. Rather, these are now days of special penitential prayers, charity, and kindness. It has become apparent that in our more affluent time, the haves find it more difficult to fast than did our have-not ancestors of previous generations.

In the epoch preceding the destruction of the second Holy Temple, there were fast days instituted by the rabbis in times of drought. An entire tractate in the Talmud, Taanit, deals with these fast days and their ritual. In those times, there were also many days on the Jewish calendar when a fast day was forbidden. These were special days that were anniversaries of miracles and glorious victories for the Jews against their foes. The record of these days was kept in a special book called *Megillat Taanit.* This work is still extant, but since the destruction of the Temple and the loss of Jewish sovereignty, it is no longer empowered to prevent the declaration of fast days by the Jewish community.

It has always troubled me that a special fast day in commemoration of the Holocaust was never instituted. The Chief Rabbinate of Israel wished to have Yom Hoshoah fall on the day of the Tenth of Tevet, so as to have a fast day as part of the remembrance of this major tragedy of Jewish history. The Israeli Knesset, in one of its less wise decisions, instead instituted a moment of silence on the twenty-seventh of Nissan as the memorial for Holocaust victims. This secular remembrance, devoid of any connection to Jewish tradition, has created a further rift in Israeli society, so that instead of being a day of unity – which a fast day such as the Tenth of Tevet would have been – Yom Hashoah has become a day of dissension and further pain in Israeli public life. Perhaps a "fasting" day of silence, instead of only two minutes of silence, would have been more appropriate.

Disaster and Rebirth – Tisha B'Av

Most nations of the world do not commemorate the anniversaries of their defeat. Conquest and victory are usually celebrated, while embarrassing losses are expunged from memory. Yet those empires that once conquered us and exiled us from our own land have long ago decayed and dissolved. The Babylonian empire and later the Greek and Roman empires are no longer around to commemorate their day of triumph over us. They are remembered only by those whom they conquered.

At first glance, this would seem to be incredibly ironic. It is the Jewish people who have kept the memory of our enemies alive and fresh in our minds, hearts, and calendar over the ages. Remembering that we are bidden to erase the memory of Amalek from our midst has served to constantly remind us of its presence in the world and of the danger that it still poses to us and to all civilization. Apparently, it is only by remembering our enemies that we are able to truly erase their legacy.

Paradoxically, commemorating the days of our disasters is the method of preserving our hopes and commitments to rebuild ourselves and our homeland. In my father's synagogue in Chicago, an appeal for funds to support the fledgling and struggling institutions then being created in the Land of Israel took place the afternoon of Tisha B'Av. As a child, I thought that it was rather incongruous for this collection to take place on that day of mourning and sadness. Now I realize the genius of that custom: it contains within it the secret of our survival and a profound understanding of the miraculous rebirth of the Jewish people over the past century. Matching all of the miracles that constitute the natural world of the planet is the unending and inexplicable miracle of the survival of the Jewish people over the millennia of exile, despite the disasters which have constantly befallen us. One has to be almost willfully blind (or spiteful) to be able to ignore this singular event in all of world history.

The rabbis have taught us that the Ninth of Av is destined to be a holiday, a day of rejoicing over the vindication and confirmation of our history and destiny. Therefore, even though it is still a day of mourning and sadness, it contains the seeds of its future greatness and hope. Jews always viewed this day of near-despair as a day of renewal and a foundation for rebuilding our world, our Land, and our mission. No penitential prayers are recited on this day because of this nucleus of hope that the day contains within it.

Our rabbis further taught that those who mourn for Jerusalem will be able witness its rebirth and restoration. The idea here is that those who truly care for the welfare of Jews immediately see in their act of mourning the beginning of the re-establishment of Jerusalem and the Jewish people to prominence and prosperity. So, in a strange way, it is a day of mixed emotions and split vision – one of a difficult and troubled past and the other of a glorious and meaningful future.

The observance of the fast day may weaken us physically, but it strengthens us emotionally and spiritually. The Shabbat immediately following the Ninth of Av already brings us comfort and hope. Our generation has seen wondrous events; surely we will be privileged to gain hope and commitment from the day of disaster and destruction.

Menachem Av

Though the month of Av carries a title – *menachem*, meaning comfort and consolation – it nevertheless remains the most cheerless and disturbing month of the Jewish calendar. Comfort is a lofty and necessary concept, but as a reality it is very difficult to obtain. This is particularly true for individuals reeling from the loss of a loved one, but it also applies to the national entity of the Jewish people. As yet, there has been no comfort, no closure, regarding the terrible national tragedy of the Holocaust, even though more than seven decades have passed since that time.

This lingering sadness should come as no surprise to Jews, for to a great extent we have yet to be comforted for the destruction of our Holy Temple and our exile for almost two millennia. No person or institution in Jewish life is indispensable; but neither are they replaceable. It is the void that is left because of this irrepaceability that prevents true comfort from taking hold. So we remained restless, and often even disoriented, over the long exile that we have endured. The sorrow of the first ten days of Av permeates our lives and resonates within us precisely because the sense of closure has eluded us.

The Talmud states that there is a Heavenly decree that engenders forgetfulness of the departed by those still living. However, if the object of grief is not truly dead but is only absent – as was the case regarding Jacob's grief over the loss of Joseph – this sense of closure and comfort remains absent as well. That is why the Torah records the inability of Jacob to accept solace from his family and friends. Joseph was not dead; the Heavenly decree of forgetfulness that allows comfort was inoperative in his case. So consolation could not come to Jacob.

I believe that in an ironic and odd way the fact that the Jewish people still suffer from the anguish of the Holocaust is because of the intense efforts made by our community to prevent it from fading from our consciousness. We keep it alive, though it pains us. (It is the Holocaust-deniers and their ilk who wish to lull us into a false sense of comfort, by proclaiming that it never happened or that it is over and that bygones should be bygones.) The Bible records that our mother Rachel refuses to be comforted over the exile of her children because she is convinced that they are not permanently lost or exiled; they will return. There is a positive side, therefore, to not being consoled. It allows for a connection to an unknown future that will not only provide comfort but also replacement of what and who was lost.

The grief and tension of the first part of the month of Av are still with us – centuries after the destruction of the Holy Temple – simply because deep within the heart and psyche of the Jewish people the Temple is not gone: it is only missing. The entire enterprise of the return of the Jewish people to the Land of Israel in their millions over the past two centuries and the establishment of the Jewish state in our ancient homeland are testimony to the fact that to us the Land of Israel and the Temple were not dead issues. Those Jewish communities and individuals who proclaimed that "Berlin is our Jerusalem" and therefore sought permanent relief in being good Germans, Russians, Poles, etc. did not fare well in God's world. False comfort is far more damaging than no comfort at all. It remained for those Jews who did not forget that they were from Zion and Jerusalem to arise and help the Jewish people survive the worst and bloodiest century in its long history.

Scripture warns us against being "comfortable in Zion." Living in the Land of Israel is not a comfortable experience, though it is a holy, challenging, and inspiring one. For living in the Land of Israel makes us aware of what we have achieved against all odds, and at the same time to appreciate what is still missing. The awareness of what is missing is what prevents us from being "comfortable in Zion."

The month of Av symbolizes this angst and challenge of living a Jewish life, of being grateful for what we have, and yet maintaining a sense of loss for what we are still missing. May this month yet bring us the feeling of *menachem* – of a better time and the eventual comfort promised to us by God through His prophets.

Shabbat Chazon

The Shabbat preceding the day of mourning of Tisha B'Av is traditionally known as Shabbat Chazon. The name derives from the opening word of the *haftorah* from the prophet Isaiah that is read on that Shabbat in the synagogue. *Chazon* means vision or prophecy. The word itself is one of neutral quality. It can be a positive and optimistically uplifting vision, or it can be a scathing prediction of dire events, as in this prophecy of Isaiah.

Thus, the very word *chazon* represents the omnipresent choice that faces humans all of their lives. How shall we view our future? Is it going to be a better world, in spite of all present difficulties, or are we doomed always to a repetition of failures, disappointments, and tragedies?

The Torah and Jewish tradition demand of us that we have a *chazon* – a vision of our future, a goal, and destination to our journey as a people. However, the choice of what type of *chazon* we have for the future is, as always, completely left to us to decide. Education without concurrent vision is an empty pursuit of facts. Education without proper and constructive vision – such as in Stalin's Soviet Union and other purely secular standards of schooling that exist in the Jewish world presently – destroys more than it builds, and dooms coming generations to error and defeat. That, in essence, is the message of the prophet Isaiah on Shabbat Chazon.

Faulty vision while operating an automobile is a lethal prescription for disaster. Faulty vision in leading a people toward national goals and priorities is many times more dangerous.

The prophets of Israel laid out a vision blueprint for the nation. They stressed that proper choices for the future are heavily dependent upon a sense of what has happened to us before. Even though it is foolish, if not bordering on insane, to continue following policies and ideologies that have proven to be wrong and harmful, the tendency to do so remains strong. It is difficult in the extreme to admit error; and the greater the error, the more difficult it is to face up to it. Politically and diplomatically, it seems clear that that the policies of Israel over the past two decades regarding "land for peace" and other such high-sounding mantras have proven to be damaging. Yet no one is willing to own up to these errors, and in fact the ideologues who first implemented them stubbornly cling to them, even in the face of all contrary evidence to their viability.

The search for a secular "loaded wagon" has gone on for over a century in Jewish education without producing results, except for complete ignorance of Judaism and Jewish values, resulting in rising rates of assimilation and alienation from the Jewish people and the State of Israel. The inability of those who reject Torah Judaism to articulate a more meaningful vision of Judaism has crippled generations of Jewish youth and left them stranded in an ocean of hate and despair. Bad vision certainly extracts its toll of woe.

But all is not lost, nor should we give in to despair regarding our future. The same prophet Isaiah who delineates the vision of destruction on Shabbat Chazon will follow with seven soaring visions of redemption, hope, and success in the weeks after Tisha B'Av that bring us to the High Holy Days.

We have the choice of which vision of the prophet we wish to follow. Even though on the surface the choice should be an easy and simple one to make, it will be hard to implement our correct vision, since switching to the positive one requires that we make fundamental structural changes to our educational and social systems. There are accumulated crusts of apathy, mistakes, vested interests, and shortsighted leadership that must be overcome in order to reveal a greater positive vision to the people.

It took us some considerable time to get ourselves into our current mess, and it will take immense patience and perseverance to extricate ourselves from it. We must abandon bad vision in favor of a clearer and brighter one. The Shabbat of Chazon Yishayahu crystallizes these choices and their consequences for us. As in everything else in life, the Torah bids us to choose wisely.

Lessons from History

A Parking Space

As all Jerusalemites are well aware, a parking space is a precious commodity in our holy and busy city. This is undoubtedly the case in all great metropolises in the world. Returning home from a late-night affair can become a matter of serious angst, as hope fades and there is no parking spot to be found reasonably close to home.

Parking on both sides of the road had been allowed on a street near our home for many decades. This made the drive through that street somewhat hazardous, and many a sideview mirror was broken as vehicles navigated their way. But people in our neighborhood were comfortable with that arrangement, for it provided quite a few parking spaces that were sorely needed. And then, without warning or consultation with the neighborhood's inhabitants, the authorities-that-be overnight abolished parking on one side of the street. True, it made driving down that street much easier, but it forced many residents to search fruitlessly for overnight parking.

Since I no longer own a car, I am able to survey the scene dispassionately and objectively. And since I am a rabbi, I am always looking for the Jewish connection in all events in life, no matter how mundane they may appear on the surface. And this set me thinking about parking spaces and the "Jewish problem."

Over the unbelievably long exile and dispersion of the Jewish people among the nations of the world, Jews have always searched for a place to park themselves. They parked in Babylonia and North Africa, Spain and Portugal, Provence and France, Italy and Holland, Poland and Lithuania, Germany, Austria, Central Europe and Russia, and lately in North and South America and Western Europe. Even though these locations initially seemed to be legal and attractive parking spaces, they eventually turned out to be hostile and illegal. Like the parking spaces on my adjoining street, overnight most of these countries declared that parking there was no longer allowed. So the Jews kept moving on, always looking for a convenient, safe, and acceptable place to park.

When the Jews arrived in Poland in the thirteenth and fourteenth centuries, they felt so certain of their parking space they felt that the Hebrew name for Poland – *Polin* – represented the Hebrew words *po* – "here" and *lin* – "to rest overnight." "Here we will rest in comfort until the end of the Exile," they thought. But practically overnight the No Parking sign was erected over much of Europe and brutally enforced. So has it been throughout our history among the nations.

There are not many parking spaces left in the world for Diaspora Jews. We have been all over the globe, and there are no undiscovered continents or new countries to offer us parking spaces. But in our time, our original parking space established by Joshua and David has somehow – against all odds – become available for us once again!

There are among us many who find this original parking space somewhat inconvenient. It is hemmed in on all sides by very large vehicles that prevent easy access. And there are many, even some amongst us, who dispute the fact that this parking space is legal. All city dwellers are aware that often such disputes result in violence and even murder. People are irrational when it comes to parking spaces; morals, common sense, and societal accommodation play no role whatsoever in these arguments.

Thus, there are many Jews who hesitate to leave the parking space where they are located – inconvenient, uncomfortable, and even dangerous as it may be – to return and park themselves in our rightful, legal, and ancient parking space. Usually it takes a traumatic experience to convince these Jews that they can no longer park themselves in their previously accustomed spot. I pray that this should no longer be necessary, but all of Jewish history tells me otherwise.

Jewish history and tradition are the signposts that signify where our legal, permanent, and eventually secure parking space is truly located. Meanwhile, I am delighted that I no longer own a car, even while living in my permanent parking place.

Eras End

In rabbinic literature, the book of Bereshit is known as the book of the *Avot* – the book of our forefathers and foremothers, the founders of our people and our faith. It was an era of individual greatness, of lone people in a hostile world whose pursuit of truth and loyalty to the Creator influenced their world and all of humankind thereafter.

The next era, which also produced great individuals such as Moses and Aaron, is nevertheless the era of nationhood, of forging a new society out of a disparate and large number of individuals. There is a certain exhilaration in being the lonely individual standing against the many on matters of faith and principle. It is courageous and often selfless. It entails the willingness to sacrifice and to endure indignities, and even worse consequences. Yet difficult as it is for one to be such an individual, it is infinitely more difficult to successfully engage in the task of nation building. An individual has freedom of choice and need not worry about the others in his world. Not so one who is forced into forming societies and directing them once formed. The great era of the *Avot* ended, but the gargantuan task of building a people with a common sense of purpose and values demands a new era of greatness and leadership. And that is the message of the change in nuance and emphasis of the Torah from the book of Bereshit to the book of Shemot.

The long and painful era of Jewish exile was not so much a time of building societies in the Jewish world as it was simply a time of struggling survival. It required special mechanisms and social pressures to maintain a semblance of organized Jewish life. But to a great extent, especially here in Israel today – and perhaps even in large areas of the current Jewish Diaspora as well – these mechanisms, tools, and outlooks are no longer really productive or relevant. The era of nation building cannot rely on bans, pronouncements, and impractical policies that may have had validity in a different era but are no longer effective in this one.

The Torah and its halachic standards do not change with the whims and fashions of the time. But attitudes, goals, and policies to create a Torah nation and physical entity do change, and change they must. People often quote personal opinions of great leaders of the past on societal matters – not *halachah* – and attempt to elevate them to the level of *halachah*, to make them the law today as well. My feeling always has been: How do I know what these great people would have said had they lived today under the circumstances of Jewish nationhood, after a Holocaust, and in the face of the modern interconnected world? And is it not slightly arrogant to think that a different era entirely would not have necessitated different responses to social and national problems, none of which are covered in the field of *halachah*?

Eras are best seen in retrospect with the perfect hindsight of history and past experiences, but they are difficult to identify in one's current time. We must try to analyze and understand the eras of every generation separately. Yet the Torah also bids us to be aware of the fact that eras change and that time is not frozen. The tasks set before every generation may be the same in broad scope, but certainly differ in nuance and detail.

The mission of building a Jewish society here in the Land of Israel is the same as it always has been, but the circumstances are not those of

1948, let alone of 1897. The adjustment to that reality has been a most difficult one for all segments of the Jewish people. We do not recognize clearly the demarcation line separating one era from the next. But surely that line does exist and, more importantly, an attempt must be made to recognize it and deal with it.

The secret of the Jewish world that has allowed it to survive has been its resilience and practicality combined with faith and tradition. We have navigated many eras of change successfully, and basically we have remained true to our original identity and purpose. I am certain that this will be the case regarding our current era as well.

Kristallnacht

Most of the time evil cloaks itself with some form of outward righteousness. Lenin, Stalin, Pol Pot, and Chairman Mao killed millions for what they claimed were just causes that would benefit humankind. Many in the Moslem world cloak their terrorism with religion.

To a certain extent, however, the brutal evil behavior of the Nazis and Germans towards the Jewish people was an exception to this rule. Here was raw evil, unmasked and unashamed, with no excuses presented and no justification advanced. And this clear revelation was on world display on Kristallnacht, November 9–10, 1938. In Germany, Austria, and East Prussia, 267 synagogues were burned to the ground; scores of Jews were killed; 30,000 were arrested and sent to concentration camps; Jewish stores and homes were destroyed and vandalized. It became clear to all who yearned to see it that the Final Solution was going to become a reality.

Kristallnacht was the watershed event in the destruction of European Jewry. The only question the next day was whether anything could be done to save European Jewry from Hitler's carefully planned disaster. Unfortunately, the practical answer to this question of life and death turned out to be one of helplessness and near surrender.

This shocking, thorough, and coordinated event should have removed the blinders from the eyes of the Western world as to what awaited them from Germany a few short months later: a world war that would destroy tens of millions and shatter Europe for generations. Part of the tragedy of Kristallnacht is that it was not taken as an effective wakeup call to those who could have yet stood up to Germany. And so the deluge arrived.

The Nazi regime in Germany was basically anti-religion and anti-God. It was not a random event that synagogues were destroyed and Torah scrolls were desecrated. The Jewish people represented (and still represent) faith and awe of the Almighty. Even though millions of Jews had abandoned traditional Jewish practice and belief, they were nevertheless caught in the net alongside those who had remained faithful to the Torah.

Most of the Jews in Germany were assimilated, proud Germans who placed their Germaness over their Jewish ancestry. But Hitler came along and stated that the Jewish problem was genetic and not one of individual belief or behavior. The fact is that Jewishness can never be separated from Torah, and if there were Jews who did not understand this, the Nazis certainly did.

Jews were always persecuted not for their own personal behavior or human failings but for the faith and value system that they represent. Judaism was the antithesis of all that Naziism and its barbarism stood for. And therefore Kristallnacht marks the beginning of that all-out war against Judaism, the Jewish people, Torah, and the God of Israel.

We can say of Kristallnacht what the brave martyr of Roman times, Rabbi Chanina ben Tradyon, said of the Torah scroll in which he was wrapped and burned alive: "The scrolls and parchment may burn to ashes, but the letters of the Torah still float in the air." The synagogues and Torahs of the Jews were reduced to ashes and the Jews were killed, but the words and values of Torah and the souls of the murdered still float in the air, still giving the world's conscience no rest.

Kristallnacht demands of us to strengthen our ties to the Torah and

Judaism and to stand strong on behalf of Jews the world over and in defense of the Jewish state. It is tragic beyond words that Hitler should gain posthumous victory over Torah and the Jewish people.

Saying "never again" is wishful and in itself impractical. Only actions and constructive efforts can guarantee "never again" as a reality. Every Jew has a responsibility to himself or herself, to the family and nation, as well as to Jewish history and destiny, to strengthen attachment to Judaism and the Jewish people. The fires of Kristallnacht must be converted to the fire of Judaism and Jewish life within the souls of the Jewish people. Fire destroys and fire warms; it can be constructive or destructive. Those choices remain with us, and Kristallnacht focuses our attention on these choices. May the memory of Kristallnacht light the fire of a greater Jewish future within all of us.

A Family Fight

There is no fight quite as bitter and harmful as a family fight. The very closeness of the relationship between the parties involved intensifies the feelings of personal hurt and deep insult. Closeness always emphasizes the differences that exist, and clouds over the basic agreements, shared values, and common worldview.

The Bolshevik Communist government of the Soviet Union hated and persecuted the Menshevik Communists, Socialists, Trotskyites, and other assorted Marxist leftists to a greater degree than they hated even their so-called capitalist foes. It was a family fight and family fights become violent, illogical, and very long-lasting.

The history of the past century has shown that the divisions in the Jewish religious world are deep and seemingly unbridgeable, even though the differing sides agree on the basic principles of faith and moral behavior. They disagree on clothing, customs, political matters, and how to share the pie of jobs and welfare, as well as governmental and private largesse.

Great institutions of Jewish learning have been broken up by internal disagreements as to the precise methodologies of study, the rights of succession, and differences of personality. Rarely do these disputes involve true ideological differences; they almost always descend into personal feuds that are eventually intractable.

From my long experience in the rabbinate, I can unequivocally state that the bitterest disputes I witnessed and attempted unsuccessfully to solve were between members of the same family. The clash was usually over inheritance rights or other family matters that to the outside observer seemed relatively petty and unimportant. This is certainly an example of the sometimes perverse side of human nature.

Our rabbis have often taught us that the bitter internal disputes that plagued Jewish history over the ages, and are all too present in our current society, can all be traced to the genetic imprint created within us by the proceedings between Joseph and his brothers. Joseph is insensitive to the feelings of his brothers, suspects them of deeds they have never committed, and slanders them to their father. They, in turn, see in this young teenage brother of theirs a threat to their very existence and to the future of the house of Jacob. Misunderstandings cause personal enmities to develop. The ten brothers cannot speak peacefully or civilly to Joseph, so deep is their antagonism to him. They harden their hearts and stop up their ears as he weeps and pleads with them to save him from the pit of snakes and scorpions. Finally, he is sold as a slave into Egyptian bondage. They are able to fool their ancient father, witnessing his decades-long grief without revealing to him their culpability in Joseph's disappearance. Wrongdoing always leads to further wrongdoings, and a lie must be inevitability covered up by further numerous lies. And all this because of a family fight over misinterpretations and erroneous assumptions about the motives and behavior of others who were bound together by blood and family.

It takes many years and very changed external circumstances to reconcile Joseph and his brothers and make the house of Jacob whole again. And we see this pattern repeating throughout Jewish history.

Common existential dangers, the enemy from outside, usually have a sobering effect on simmering internal disputes. Only diehard ideologues continue to whistle past the graveyard, oblivious to real dangers.

It seems that unfortunately we need a discernible external and immediate threat to allow us to forget and forego our internal squabbles, at least temporarily. Let us hope that we will find a wiser and better way to deal with our family fights, both personal and national.

Echoes from the Past

Despite all claims to the contrary by its biological and spiritual descendants, Eastern European–style Jewish life has passed from the scene. The social, religious, and political movements that dominated pre-Holocaust Eastern European Jewish life are no longer active, and are perhaps even inoperable in our current society.

The yeshiva system of education that was prevalent in nineteenth and twentieth century Lithuania was built only for the elite, concentrating on memory retention and creative commentary upon existing texts. It was a system that was never intended to include the "average" student; therefore, the numbers attending these yeshivot were relatively small, certainly in comparison to the tens of thousands of students attending yeshivot today in Israel and the Diaspora. Though today's yeshivot attempt to perpetuate the legacy that they have an elite student body, the truth of the matter is that this is no longer true. In our world, a yeshiva education has become mandatory even for the "average" student. In fact, without a yeshiva education it is unlikely that a young man will grow up to be a truly observant Jew. The Lithuanian yeshivot once produced almost all of the great rabbinic leaders of Israel. Today those institutions frown upon producing rabbis and many of them do not even have a rabbinic ordination program. Along its entire broad spectrum, the yeshiva world has changed radically from what it was a century ago.

The Bais Yaakov women's school system begun in the 1920s by Sarah Schenirer in Cracow, Poland, was originally intended to produce teachers for the Jewish world. It also aimed to help stem the tide of radical assimilation and anti-religious ideologies that were sweeping the Jewish youth, especially women, of that time. Today's women's seminaries, though still advocating the the goal of producing teachers, concentrate on preparing their students to marry Torah scholars and become the primary breadwinner of the family. They are to be the superwoman of our time – wife, mother, breadwinner, housekeeper, good neighbor, and moral force of the family, all at one and the same time.

Since there is a large surplus of female teachers everywhere in the Jewish world and the pay scale for such employment is usually quite low, the seminaries are forced to facilitate programs that will allow most of their students to enter other fields of endeavor commensurate with current employment opportunities available in broader society. These young women are thrust from a most sheltered environment and many years of gender-separated education into the rough and tumble of today's workplace. And women who wish to pursue an academic or professional career face the challenge of academic life and the environment of its educational institutions. (Not surprisingly, many opt for online educations leading to college degrees.) The challenges are formidable and varied, and most of them were completely unimaginable in Cracow of the 1920s.

Even the most influential ideological movements of the past centuries have been consigned to the ash heap of history. Marxism, in all of its permutations, has proven to be a false god. The Left still pays lip service to its ideals and axioms, but it really only wants more benefits, wealth, and political power for itself. Most of the rhetoric about fairness in society really means "give me more of the pie." The kibbutz movement has largely become privatized and capitalistic; and no one looks to North Korea or Cuba as a role model for a fair and just society. The Zionist movement in its various forms has also apparently shot its bolt and no longer commands the loyalty of the Jewish street, even of many Jews living in the

Jewish state that it so heroically created and fashioned. Jews have become blasé about Israel, and there are generations that no longer remember the Diaspora or the War of Independence.

The impressive movements that shook and motivated the Jewish world a century ago have passed from the scene; only their echoes remain with us. History teaches us that past solutions and tactics fade in the face of different circumstances and changing societal pressures.

Though our future always contains an element of uncertainty, we can be certain that the Jews of today and tomorrow will have to develop answers to new problems. In particular, the process of nation building in Israel will require ongoing innovative thinking and clever implementation in order to succeed. But succeed we will!

Government and Religion

Over the span of the millennia of recorded history it is obvious that governments either opposed or corrupted religious beliefs for their own benefit, or forced religion to conform to the politically correct ideas and norms of a time. In the ancient world, governments relied on paganism to strengthen their hold on the people and to create tyrannies. The Roman emperors felt compelled to proclaim themselves gods in order to guarantee the obedience of the masses. The half-mad Roman Emperor Caligula even had his horse proclaimed a god by the Roman Senate. And later, it was the power of government in the Roman and Byzantine empires that Christianized Europe by force; little intellectual convincing was necessary for a mainly illiterate population.

Throughout the Middle Ages, the contest was between the authority of kings at odds with powerful religious authorities. In effect, it was the government that told its hapless subjects what to believe and how to believe. The unholy alliance of church and state became the norm in Western society, as well as in the Moslem world.

As the Enlightenment took hold in Western Europe, the power of religion was severely weakened; and government moved in to fill the vacuum. The United States and France, after their respective revolutions, declared themselves to be countries where church and state would be separated, where religion would have only moral sway but no temporal power to enforce its beliefs. This example was followed by other nations in due time.

As Western civilization became more and more irreligious, and as secularism became the dominant intellectual force, governments became increasingly less tolerant of religion. Governments often feel a compulsion to oppose religious beliefs and practices, to legislate against them, and to enforce decrees intended to make observance more difficult. Naturally, all of this is done in the name of progress, equality, and other high-sounding words and phrases. But the bottom line is that it ends up being a dictatorship over what people can believe and practice. By enforcing rules such as gender equality, and carrying these rules to an extreme – mandating same-sex bathrooms and a refusal to identify a newborn infant as male or female – the heavy hand of government stifles religious expression and beliefs.

The power of government is so enormous that it can and (often does) infiltrate every aspect of its citizens' lives. The Soviet Union enforced atheism as the national "belief" of its millions of citizens, actively destroying the infrastructure and leadership of religion in that country. In the United States and in Israel, the arbiters of which religious expressions are to be allowed are the unelected members of the Supreme Court. For example, fierce debate regarding the legally protected right to abort a living fetus has been raging without end for the last seventy years, as religious beliefs and governmental policies clash. And this is only the tip of the iceberg.

If government would be truly neutral regarding religion, it would not be viewed as an enemy of religion. However, since governments in the Western world, and at times in Israel, are hardly neutral in religious matters, tension between government and religion remains high and volatile.

History has taught us that in spite of their apparent power, governments come and go. That what is accepted social policy in one generation may be determined to be criminal activity in another generation. Though religion also experiences change and social evolution, it does so slowly and in a very conservative manner. As such, it provides stability to a social environment that otherwise sways radically from one extreme to another.

No one should advocate a theocracy, for history has shown us that this create a dysfunctional nation; witness Iran, Saudi Arabia, and other such states. At the opposite extreme, governments should stay out of advancing policies that weaken the religious beliefs and systems that function in their societies.

A great deal of wisdom is required to achieve the necessary balance between religion and government, and we all know that wisdom is at a shortage. Nevertheless, this problem should be realized and considered before governments adopt policies that are inimical to religious norms.

It's the Zhids

One of the more uncanny peculiarities in human history has been that the Jews are immediately sought out as the scapegoat whenever a sinister event occurs. Unfortunately, there is a very long and bitter history to this phenomenon. It is so deeply ingrained in parts of the non-Jewish world that even in our time, against all logic and facts, this canard still persists.

Consider the amazingly unbelievable statement made by Vladimir Putin that the Jews somehow rigged the US presidential election in 2016. This comment was immediately followed by the pious disclaimer that it could not have been the Russians because such a nefarious scheme and its execution were beyond the capabilities and imagination of the Russian government. I am reminded that after the terrorists attack against the United States that destroyed the World Trade Center, many in the Moslem world – and even in parts of the Western world – attributed this act of wanton murder to Zionist Jews. Their claim was that it was far too sophisticated and well-planned to have been executed by Arabs. It could only have been done by Jews, who are clever enough, sinister enough, and amoral enough to conceive and execute such mayhem. The fact that such nonsense can continue to be disseminated by supposedly responsible and intelligent people only shows how deep the anti-Jewish virus is implanted in our current world.

The Russians have a long history of blaming the "Zhids" for their woes. Czar Nicholas II blamed the Russian defeat in the 1904 Russo-Japanese war on the Jews. He further attributed the popular uprising and revolution of 1905 to the Jews. In fact, all of the mounting woes of the Romanovs were ascribed to the Jews. The "Jewish question" was predominant in all Russian government circles in the nineteenth and twentieth centuries until the Bolshevik revolution.

During World War I, despite the fact that over 100,000 Jews served in the Russian army and many thousands were killed in the war, the Russian government treated the Jews not only as enemy aliens, but also as spies and traitors. It was an ingrained belief of the czar and his army general staff that Russian losses were not because the German army was superior, but because Jews in the service of Germany had betrayed the Russians. Because of this accusation, many hundreds of thousands of Jews were expelled from their homes and forced to resettle deep in disagreeable areas of Russia. This draconian policy, together with repeated and systematic pogroms committed by Russian forces, accounted for the deaths of more than 250,000 Jews before the Bolshevik revolution and the later civil war, which in their turn would annihilate thousands more.

It is almost futile to argue logically against wildly anti-Semitic conspiracy theories. The poison spread by the Russian Secret Service in the 1890s with their pamphlet on the fictitious "Elders of Zion" running the world took root and is tragically alive and well in much of the world today. All protestations of our innocence and the fact that all of this is pure bunk simply lands on deaf ears.

The Syrians blame their woes on Israel, even though Israel has nothing to do with the Syrian civil war or the brutality of the Assad regime. It is not reported widely, but after almost every chemical or air attack that the Syrian government mounts against its own citizens, the Syrian media blames Israel. The fact that there is chaos in Gaza, that there are shortages of fuel and electricity there, is attributed to Israel and not to Hamas or the Palestinian Authority.

We live in an Alice in Wonderland world where everything is seen through a distorted mirror. The problem is that the world is so accustomed to viewing itself through that mirror it believes that it actually reflects reality. But the world is not an amusement park and skewed vision and preposterous conclusions are dangerous. So we must continue to speak out against ridiculous accusations and demand that some modicum of reality enter into the world's dealings with the Jewish people and the State of Israel. History has shown that it will not be easy.

Europe Is Gone

What can one say about Europe? I imagine that if we want to be bitterly truthful, we could say that Hitler has, in effect, triumphed. He branded the Jews as the root of all troubles and proclaimed that the "final" and only solution to the "Jewish problem" was to eradicate all Jews from the face of the earth. And as we all know, he followed through on his genocidal program. A great deal of Europe, its leaders, intellectuals, and common folk, willfully and almost gleefully cooperated in this genocide. Many did so actively, while many more did so passively.

Once the horrors of the Holocaust were revealed after the war ended, this irrational and pathological hatred of the Jews went underground. After all, it was too shameful to admit that the continent that prided itself on the advancement of civilization could be guilty of organized, government-sponsored inhumanity and cruelty. So most Europeans shielded themselves from guilt by simply stating that they were ignorant of what was occurring. The Vatican and other Christian churches aided many Nazis and other war criminals in escaping from Europe and settling rather comfortably in other continents, notably South America.

As penance for their atrocious behavior, many European countries, though not all, voted at the UN in 1947 for the establishment of the State of Israel and granted the nascent nation diplomatic recognition and economic help. And there the matter seemed to rest during the decade of the 1950s. But the State of Israel, always the burr under the world's saddle, would not let the matter rest. The wound was too deep and raw, the losses too great; the world would not be allowed to so easily forget what had happened.

When Israel captured Adolf Eichmann (a Nazi high in Hitler's hierarchy) in Argentina, he was placed on trial for his crimes against the Jewish people and humanity. The trial, beginning in April 1961, lasted almost a year, and revealed through eyewitnesses in a stark and graphic way what had happened to the Jewish people on European soil from 1939 to 1945. Thus, it was not only Eichmann and the Nazis who were the defendants in that most bruising and bitter trial, but in a very real sense, Europe itself was on trial. And when Eichmann was justifiably found guilty and executed for his crimes, subliminally Europe was also judged guilty and complicit in the horror of the Holocaust. Europe has never forgiven Israel for that trial and verdict.

Europe rues not so much the Holocaust itself, but that because of it the Jews were allowed to create a nation state for themselves. Therefore it will build Holocaust memorials and museums, but objects to the inclusion of the State of Israel in that story.

And in line with its time-honored obsession with the Jewish people and its innate necessity to scapegoat Jews for all of Europe's problems, Europe has turned its enmity in an unremitting fashion against the Jewish state. Israel should be pilloried and boycotted, delegitimized and isolated, while the noble Palestinians – fomenters of worldwide terrorism, intifadas, and recurring wars – are worthy of diplomatic recognition, media support, financial aid, and moral justification. Hamas is no longer a terrorist organization as far as Europe is concerned; but Israel should be hauled before the International Court of Justice at The Hague. This is Europe's revenge against the Jews for surviving the Holocaust, instilling the unease and guilt that Europe feels towards Jews, Judaism, and the Jewish state.

To use a Christian phrase, Europe is sorely in need of redemption. Catholic countries such as Ireland, Portugal, and Spain have not digested the lessons of history vis-à-vis the relationship of the Church and the Jews over the centuries. And it is no better with the liberal Left, which refuses to deal with the history of oppression and anti-Semitism that Marxism, the Soviet Union, and the Left generally has inflicted on world Jewry. And that leftist agenda marches on: country after country bans kosher slaughter and attempts to ban circumcision, all in the name of some lofty ideals of animal and infant rights. Perfidious and hypocritical as it is, Europe claims the high moral ground for its "progressive" attitudes, sneering condescendingly at the United States.

Even George Orwell would be astounded to see how skewed European vision and policies are today. Only time will tell if Europe is ever able to right its perverse attitude towards Jews and Israel. History teaches us that it will be doomed if it does not.

Promises

It is apparently impossible to be elected if one has not strewn the electoral landscape with promises. "Vote for me and I promise that I will do great things for you and for our party" is the candidates' mantra. But by now any voter with a modicum of sense knows, or should know, not to believe in the promises of political candidates. As cynics so wisely noted, promises are made in order to be broken.

Rabin was elected because he promised to smite the PLO "foot and thigh." Instead, he brought them back from Tunisian exile and installed them in corrupt power that still plagues us today. Peres promised us a new Middle East, a veritable Garden of Eden. But it is the old Sunni-Shiite Middle East that still confronts us. Sharon promised to defend Israel's right to build anywhere in the Land of Israel and instead evacuated Gaza, causing wars, deaths, and untold privations to thousands of innocent, hapless Israeli citizens. Obama promised Americans that under his health plan law they could keep their current health insurance policies. That has been proven to be blatantly untrue. The elder George Bush promised not to raise taxes – "Read my lips," he famously said – but once in office, he did raise taxes, no matter what his lips said. The list of broken diplomatic, military, and governmental promises made and broken is endless.

Our prime minister now promises us that he will not allow Iran to obtain nuclear weapons. I hope and pray that he is somehow able to keep that promise. But I am wary of any human promises. Humans are often unable to fulfill their promises, no matter how well-intentioned. The Talmud warns against making a promise to a child and not fulfilling that promise, for it will teach the child that it is acceptable to lie.

So great caution should be employed in making promises. The observant Jew always qualifies a stated commitment to others with "*bli neder*" ("without a vow intended"), which, in effect, softens the promise and weakens the commitment. It allows for the possibility of unforeseen circumstances that may not allow the promise to be actualized. This is not meant as a cunning loophole to escape the fulfillment of one's word.

Rather, it is an admittance of human frailty and impotence in the face of the unknown and ever-changing future. For who truly knows what tomorrow may bring? The Psalmist exquisitely asserted, "There are many plans in the hearts of humans, but only God's plan will truly arise."

All of this unpredictability should engender in every one of us – and especially in those who purport to be our leaders – a sense of humility and caution. That is one of the ideas that lies behind the rabbinic advice that "the words of the wise should be said softly." The wise have also been found to have been mistaken in their assessment of the future, and even in their own capabilities to influence that future.

I am always skeptical of those who claim that they can somehow read God's mind, so to speak, and predict future events or trends, making promises contingent on them. Caution in behavior and in speech always pays dividends.

Promises easily made are a sign of arrogance and hubris. And yet, people who assume leadership roles must have some smattering of arrogance. The Talmud allotted them one-sixty-fourth portion of arrogance in their personality makeup. But that is a limitation too confining for those in political leadership. It is arrogance that leads to scandal and criminal behavior among the high and mighty, for they view themselves as being above the law. Often, this corruption is due to the attempt to fulfill unattainable goals and foolishly made promises.

Hitler promised a thousand-year Reich. Khrushchev promised that the Soviet Union would bury the Western democracies. In most areas of human life, less is more. So it is with promises as well.

Individuals and History

Douglas Southall Freeman was recognized as one of the premier American historians of the twentieth century. He was a confidant of presidents, a noted author and Pulitzer Prize winner, and a man of great charm and character. During the Cold War he was the thorn in the side of leftist acamedicians, who insisted that the inexorable tide of history was on the side of the Soviet Union and that the West was doomed to witness the victory of the "progressive" forces of the world. This Marxist view of history, which allows little room for individuals and sees all major human events as being steered by ill-defined, unseen, but all-powerful social, historical, and economic forces held sway in the halls of Western academia for decades. Not even Stalin's ruthlessness and the ineptness of the Soviet economy could sway the true believers from discounting the role of the individual in shaping events. To counter this Marxist idea, Freeman wrote: "The influence of personality in History cannot be overestimated. While there are always great events that stir humanity, it will always be found that these events center around one man, and in him have their life."

Freeman's view of history corresponds with the traditional Jewish view on the same matter. It is interesting to note that the Bible records the great sweep of history over more than a millennia of time, but it does not deal with abstract, impersonal forces that push individuals around and into the corner of the story. Rather, it depicts almost exclusively the stories and lives of individuals. And it is clear from the biblical narrative that these individuals – through the exercise of their Divinely granted freedom of will – created the events that we call history.

To a great extent, Marxism absolves humans of any responsibility for their actions. It postulates that things must happen in a certain way and that humans are powerless to stem that tide or defeat those forces that guide history. In contrast, Judaism postulates that God grants humans ultimate free will and freedom of action, making humans responsible and acutely accountable for their decisions and actions.

So humans – individuals like you and me – are the true creators of history. The individual is not a passive pawn in shaping events that affect human life. Rather, humans are the active catalyst that creates events, propelling the story of human history onward.

This point is discussed in commentaries to the biblical narrative of Abraham being told by God that "your descendants will be strangers in a land that is not theirs. They will be enslaved and afflicted there for four hundred years." The question that is raised there is, if God predicted this event, why were the Egyptians punished for enforcing His decree? Nachmanides answers that they were punished for their cruelty in "overdoing" it. However, Maimonides cites the principle of free will. No one commanded the Egyptians to enslave the Jews. God's prediction in no way removed their freedom of choice. In fact, they should have treated the Jews nicely out of gratitude to Joseph, who saved them in the years of famine and established Egypt as the dominant economic empire of the time. This is what the Torah means that an Egyptian king arose "who knew not Joseph." He made himself not know Joseph. That was his personal decision, and his people went along with it, much as the German people went along with Hitler's murderous policies.

The Lord grants freedom of will and action to even the most evil and malevolent of human beings. But He also holds all human beings responsible for their choices and behavior. That is the essence of Jewish belief. All other interpretations of human behavior and history are rejected forcefully by Judaism. It is no wonder, then, that the "dialectical materialism" explanation of human history fostered and advanced by the Soviet Union turned it into an anti-Semitic state and a hater of Judaism and traditional Jewry.

Many in the modern world treasure their right to individual free will and freedom of behavior. Yet many of these same individuals are loath to accept responsibility for that behavior and its consequences, both individually and nationally. Judaism does not allow humans to wriggle off of that hook easily. The Torah commands individuals in correct behavior and policies, but allows the individual to choose. It is the behavior of those individuals – of each and every one of us – that creates our history.

Regressing

One of the unfortunate delusions that besets both our general and Jewish societies is that we are somehow advancing in an unbroken line upwards towards better times. We gaze triumphantly at all of the impressive technological gadgets and medical advances that give us such satisfaction and pride. In the Jewish world, we revel in the new freedoms that we now routinely expect in our reviving numbers and material affluence.

It should be fairly obvious to all by now that the Holocaust as a moral lesson and as an historical reminder is already passé and irrelevant. Anti-Semitism, certainly in Europe, has reached the level of the 1930s. No one is embarrassed to be anti-Jewish and anti-Israel. Just as Germany advocated and enforced boycotts against Jewish commercial establishments, so too is this the tone of European society today regarding Israel and its economy. Just as Germany and Poland in the 1930s banned *shechitah* and ridiculed circumcision and other Jewish beliefs and rituals, so too is this wave of hatred – cloaked in the piety of animal and human rights – sweeping Europe today. As far as the Jews are concerned, so-called democratic Europe has regressed back to where it was eighty years ago – a weak, feckless institution inimical to Jews and Judaism. Appeasement, though by a different name, is the policy of Europe and the United States to all aggressions, and the United Nations is proving itself a worthy successor to the impotent League of Nations when dealing with crises and armed conflicts. Despite our gains in other areas, generally speaking, the world has regressed in its policies and attitudes towards evildoers, haters, and bigots.

The Arab world also has apparently learned nothing from the events of the past century. One cannot say that it has regressed to its original position of not acknowledging the existence of the Jewish state, since it has never left that position for more than seven decades. (Only Egypt and Jordan are the tenuous exceptions to this mindset.) The opportunity for a Palestinian state existed in 1948, again in 1967, in 1991 with the Oslo agreements, with Ehud Barak's proposals at Camp David, and later with Ehud Olmert's far-reaching concessions – but all to no avail. So in effect, in spite of all of the efforts and optimistic statements, and all of the pressure placed on Israel for more and more concessions, we have really gone nowhere as far as this so-called two-state solution is concerned.

In the Jewish world we are also witness to a tide of regression. The Jewish Left has apparently learned little or nothing from the events of the past century. It has whitewashed the Soviet Union and demonized the American victory in the Cold War. It opposes Israel and its policies of self-defense, and portrays it as the main obstacle to world peace and societal serenity. It has learned nothing from the foolish unilateral withdrawals that have brought only grief and death to thousands of Israelis over the years. It is relentless in its condemnation of Israel, and has nary a good word to say concerning traditional Judaism or the destiny of the Jewish people. Its political correctness stifles all dissent.

In my opinion, much of the Orthodox Jewish world has also regressed. For many members of this society, and for many of its educational institutions, we are still living in 1920s Eastern Europe. It is as though the Holocaust never occurred, and if it is acknowledged, it is as though no practical lessons are to be learned from it. It teaches us no lessons to be applied in today's society. And certainly as far as the State of Israel is concerned, it is still embroiled in the battles over Zionism that so roiled the Jewish world a century ago. The reality of the existence of the State of Israel – that it is now home to over six million Jews and that the Jewish future everywhere is inextricably bound to its welfare and success – is completely ignored.

It revels in fighting battles that have long since disappeared from relevance. Constructing a fantasy world of false history, legendary biographies that have little basis in fact, and ignoring the moral and societal implications of the isolationist behavior of much of Orthodox society have created an enormous disconnect between it and the rest of the Jewish people. Parochial interests, political power, and the budgetary pie have resulted in a regression from the nobility of Orthodox life of seventy years ago and returned us to the bitter divisions and internecine warfare of Eastern European Jewish life in the 1800s. One would hope that this disconnect can somehow be bridged before it brings complete disaster upon all of us.

Infanticide

There are many things in current society that are not particularly to my liking, but I'm willing to allow them to exist without any necessity for me to comment upon them. However, the latest dangerous legal insanity of infanticide should not be allowed to pass without comment and passionate objection.

Slowly but surely, the acceptance of abortion at will and as a "right" of a woman to govern her own body has been strengthened and become societally normative. In the United States, this process began with the famous Supreme Court decision of *Roe v. Wade* almost a half-century ago. Here in Israel, in the secular Jewish community abortion is widespread and considered unremarkable.

The Orthodox Jewish communities, both in Israel and the United States, have opposed abortion at will, with practically no fanfare and true passion, but with little success. The governments of the United States and of Israel – and undoubtedly within the European Union as well – finance abortion groups and their agendas. These groups always have high-sounding names such as Planned Parenthood, which mask the fact that that they are really about killing babies, and in many cases making a gruesome business out of selling the body parts of their infant victims. But lately, especially in the United States, as the Left has become more extreme and virulently vocal, abortion has morphed into the actual killing of blind babies during any stage of pregnancy, even in the birth canal, and there are proponents of the rights of the mother to kill the baby immediately after it has, in fact, been born. The barbarity of this position does not deter the Left, the media, and extreme feminists from insisting on this type of murder is a constitutional right.

The legislature of the state of New York recently passed a bill into law allowing for abortion to take place even when the mother is in labor giving birth to the baby. There is no doubt, medically or empirically, that the baby is then a living human creature. When this bill was finally passed, the majority of senators rose and applauded their work. Thus, infanticide has become legal in progressive modern-day culture. Add to this the fact that the governor of Virginia, who ironically is a doctor, stated that under a bill that was proposed in the legislature of that state a woman would have the right to terminate the life of an infant that had been already born, if she and the doctors wish to do so. Of course, he added that the baby would be "made comfortable" before being killed.

Woe to such a society as ours that has reached such depths of legal depravity! This is a throwback to ancient militaristic Sparta where unwanted children were taken out into the forests and left there to die. As they would not have made good soldiers, they would become a burden on Spartan society. It is also a throwback to the decrees of Pharaoh in ancient Egypt to cast all of the male Jewish infants into the Nile River so that they would be devoured by the crocodiles, ending what he considered to be "the Jewish problem" in his time. In the upward climb of human society to become more civilized and compassionate, the current approval and applause of infanticide is a gigantic step back towards the cruelty, violence, and murder of past generations.

In the nineteenth- and early-twentieth-century supporters of Social Darwinism, one could detect the trend to adopt murder as a means of improving the lives of the elite society who "deserve" to live and prosper.

These ideas led to the movement of eugenics, which allowed for the murder of tens of thousands of human beings who were considered mentally unfit and a burden on society. In the United States in the 1920s, there were many thousands of such murders committed and sanctioned by the state and federal governments. One of the most disturbing ironies regarding the movement of eugenics was that many medical doctors who had taken the Oath of Hippocrates, pledging to do no harm, participated in this slaughter of innocents.

When they came to power, the Nazis emptied the insane asylums and systematically murdered (by many estimates) at least seventy-five thousand people. There did arise a popular protest against this practice, but Hitler had proven that unwanted people could be disposed of by murder, and that his Nazi government could easily survive any objections to its tyranny by using terror and coercion. As he could destroy so many thousands of perceived burdens to society, he felt that he could also implement the "Final Solution" and destroy millions whom he could unilaterally declare to be subhuman and not worthy of life.

Some decades ago, a noted conservative radio personality spoke to a largely Jewish audience at the 92nd Street Y in New York City. Most Jews in that typical New York audience considered themselves very liberal. In fact, I would say that they were liberal first, and only then Jewish, if Jewish at all. The speaker made the unforgivable mistake of linking the demand for unlimited abortion at any stage of pregnancy (even during birth labor) with the Holocaust. While all hell broke loose, he was booed and practically driven off the stage by the audience. He later remarked that he was surprised at the reaction: he had thought that a Jewish audience would appreciate the logic of his connection, and be aware of the dangers that could ensue from murdering babies, simply because they are not wanted. His surprise was because he did not understand the mindset of the liberal, secular Jew who is usually quite ignorant of Judaism and Jewish values; he is interested only in fixing the world in his or her image, no matter the cost to others.

People who can stand up and applaud a law that approves the killing of infants for the convenience of others are very dangerous; they are already well down the slippery slope of murdering others who simply do not agree with them or are different than they are.

I doubt if this essay, no matter how persuasive it is, will have much of an effect on Western society. But I simply cannot let the matter pass without expressing my opinion.

Ideology and Reality

The Torah describes itself as a *Torat chayim* – a Torah of life and living. There are many possible interpretations of this phrase. It can refer to the fact that the Torah is eternal, it is vibrant and ever-renewing, it is the source and fountain of life – it is a living Torah. To my mind, this phrase implies that it is also, if not primarily, the Torah of practicality and reality. It is fashioned to fit the world that it preceded. It does not demand the impossible, nor does it deviate from the norms of human and natural existence. Therefore, it is not only a living Torah, it is also a realistic and practical guide to human life.

Though the Torah is built upon the bedrock of faith, it is not ideological in nature. Though it espouses a monarchial system of government, it advances no ideological political view, no grand economic plan; it is rather humble in imposing set forms and ideas upon human society. Throughout the biblical period, when there were many prophets who lived and guided Jewish society, they almost unanimously spoke of moral behavior, justice, kindness, and tolerance. They emphasized the practical dangers that the Jewish kingdoms faced, and warned against hubris and provocations. The prophets of Israel did not advance capitalism, socialism, communism, nationalism, universalism, or other ideological doctrines or restraints.

Sooner or later, all ideologies infringe upon individual rights and create tyrannical societies that propagate evil in the name of a higher good. Ideologues are always able to justify injustice in order to achieve their imagined perfect goal. We are painfully aware of where the ideologies of the past number of centuries have led us.

When ideology combines with religion and incorporates that ideology as part of the faith basis of that religion, it becomes doubly lethal. Religious wars throughout the centuries have really been wars of ideology, territory, power, financial gain, and dominance rather than struggles of faith and soaring belief.

The Torah contains 613 commandments. One would think that that would suffice. Nevertheless, in our time it has been overlaid with conflicting ideologies that have taken on the aura of principles of faith. To the fringe anti-Zionists among us, denigrating and defaming the State of Israel is equal to observing the Sabbath and eating kosher food. Their ideology has made them haters and hated. That cannot be the state of being that the Torah had in mind for Jews, nor for human beings generally. To many Zionists, settling in the Land of Israel is the prime ideology that rules all else. It must be admitted that the extreme application of this ideology flies in the face of current experience. And the Torah, if it is nothing else, is reality personified and applies in all situations. Apparently, human beings cannot live without an ideology to sustain their political beliefs and societal programs. But care must be taken that ideology does not fly in the face of practical certainties. In instances when it does, no good occurs.

We see throughout the books of the prophets that reality was the lodestone that guided them. The prophet Samuel hesitates, even when commanded by God, to go to the house of Yishai to crown the new king of Israel. He says: "But King Saul will hear of this and will slay me for being disloyal to him." The Lord takes this truth into account. He instructs Samuel to take animals with him to sacrifice publicly in Bethlehem as a cover for his real purpose in going there. This strong sense of reality informs the words and dominates the views of all prophets of Israel.

In Second Temple times, most of the great rabbis of Israel did not support the rebellion against Rome. They felt it was futile and that it would only result in the destruction of the Holy Temple. The actuality of Roman power overrode the ideology of Jewish messianism during that era. Sixty years later, most of the rabbis again dissented from the ideology of Bar Kochba and Rabbi Akiva, opposing this further rebellion against Roman power because it was doomed to failure.

We should be cautious not to confuse ideology – which is not necessarily a tenet of our faith – with the realities that we face. We should pray that the Lord gives us the wisdom to be able to discern and apply this historical truth to our times and situations.

Rabbi Isaac Halevi Herzog

I once attended an all-day conference in Jerusalem commemorating the one-hundredth anniversary of Rabbi Isaac Herzog's seminal PhD thesis that he submitted to the University of London. It was a scientific, historical, and halachic review of the source of the ancient dye used to produce *techelet*-colored wool for the priestly garments and for the *tzitzit*/fringes of four-cornered garments worn regularly by Jews. The conference, attended by a large and diverse audience, was most interesting and informative. But this article is not about *techelet* blue, indigo, or purple dye; it is about the author of that thesis, one of the eminent rabbis of the past century who, in my opinion, has never been given his proper due.

There are probably many reasons for this lack of knowledge and approbation about him and his accomplishments. But I feel that the main reason is that he was unique. He was out-of-the-box, apolitical, and fearless in his views and decisions – while at the same time he was humble, self-effacing, and modest to an extreme in his private persona. For various reasons – psychological, theological, and historical – the

Jewish "establishment" does not easily tolerate such people. They make us "normal" people – conditioned by dogma, preconceived notions, and societal conformity – uncomfortable, and force us to think. And that can be a painful experience.

Rabbi Herzog was a linguist with a grasp of a dozen languages, including many ancient ones such as Sumerian and Akkadian, as well as classical Greek and Latin. He was a biblical scholar of note, a Hebrew grammarian, and a scholar of enormous proportions of Talmud, rabbinic writings, and halachic decisions. His memory and genius were of a prodigious nature. He also explored the sciences, including zoology, botany, astronomy, physics, and chemistry with diligence and perspective.

But his main commitment and passion, intellectual and emotional, was Torah, in all of its variety and ramifications. His many volumes of responsa, as well as his opinions on halachic issues and cases brought before the High Court of the Chief Rabbinate here in Israel during his years as its head judge and chief rabbi, are a treasure trove of Torah erudition, hard-headed logic, and a practical, yet compassionate, worldview of life, people, and Jewish society.

Worldlier than Rav Kook, his predecessor, Rabbi Herzog was the chief rabbi during one of the most turbulent and decisive times in Jewish history, from 1936 to 1959. He saw the Jewish world destroyed and rebuilt during his tenure in office. He never flinched nor faltered when facing pressures exerted upon him by the non-Jewish world, the Catholic Church, the militantly secular Zionist leadership of the emerging state, the violent zealots of Jerusalem (who opposed him without truly knowing him), the British rulers of the country, and the complexities of being the chief rabbi for hundreds of rabbis of different personalities, ideologies, and ambitions. His gentle personal nature belied his iron determination and stubborn love for Torah and the Jewish people.

The Chief Rabbinate of Israel today is no longer that of Rav Kook or Rabbi Herzog. Though always subject to political competition – Rabbi

Herzog had to defeat Rabbi Yaakov Moshe Charlop in a hard-fought election campaign in 1936 to become the chief rabbi – it has further deteriorated. It is now seen by many as almost a purely political office instead of one of spiritual vision and national leadership. Unfortunate scandals that have surrounded the office have only further diminished its original luster.

There is always nostalgia when looking back at previous generations and their leaders. Yet I believe that no one would disagree with the statement that the Chief Rabbinate of Israel has never again achieved the dignity and widespread support of all sections of the Jewish world that it had during the tenure of Rabbi Herzog. And we are all the poorer because of this decline of an important institution in Israeli and Jewish life.

The Talmud teaches us that superior people are not a commonly found commodity. The Lord, so to speak, scattered them throughout the ages and implanted them in separate generations. Rabbi Herzog was just such a superior person, gifted to us by God in a special generation of Jewish life and history. His contributions to Jewish scholarship, life, and rebirth remain today, and we are all in his debt.

Jewish Mail

The postal systems that exist in our modern world – governmental postal services and private businesses delivering mail and cargo – are highly developed and sophisticated enterprises. Tens of millions of letters, documents, and packages flow through them; and an amazing percentage of them actually get delivered to their desired destination. In the centuries before electronic communications, the necessity for such a system was obvious: people from one place had to be able to communicate with people living somewhere else. Some rudimentary postal system was probably always in place.

In the ancient world and through the period of the Middle Ages, there were couriers who risked their lives to deliver messages to far-flung outposts of empires. Diplomatic pouches and couriers date back at least a millennium. The rudiments of a modern postal system existed in England in the seventeenth century with the advent of postage stamps, and official postal authorities arose in the next century.

There was always a Jewish postal system, though never officially established and authorized. Throughout the ages, important legal and scholarly documents had to be transmitted from one place to the other in the Jewish world. The delivery of "mail" was usually entrusted to two types of travelers: merchants who traveled for commercial reasons, and the representatives of yeshivot and other Jewish institutions who traveled to gather funds from other Jewish communities to help support their endeavors. There were also official agents or bailiffs of Jewish courts who traveled to deliver legal documents – such as bills of divorce – from one community to another. And then there were special couriers who delivered books and Torah writings to the outposts of the Jewish world. Amazingly enough, this ad hoc type of delivery system was efficient (given the circumstances of travel), timely, and honest. Jews trusted each other with the delivery of important personal and commercial documents. And this trust was backed up with an official ruling.

In the tenth century, Rabbi Gershom, known as the "Light of the Exile," the head of the yeshiva in Mainz (France-Germany), promulgated a number of ordinances that affected Jewish life greatly. The most famous one was the ban on polygamy. However, one of his other, "lesser" ordinances forbids opening, reading, or using any information that was in a letter or document with which one had been entrusted for delivery to another person. Till today, a Jew is not allowed to open a letter addressed to someone else. This ban strengthened the Jewish mail system greatly, for Rabbi Gershom buttressed his ordinances with the power of a *cherem* – a ban of anathema and exclusion from the Jewish community for anyone who disobeyed the ordinance. I have personally known Jews who were completely unobservant of many important *mitzvot*, yet they remained scrupulously observant of Rabbi Gershom's ordinance because of the *cherem* attached to it. In any event, the flow of Jewish letters and documents continued unabated in the Middle Ages and until modern times, independent of any official postal delivery system.

Rashi's great commentaries, written in eleventh-century Troyes, were known soon after their writing throughout the Jewish world. Maimonides sent special couriers to France and Morocco, as well as to Yemen and Iraq, to bring his important works to the attention of those Jewish communities and their scholars. It is truly amazing how his works were so rapidly disseminated. His communications to and from the rabbis of Provence and Iraq have been preserved as testimony to the impact of his writings on the Jewish world of the twelfth century.

The famous Cairo *genizah* – a storehouse of discarded documents, usually of holy writings – contains copies of letters sent to the Jewish community of Cairo from rabbinic figures throughout the Middle East and Europe. Since Jews were always active in mercantile trade and traveled extensively, it seems there were always couriers available to deliver Jewish mail around the world.

This habit of private mail service is so ingrained in the Jewish psyche that it continues, despite modern postal services. Who among us has not been asked to take some mail or a package for someone when embarking on a trip to another country or city in which there is a Jewish community? The Jewish mail system, like most Jewish habits and traditions, remains strong and operative even today!

Jewish Heritage

The Universal Jew

The modern liberal Jew has redefined Judaism as a religion that has no fixed laws, that is built on vacuous slogans (such as "*tikun olam*"), that embraces moral relativity, abhors tribal loyalties, and defines itself in purely currently acceptable universalistic terms. This type of Judaism has removed all the uniqueness of Jewish life and tradition, and it seeks mainly to appeal to the non-Jewish world by showing that we and they are really the same; that there is nothing special about being Jewish nor anything unique about the beliefs of Judaism.

Commentary magazine once quoted a young Reform rabbi in Los Angeles: "Don't keep kosher, that's fine; don't keep Shabbat, that's fine; marry a non-Jew – whatever. But understand that it will take away your Jewish identity if you don't fight for justice." The fatuousness of this remark is breathtaking. Judaism is now reduced to a struggle for an undefined, almost indefinable, universal concept called justice. And somehow this idea is to become the core of one's Jewish identity. Is there any hope for Jewish survival with such redefinitions of Judaism prevailing?

The liberal Jewish community in America and elsewhere has turned Judaism on its head in its public and principled support of unlimited abortion; gay marriage; unwarranted and untrue accusations against the State of Israel, questioning its very right to exist; and the complete abandonment of observances of Jewish law. Whatever this liberal hodgepodge of ideas may be, it is certainly not Judaism.

This idea of Jewish universalism versus Jewish particularism is an ancient one, disproved many times over by the events of Jewish history. The leaders of the Jewish exiles in Babylon two thousand five hundred years ago came to the prophet Ezekiel and declared their intention that the Jewish people – the "House of Israel," as they phrased it – should be identical in outlook, behavior, and goals with the rest of the non-Jewish world. The Lord informed the prophet that such an arrangement would never take hold – not because the Jews weren't willing, but because the non-Jewish world (the instrument of God's wrath, so to speak) would never permanently agree to such an arrangement.

It is the very particularity of the Jewish nation that makes it valuable to all mankind. The more German Jewry became German, the more the Russian Jews became Soviet Marxists, the more fertile the ground became for hatred of the Jew. As long as Jews insist on being liberals first and Jews second, or not at all; feminists first and Jews second, or not at all; environmentalists first and Jews second, or not at all, etc., a large portion of those groups of Jews will eventually disappear. As long as attending Harvard or Yale is more important to Jewish parents than giving their children a basic Jewish education, and the ephemeral pursuit of utopian world justice is more important than Shabbat or marrying a Jew, the disappearance of large swaths of American Jewry is guaranteed.

It is the modern liberal Jew that is loathed throughout the non-Jewish Western world today. The Israeli government's foolish secular message that "we are just like you" has little resonance in the European Union or the United Nations. The support that Israel receives from many Christian groups is based on their perception of Israel as a Jewish state, biblically ordained, and not as a universalist, liberal, fixing-the-world bunch of Jews living in the Middle East.

The Jewish liberal establishment preaches inclusion of non-Jewish partners, but wants very little to do with the Orthodox Jewish world. That is somehow outside of the pale of inclusion, despite the expanding numbers and growing influence of Orthodoxy. When one is occupied with fixing the world, one has little patience for one's brethren who still are unwilling to countenance the public desecration of Shabbat and intermarriage with non-Jews. Being busy with the universal leaves little time to be occupied, or even interested, with the particular.

I am fascinated by the fact that there are two main groups within American Jewry who voice vociferous opposition to the State of Israel. One opposes the state because it is not Jewish enough, and the other opposes it because it is too Jewish.

The universal Jew is ashamed of the Jewish state. It is too small, too parochial, too mundane, and certainly too narrowly Jewish. But Jewish survival – a worthy end in itself – will never be assured through the ideals of universality for the sake of universality alone.

Back to School

I think that even though we can all agree that school is a very necessary part of our society, there is still a downside to it. Not all children do well in school, yet their poor performance is not a true indication of their abilities and talents. School often fosters a sense of inadequacy, frustration, and lethargy in many of its students. Packing a large number of students in one classroom almost automatically guarantees that some of them will not do well. Inspirational teachers, perfect classroom settings and size, and elite, motivated student bodies are not easily found in the mass educational systems that comprise modern society.

This fact is true not only in the area of general studies, but also – and especially so – in the area of Torah studies. For there it is not only knowledge that must be transmitted but more abstract – and yet extremely vital – goals such as faith and life values. And for those abstract goals there is no set curriculum, no perfect text that can help achieve success in the mind and soul.

To be a Torah Jew requires study and knowledge. Yet knowledge alone is no guarantee of being a Torah personality. Nachmanides expressed the tragedy of creating a person who is a *naval* – wicked and obscene – who nevertheless has Torah knowledge and lives within Jewish society.

The great religious movements of Chassidut and Mussar aimed to supplement Torah knowledge with a societal value system that would create a whole person, formed in the image of the Creator. There was great opposition in the past to these ideas and new curricula. And there are still many in the observant Jewish world who maintain that knowledge and study alone are sufficient to form a pious and holy person. Yet opposition to Chassidut and Mussar in our time has become more subdued, partly because those movements have in themselves changed. Mussar, for instance, is still taught in many, if not most yeshivot, yet there no longer exist any truly Mussar yeshivot as existed in pre-World War II Eastern Europe. And there are some who would argue that Chassidut as well has become more a matter of form, political ideology, dress, and custom than of strong spiritual substance, personal development, and inspiration. It seems that atrophy and conformity has invaded observant Jewish society and has naturally spilled over into its classrooms. This is not the sole reason for the "children at risk" syndrome which plagues so many of our families, but it certainly has a causative effect in creating that troubling situation.

But the schools are not the only educators of our children. Parents play a pivotal role in educating and raising the next generation. The values and inspiration that are not found in the school can yet be transmitted at home. A great person I once knew, who was clever, astute, and highly practical, always counseled parents to keep their teens in the local school so they could live at home, even if the local school was inferior to other schools out of town. He often told me that children need parents even when the children are fifty and sixty years old, certainly when they are still in their formative teenage years. He was going against the grain of the accepted norms of the generation. Yet I believe that, in most circumstances, he was correct: parents impart not only knowledge but also a sense of values, tradition, family, continuity, and confidence which no school, no matter how well run and educationally advanced, can ever provide.

In our time, when the Lord has blessed many of our families with grandparents and even great-grandparents, it is the task of this older generation to provide for their offspring the values of Torah and the continuity of families and generations. By so doing, we reunite the young child wearing his first backpack to school with the experience of Sinai and the eternity of Israel.

Gratitude

One of the basic values of Judaism is *hakarat hatov* – gratitude to others for favors and help. This concept is embodied in the relationship of a Jew with his Creator. Ingratitude towards the Creator, Who has granted us life and all of its benefits, is reckoned in Jewish ethical thought as a primary sin of attitudes and bad values. We find in the Torah that our father Abraham and his descendants are held to account for Abraham having said to God: "What are You giving me?" when entreating Him for a child.

Part of the rationale for the principle of honoring one's parents, as articulated in the Ten Commandments, is that it is an extension of this concept of appreciation to those who have given us life, and in most instances raised us and protected us from misfortune. Furthermore, Judaism does not view this debt of gratitude as a one-time event (and now let us get on with our lives). There is an ever-continuing obligation that does not automatically expire because of changing times and circumstances. And in Jewish thought, this value transcends generations. My children, if they are aware of others' past favors to me, are also bidden to acknowledge that goodness and to attempt to repay it in kind. There are numerous incidents in the Talmud that point out this intergenerational duty.

Here in Israel, an Arab Israeli was arrested for plotting, and almost executing, a mass murder of Jewish Israelis – civilians whom he did not know and had done him no personal harm. It was revealed that the young daughter of this would-be terrorist murderer had only three weeks earlier undergone life-saving surgery at Hadassah Hospital in Jerusalem, and the surgery was performed gratis by an expert group of Jewish medical personnel. One would have thought that a shred of decency, a whiff of gratitude, would have swayed this plotter to refrain from his nefarious intent to kill innocents. But hatred warps all logical and normal emotional responses. Proud as he is to be a martyr for his faith and devoted as he is to his hatred of Jews, there is no room left in his psyche and soul to consider a smidgen of gratitude towards Israeli Jews.

After the evacuation of Jews from Gush Katif, American Jews – well-meaning and naïve in the extreme – raised fifteen million dollars to purchase (from the UN relief organizations) the greenhouses and hothouses of the flourishing Israeli agricultural triumph there. Hamas-led rioters destroyed all of this infrastructure completely and willfully on the specious claim that they did not want to be beholden to Jewish generosity. Needless to say, none of the hothouses or greenhouses have ever been rebuilt. Only complaints and false weeping about being under siege and remaining impoverished emanates from official Gaza. It is difficult to make peace with people who do not have any sense whatever of gratitude towards others for help extended to them.

The prophets of Israel long ago lamented the lack of gratitude that our ancestors exhibited towards the Creator. God says to them, in a manner of speaking: "You took the gifts of wealth and life that I granted you and used them to fashion idols and promote evil." It is not only the idols and evil, but the sheer audacious cold-hearted ingratitude that drives that behavior and brings down God's wrath against His people. The prophet Isaiah points out that even a domesticated animal recognizes its owner and provider of food and care. But "My people knew not," says God; and that ingratitude led to the destruction of the Holy Temple, Jewish exile, and dispersion.

There is an element of ingratitude in the relationship of certain segments of our current society to the temporal State of Israel. Is it not unseemly to take sustenance and benefits galore from the state and yet revile it at the very same moment? How does that square up with Jewish values and true Torah behavior?

A person with a sense of gratitude can feel contented with his or her lot in life, no matter the circumstances. An ungrateful person always feels deprived, frustrated, and angry at the world and everyone in it. We should all develop the mindset of gratitude so we can learn to say a proper thank you, and to really mean it.

Civil Argument

One of the strong points about Jewish life throughout the centuries has been its lack of conformity. Diversity is not the same as pluralism, which intimates that everybody and every belief (or lack of belief) are "right" and acceptable. Rather, Judaism and everyday Jewish life operated within a framework of belief in monotheism and the Revelation at Sinai, the Divinity of the Oral Law, the importance of traditions and customs, and tolerance of a flexible spectrum of Torah observance. Within this framework, there still was plenty of room for differing customs and halachic opinions. And there were varying responses to the pressures and ideas of the far larger non-Jewish world in which Jews lived. Much of the time, these debates were conducted in a civil and scholarly fashion. However, there were instances when the disagreements got out of hand, resulting in verbal and social abuse, and sometimes even physical violence.

This volatile response was especially likely when new forces and ideas emerged, again all within the general framework of the Judaism described above. The rise of the Chassidic movement in eighteenth-century Eastern Europe, of Hirschian neo-Orthodoxy in nineteenth-century Germany, the Yeshiva movement, and later the Mussar movement that came to dominate the nineteenth- and early-twentieth-century yeshivot, all were sources of controversy and fierce debate within the ranks of traditional Ashkenazic Jewry.

The great Jewish mantra that what common sense cannot accomplish, the passage of time eventually achieves, certainly proved true in all of these cases. These matters have been pretty much settled or reduced to scholarly discussion.

The rise of Reform, Haskalah, and secular Zionism, however, created a much deeper rift within the Jewish world. These movements were operating outside the framework of traditional Jewish thought, belief, and practice. They denied the basic premises of millennia-old Jewish life. The Torah was no longer Divine, the Oral Law was a fiction of the rabbis, observance of tradition and ritual was unnecessary – saying in effect that in all of the previous generations our ancestors were liars and fools.

Because of the radicalism inherent in these assertions, opposition from the traditional camp to these new groupings was fierce, prolonged, and basically uncivil. In the rough-and-tumble course of human interaction, insult begets insult, and violence begets violence. Civilly conducted disagreement upon basic points of faith, as well as definitions of Judaism and the Jewish mission in the world, became almost nonexistent. These struggles spilled over secondarily into the traditional Jewish world as well, with quarrels between Jewish leaders and scholars about how to deal with these challenges.

Of course, there had been numerous internal disputes before the rise of the modern radical movements. The Sadducees, Karaites, and false messiahs engendered fierce opposition in the Jewish world because of their radicalism and the threat that they posed to traditional Jewish beliefs and way of life.

In recent times, the tradition of civil dispute was greatly undermined by the split within traditional Jewry over the Zionist movement.

Religious Zionism became the main focal point of disagreement in Eastern European Jewry in the years before World War II. The deeply held convictions on both sides and the looming importance of the issue intensified the debate.

The ideological and social disputes of the past became entrenched in the political party system of the State of Israel. The pressures of constant elections and the struggle for power, patronage, and budget allocations – the stuff of modern-day democratic electioneering – soured hopes for civil disagreement in our country. Negative campaigning, smears and innuendos, populist slogans, spin doctors, and pollsters created an atmosphere that does not easily allow for sincere debate of programs and policies. Instead, a shouting match ensued, and has lasted for the entire existence of our state.

The Torah allows for civil debate and disagreements. But it always reminds us that "its ways are the ways of pleasantness." We would do well to remind ourselves that our country needs a good deal more "pleasantness." And we must attempt to have civil discussion of the issues, even though there are broad disagreements about them and the possible solutions to our problems.

On Being a Rabbi

Because the Lord has blessed me with long years far beyond my original expectations, I am now able to look back on well over sixty years of service as a rabbi. Even during my nine years as a practicing attorney in Chicago, I served as a Shabbat rabbi, voluntarily of course, in a small congregation of about thirty families in a storefront synagogue. This was after I was an official rabbi for six months in an established synagogue in the neighborhood; but I became embroiled in a dispute in that synagogue and left.

But even as I made my living as an attorney, most of the time I truly loved being a rabbi. And because of that feeling, I left the legal profession and moved to Miami Beach to take a rabbinic position. I have served as a rabbi and teacher, the head of a yeshiva, and the director of an educational foundation. Being old and grizzled, I have had the opportunity lately to discuss the profession of the rabbinate with a number of young rabbis from the United States. It is obvious to me now, as it was when I was much younger, that, like other professionals, rabbis also require a senior rabbi to talk to, someone who will understand their troubles and vexations. I am mindful of the words of the rabbis: "If wisdom is not here, at least old age and life experience are present." So I have had the ability to think about the rabbinate and its vicissitudes, challenges, and opportunities.

For over half a century I have developed a number of insights into the rabbinate that have governed my behavior. I feel they are true and valuable to anyone in the field or contemplating becoming a rabbi. The first, and perhaps the most important, principle is to realize that one is not an employee of the congregation and is not working for the officers, board of directors, or membership of the congregation. One must develop a global view of the position: you are laboring on behalf of God and the eternity of the Jewish people. In my opinion, the rabbi must convince himself that this is the case. This requires a very secure and self-confident view of one's self. The profession is not kind to those who are insecure in their own skin. If the rabbi truly believes that even though the congregation may be paying his salary he is not their employee, but is accountable to Heaven – and can communicate this to his congregation – a great deal of stress will fall away from him personally, and there will be a more wholesome atmosphere in the synagogue generally.

A rabbi must know that a great deal of the criticism and strife directed towards him by individuals in the congregation is not to be taken personally. They really do not mean him. Because of circumstances at home or in the workplace, they are inhibited from expressing their frustrations or disappointments, so they redirect their anger towards a target that usually cannot counter them. I remember that a member of one of my congregations once remarked to me that he did not like my sermon. I responded that I didn't like it either, but that I had to speak, and at that time that was the best I could do. I knew that this person was going through a very difficult time at home and that he really was not commenting on the quality of my sermon; he was expressing his exasperation at his current life experience. By not taking everything personally, one is able to ignore difficulties and retain a sense of the big picture, which in my opinion is so necessary for a successful rabbinical career, both physically and spiritually.

I also noticed a tendency amongst some rabbis to micromanage their congregations. Every little detail of the physical plant and of the distribution of honors during the synagogue services must be supervised and approved by the rabbi. I am a firm believer in allowing the officers and members of the congregation to run the everyday operation of the synagogue and its finances. Naturally, every rabbi is a fundraiser in one way or another. It is important for a rabbi to realize that fundraising, whether direct or indirect, is part of the job description. But he has to judiciously leave the financial end of synagogue life to the officers and members of the congregation. Not every detail of synagogue life is necessarily worthy of rabbinic opinion or guidance. As in all facets of human life, less is more. Many times micromanaging stems from the inherent personal insecurity that I mentioned above. If the rabbi is not able to step away from the details of synagogue life, he will be doomed to constant stress and frequent disappointment.

I have always been grateful for the opportunity to serve as a rabbi. Even in some of the darker moments of my career as a congregational rabbi, I was always aware that this is the only profession that pays a salary simply for observing the rules and values of the Torah. This type of mindset is needed for a fruitful career as a rabbi and a servant of God and of people.

The Jewish nation (and the world generally) will always need good and talented people as rabbis. History has shown us that such people will always exist and will be willing to shoulder the burden and privilege that define this noble career.

Prayers – Answered and Unanswered

In its most formal sense, prayer comprises an important part of daily Jewish life. The rhythm of daily morning, afternoon, and evening services are the staple of every synagogue and home throughout the Jewish world. And perhaps no subject has been explained and scrutinized as closely in the writings of the great Jewish scholars throughout the ages.

There are many dimensions of prayer in Jewish tradition and thought. It is at one and the same time composed of rigid formality with set halachic rules and personal emotion, devotion, and intent. Reconciling these two apparently contradictory motives is a daunting task for the individual Jew who prays every day. On one hand, it can become purely a matter of rote and habit, something that one does in a mental state of stupor and absentmindedness. On the other hand, there are times when one experiences intense emotional feeling – and this is especially true when there is a necessity for a particular personal request before one's Creator.

Devotion and mindfulness during prayer should be present at all times, even in the most formal settings and circumstances. I think that we can all agree that achieving meaningful and spiritually satisfying prayer on a regular basis is a most challenging and taxing goal.

Basically, prayer has two components. One is the concept of praise, wonder, and awe that characterizes our relationship with the Almighty. It is an acknowledgment of our faith in a universe created ex nihilo by an omniscient and omnipotent Supreme Being, a daily recommitment to the essential belief of Judaism in a universal and active God.

The second element of prayer is our request from Heaven for earthly blessings and personal wishes. Though even these prayers are formal in language, the requests are decidedly personal. And there is latitude for even more personal and individual formulations of wishes for health, family, prosperity, and the like. There are also requests for national salvation of Israel and for the betterment of all mankind. Part of the sophistication and elegance involved in the formulation of traditional Jewish prayer over the millennia has been the ability to blend these two differing purposes of prayer into one almost seamless whole. Prayer is always meant to be a serious exercise in thought, life-analysis, and faith. It is also meant to be emotional and meaningful, soulful and exalted. (It never was intended to be easy on the mind and the clock, nor was it necessarily supposed to be entertaining or "cool.")

In order to achieve this precarious equilibrium, rules of *halachah* were formulated to govern prayer. Deviating from these regulations engenders a loss of prayer's essential balance and forfeits its holy aura.

But what are we to think when our prayers seemingly go unanswered? It is painful in the extreme to be ignored or rebuffed. And yet we never have any guarantee that our particular requests will evoke a discernible response from Heaven. In fact, at certain moments of our lives we all feel that our prayers have gone unanswered. There are those who say that "no" – being ignored – is also an answer. But that explanation only begs the question.

So it is obvious that we should not deal with prayer as an application to Heaven that must be immediately acted upon. The rhythm of Heaven is not that of our earth, and prayers that seemingly go unanswered for centuries suddenly and unexpectedly receive response and fulfillment. Though intended most often by the person praying to be short term and immediate, in reality prayer is always long term and can affect generations yet unborn.

Prayer, therefore, is part of the inscrutable nature of all things governed by Heaven and Divine Will. It is our task and obligation to pray and request, to praise, and to renew our faith in our Creator. Heaven will deal with our prayers in Its own perfect and beneficial way.

My Unseen Minyan

Last week, for various reasons (none of which were connected to my piety) I arrived at the synagogue for the morning service very early – so early, in fact, that I was the one who unlocked the gates. As I sat there alone, waiting for the rest of our faithful minyanaires to arrive, I looked around the *shul*.

In my mind's eye, I was no longer alone, for now I glimpsed all of my *minyan* companions over the past many decades in Chicago, Miami Beach, Monsey, and here in Jerusalem. I was amazed that I accurately remembered so many of them: their appearances, words, habits, individual traits, and peculiarities. Eerily, but also comfortably, I no longer felt alone in that spacious empty room. I believe that such hallucinations are indicative of the years that I have achieved, but nevertheless they were of strong effect and importance to me. They reinforced my lifelong belief that a Jew should never feel utterly alone and abandoned. The unseen *minyan* is as significant to our souls and well-being as is the visible one.

Over the last few years, the inexorable fate of time has transferred many of my friends from the seen *minyan* to the unseen *minyan*. But now, suddenly, in the early morning light of that synagogue room it was the unseen *minyan* that I experienced. I saw them in their prayer shawls and *tefillin*, in their contributions to the charity box, and in their friendly countenances and good cheer. I saw my teachers and students, my father, my congregants and synagogue officers, my teaching and rabbinic colleagues – the *shul* was crowded and full.

As the members of the visible *minyan* arrived and prayer service commenced, the unseen *minyan* faded away. It is difficult to hold on to an apparition when tangible life is actively functioning all around you. It occurred to me that no Jew prays alone. Aside from the active *minyan* surrounding you, there is also an unseen *minyan* participating in your prayers. And its influence can be very great.

It is this chain of past associations that has shaped each and every one of us. As people I knew transfer to the unseen *minyan*, their relationship to me changes. It seems to me that they now have the right to be judgmental, and I wonder if they approve of my prayer, or even of me personally, as I now am. And to me, they have become examples and role models, no longer the members of my former peer group. None of them were perfect, for there are no perfect humans, but each one of them had a special quality that deserves to be remembered and emulated. In fact, that is the efficacy of every *minyan* – it combines all of the special qualities of those assembled and ignores their individual human imperfections.

When I recited the *Amidah* that morning, I understood why the Men of the Great Assembly began that prayer by referring to the God of Abraham, the God of Isaac, and the God of Jacob. I realized that our forefathers are the original founders of our unseen *minyan*. It is they who are our role models and the main influences in our lives and aspirations. Our real *minyan* cannot function well without their presence in our *shul*, and in our hearts and souls.

In fact, it dawned upon me that our unseen *minyan* numbers in the thousands and millions. All of the generations in Jewish history come to pray with us, strengthening us in continuing the chain of Sinai. Once we grasp that we are not alone in this endeavor – that it is not only the ten or twenty people who comprise our visible *minyan* in the room, but that we are aided by so many preceding generations who form the great unseen *minyan* – we can view our challenges with greater equanimity and confidence. Knowing and believing that we are never truly alone, that together with our unseen *minyan* God also accompanies us on our life's journey, will certainly enhance our prayers and improve our outlook on life.

Charity

Helping the needy, acting in a kindhearted way towards people who need our help, is one of the pillars of Judaism. We are trained from our earliest days to share our wealth with those suffering hardship. The Talmud places considerable stress on giving charity, and doing so in a regular, compassionate, and honorable way. It also recognizes, however, that this commandment to give charity allows for all sorts of nefarious schemes and questionable behavior. It ruefully notes that one should have gratitude to the frauds among us because they provide us with an excuse for not fully fulfilling our charitable obligations.

Life presents us with many puzzling situations. We always want to do the right thing, but it is not always clear what the right thing is. Perhaps like many people who read these words, I have often been scammed by rogues who claim to be asking for donations for charitable causes. I have tried not to allow these experiences to turn me into a jaundiced critic of all charity collectors or to develop a cynical attitude towards those who might really need help. But I must confess that I have great misgivings after giving a contribution to someone whom I suspect is a charlatan, even though I have no evidence. And when, upon reflection, I am convinced that I was scammed, it affects me emotionally and spiritually. No one enjoys being made a fool.

This past week a man with the outer appearance of an observant Jew was waiting for me when I left my home to go to the synagogue. It was a Friday morning, and he approached me immediately. He spoke perfect English, said that he was from England, and that he was collecting money for a family that needed to buy food for Shabbat and literally had no money to do so. He pressed me to give him a one-hundred-shekel check, which he said would suffice. The car that was going to drive me to the synagogue was waiting at the corner, and I had no time to discuss the matter further with him. So I thrust my hand into my pocket and somehow it emerged with a hundred-shekel bill. The man took it directly from my hand, put it in his pocket, and rapidly disappeared down the street. I thought about it almost all day. Disturbing vibes pounded within me. Was he legitimately collecting for a poor family, or was he just one of the many con men who prey on the goodness of others? I doubt if I will ever see that person again, and I have no way of knowing if anything that he told me was even close to the truth.

And then I thought to myself, why should I suspect that Jew of being a swindler? I have no evidence for it, and maybe he was truly a selfless volunteer trying to help a family in need. And maybe the "family in need" was his own. To put it mildly, I was conflicted by the entire incident. So I relied upon that statement in the Talmud that I should be grateful to him even if he was scamming me, for he provides me with an excuse for the paucity of charity that I give to others.

Very wealthy people are able to set up an apparatus so that their charity is distributed by others, or by people in their employ. This arrangement frees them from the burden of being personally involved and saves them from the disappointment of being scammed. When I was a rabbi in Miami Beach many years ago, a number of the members of my congregation gave me a sum of money at the beginning of the winter season to distribute to the charity collectors. These benefactors were convinced that somehow I had an intuitive sense and would never be scammed. So I found it necessary to disabuse them of this fallacy. And after a short while, I informed them that I could not warrant that every dollar was given wisely to an authentic cause.

I can never guarantee in my heart that every dollar I distribute goes to a person or institution that is in legitimate need. Yet I comfort myself with the thought that in Heaven charity is judged by the intent of the donor.

Half-Empty

I have always attempted to be a pragmatist; a realist, if you will. The advantage of being a realist is that one is rarely shocked by events as they unfold. The highs of life are not really that high, and the lows are not really that low. It becomes a matter of perspective, of patience, and, above all, a matter of faith. It is the high expectations that we harbor for our children, our finances, our social acceptance, and our success that lead to our deepest disappointments. The secret of successful therapists is that they respond only to the realities of their patients and not to their fantasies or psychotic ramblings.

Yet we are all aware that fantasies are part of our existence, perhaps even a necessary and positive part of human life. And because of this propensity to avoid genuine perspective and realistic judgments, it becomes very easy to view life as a glass that is half-empty. If this is true regarding world events, it is doubly true concerning Jewish life, Torah, and the State of Israel.

We are all aware that the security issue in Israel is a troubling one. Moreover, we know that the chances for any sort of fair and meaningful accommodation with the Arabs are quite slim. In our fantasies, we thought that such an accommodation was somehow within reach – Oslo, Wye, Annapolis, Hebron, Lebanese withdrawal, Gaza disengagement – all promised positive results, and all have disappointed, to put it mildly. People today speak of a third intifada, God forbid, and not of a rose garden here in the Middle East.

For a few decades after World War II, Jews were convinced that anti-Semitism had been finally checked. Today we know better: this was a mere illusion and a wild fantasy. On a recent trip, I visited the United Kingdom, the United States, and Canada. As in other countries, I found the prevailing mood in Jewish communities wherever I visited slightly depressing. Jews are war-weary, concerned about their future, and feel threatened, wherever they may live. So it is not surprising that Jews around the globe see their glass as half-empty.

Yet in historical perspective, the State of Israel is stronger now than it has ever been. And Jewish societies the world over are more influential and affluent than they have ever been in the history of the Diaspora. We have a lot of problems that impinge upon our serenity, but we are certainly in a better place and in better conditions than the Jewish world was a century ago. The Land of Israel was then part of the Ottoman Empire; Eastern European Jewry was ravaged by war, revolution, and pogroms; the immigrant generation was struggling to find its way in the United States; and the Great War was just beginning. In that view of history, one can easily say that our glass is now half-full.

In terms of Torah study, religious observances, and the continuity of traditional Jewish lifestyle, the glass is subject to contradictory assessments. On one hand, we have a very distressing high rate of intermarriage throughout the Diaspora. The Conservative movement in the United States is in dire decline, and the Reform movement has become the haven of the intermarried. The secular Israeli is still opposed to *halachah* as well as to representations of Jewish tradition and Torah observance in Israeli public and political life. Most Jews in the world are not committed to halachic observance of Judaism, and most Jewish children receive a minimal Jewish education, if at all. So that glass can certainly be viewed as half-empty.

Yet, in truth, the Jewish world is much more Jewish today than it was a few decades ago. The number of people involved in regular, serious, daily Torah study is probably at an all-time high. The masses of students in Jewish schools and yeshivot are far greater than in previous centuries. And the universal Shabbat Project attracts one million participants – something completely unimagined and deemed impossible only a half-century ago. So there is legitimate reason to view our "faith" glass as half-full.

It all depends on our viewpoint and mindset when we view the problems and accomplishments of the Jewish world. Like beauty, hope or despair are in the eye of the beholder.

Good Fortune

The rabbis of the Midrash stated that "everyone and everything requires good fortune – *mazal* – for successful existence." They added that this rule applies "even to the *sefer Torah* that is in the ark." Over the ages, there have been many interpretations offered to explain this enigmatic statement.

There are two most commonly quoted explanations. In its simplest form, the statement of the rabbis refers to instances when there are numerous *sifrei Torah* resting in the ark and yet only one or two of them are ever used for the public reading of the Torah. The other *sifrei Torah* that lack of good fortune are ignored, which leads to their deterioration. Another understanding may refer to the fact that a certain *sefer Torah* may have an error in it that would render it unfit to be used until the error is corrected. However, the error appears in a section of that *sefer Torah* that for some reason is never read publicly, and thus the error remains undetected for years or forever, while in another *sefer Torah* its one error is found and that Torah is immediately removed from public service. One *sefer Torah* has good *mazal* – escaping the ignominy of being declared unfit for public reading – while the other *sefer Torah*, not having *mazal*, retains its honored place in the synagogue services.

A stark and simple demonstration of the Midrash occurred at our Beit Knesset Hanassi in Jerusalem. Some time ago, a robbery occurred at a neighboring synagogue. That synagogue is located barely one block away from Hanassi and is on the same side of the street as Hanassi. In that robbery, five *sifrei Torah* were stolen. The anguish felt by the members of that synagogue was shared by all of us at Beit Hanassi when we learned of that dastardly deed. Though the police were investigating the matter, many of the members of both synagogues despaired of ever seeing those *sifrei Torah* again. There is a brisk market in used *sifrei Torah,* and tragically, stolen ones easily find their way into that market.

Last week, I noticed two suitcases in the front courtyard of Beit Knesset Hanassi. Ordinarily, I would have thought them suspicious and called the police bomb squad; its mechanical robot would have blown them up without inspecting their contents. But I just did nothing. Next morning, someone even more foolhardy than I carried the two suitcases into the synagogue. Once inside, they were examined by a number of us and – lo and behold! – they contained four *sifrei Torah*. Presuming that the thief may have been overcome with pangs of conscience and regret, we contacted our sister synagogue down the block. They immediately sent over their "experts," who were able to positively identify these *sifrei Torah* as the stolen ones from their synagogue. The joy at finding these stolen *sifrei Torah* and being able to return them to their rightful place in the ark was unbounded. These *sifrei Torah* truly had *mazal* – the best of good fortune.

If a *sefer Torah* requires *mazal*, we ordinary mortals certainly do. All of our daily activities are fraught with potential peril. As drivers or pedestrians, automobiles are certainly a hazard. Being in the wrong place at the wrong time can be disastrous.

How the Lord dispenses *mazal* is unknown to us. But all of us realize that it is an essential ingredient for success in commerce, family, and in life itself. The rabbis of the Talmud taught us, "Children, life span, and wealth are dependent not only upon our merits and efforts, but upon *mazal* as well." Many have been the comments and explanations regarding this declaration of the Talmud, but the simplicity of the statement speaks for itself. One can do everything "right" in family, career, and health matters, and yet be unsuccessful since the elusive ingredient of *mazal* is absent.

I wonder what happened to the fifth stolen *sefer Torah*. What was its *mazal*, and where is it now? All of this remains a mystery to me, as does the entire concept of *mazal*. In any event, I wish you good fortune and *mazal tov* – however that operates in this world – in all of life's endeavors and circumstances.

Spring Ahead

Numerous countries, including Israel, annually push clocks ahead one hour and go to Daylight Savings Time. The advantages of doing so are still debatable. (There even was a report in the media that the switch to summer Daylight Savings Time contributes to an increased risk of heart attacks!) But nevertheless, Daylight Savings Time it is. Aside from losing an hour's sleep, I suffered no ill effects from putting my mechanical clock – though not my body clock – ahead the one hour required by law. And I searched for some great moral lesson that I could derive from this mundane happening. After all, nothing that happens in God's world is without meaning and instruction.

I came to the conclusion that springing ahead is a good Jewish trait – even a Torah value, if you will. For Judaism always insists that we look ahead and always consider tomorrow in our plans and actions for today. Our father Jacob said, "Tomorrow I will attain my compensation and reward."

It is our nature to plan for our future, even though that future is always uncertain. We plan for our retirement and even for our eventual demise. We are always planning ahead, projecting our future onto our current activities. Our clocks are always set ahead because, as much as we live in the present, we really live in the future. This most human of all traits governs our thinking individually and policies nationally.

We are to be comforted for our lost hour of sleep by the realization that almost seven months from now we will turn our clocks back and regain that lost hour. Though there have been proposals to keep Daylight Savings Time all year long, Standard Time has not yet been eliminated. It seems that we cannot always spring ahead; sometimes we must remember to fall back.

Our future is always built upon our past. Without an understanding and appreciation of that past, the future becomes even more murky and unpredictable. Over the past few centuries, much of the Jewish world has only looked to spring ahead. It almost consciously removed its past, focusing only on the glittering future that it imagined for itself – a utopian future that in many respects has never yet come into being. And the great and good future that did come to reality, such as the State of Israel and the ingathering of the scattered exiles of the Jewish people to the Land of Israel, was really built upon the longing and devotion of generations of past centuries. Thus, without the fall back, the spring ahead would never have occurred.

The lack of historical perspective in almost all sections of the Jewish world today is one of the most appalling and disturbing features of the dysfunction that plagues our current Jewish society. By neglecting to teach our children of our past, we limit their vision and hopes for their future. But just as metaphorically we regain the one hour that we lost when springing ahead by the process of later falling back, so too can we regain our past and thereby help illuminate our future.

There is a debate raging in the Israeli Hebrew press as to the reasons why Israelis who move abroad assimilate into their new society without retaining any Jewish connection at a far greater rate than do Jews born in those countries. Without my weighing in seriously on that debate, I feel that it is proper to note that the average Israeli school teaches little about our past and therefore does not engender any feeling of Jewish self-identity in its students. It is no wonder that once the Israeli is no longer living in Israel, he or she has absolutely no moorings to the past and is extremely vulnerable to immediate assimilation and loss of Jewish identity.

Generally speaking, we live in a "now" generation, desiring instant gratification with little thought about tomorrow or about yesterday. But it is clear that "now" is never satisfied, no matter how much material wealth and abundance is heaped upon it. The nature of human beings is to find satisfaction in dreaming about tomorrow and in reminiscing about yesterday.

Only by springing ahead and falling back does our present situation in life take on some meaning and satisfaction. In any event, I am looking forward to regaining that lost hour's sleep later this year.

Career or Calling?

There was a time, not that long ago, when those entering the field of the clergy did so in response to what they felt was a calling. They had a Heavenly instinct that called them to the service of their faith and its adherents. This idea was promulgated and publicized especially after the Reformation that changed the face of religion in Europe. But its basis (as is true of much of the ideals and mores of the modern Western world) lay deeply embedded in Jewish thought and tradition.

Teaching Torah, helping those in need, leading and guiding people according to the value system of the Torah – in short, serving as a communal rabbi – is not regarded as a "career" in Jewish thought. When our teacher Moses installed the tribe of Levi as the "professional" religious leaders of the people, he admonished them: "Do not think that I am granting you power or office. I am granting you servitude!" And that has pretty much been the general attitude towards serving in the rabbinate throughout Jewish history.

In fact, the concept of communal rabbis drawing a salary from public funds does not appear to have taken hold in Jewish life until the fourteenth and fifteenth centuries in Ashkenazic Europe. And even then, many rabbis struggled mightily to earn their own sustenance and not be beholden to the community coffers. In this fashion, the rabbinate was still seen as a calling and not as a career.

Understandably, not every rabbi was the paragon of altruism and purely devoid of self-interest. Human nature is human nature, and rabbis are not immune to the pitfalls that menace all people. Yet, generally speaking, the honor afforded to Torah scholars – and especially to rabbis – was recognized as honoring Torah and not necessarily the scholar or rabbi personally.

But slowly over the centuries, the concept of the rabbinate as a career and not a calling seeped into Jewish life. We have European records from the eighteenth and nineteenth centuries of rich relatives "buying" rabbinical positions for their family members, and of the emergence of dynastic families controlling the rabbinate of certain communities for numerous decades. With the rise of Chassidut in those centuries, one can easily make the case that being a *Rebbe* also became a career for which one required training and pedigree. Naturally, there are always exceptions to this observation, but in the main the shift in religious Jewish life from calling to career was gaining momentum. Especially in American Jewish life in the twentieth century, the rabbinate became almost purely a profession requiring certain training and skills while the spiritual component of the position was diminished, and sometimes ignored. America has witnessed openly atheistic "rabbis," as incongruous as that sounds. But once the rabbinate became only a career, such incongruities are understandable.

And what about the Chief Rabbinate of Israel? In my opinion, the chief rabbi need not be the greatest Talmudic scholar – though he must certainly be a Talmudic scholar – nor need he be the most gifted orator in the land. The task involves being politically savvy, but he should not be a politician. Independence of agenda and freedom of action are necessary requirements for the job. But above all, he must view his position as a calling and not the culmination of a career.

In Avot we are told that one should not advance one's own personal interests and monetary gains through the exploitation of Torah. The careerist is most susceptible to fall into that disgraceful trap. The careerist feels answerable to humans, and humans can be manipulated and fooled. But one who feels called to public service feels answerable to Heaven, resulting in a different attitude towards the tasks and challenges at hand.

Legend has it that when Rabbi Yisrael Lipkin of Salant instructed his disciple Rabbi Yitzchak Blazer (Peterburger) to assume the position of rabbi in St. Petersburg, Rabbi Blazer told him, "Master, I am afraid!" To which Rabbi Yisrael responded, "Well then, whom shall I send? Someone who is not afraid?" The careerist is never afraid; but one who feels the rabbinate as a calling possesses the necessary trepidation to see the challenges of public service vividly.

Sermons

I have been delivering sermons on Shabbat in the synagogues where I have served as a rabbi for the past sixty years. I have always felt that the much-maligned sermon is a powerful tool in the arsenal of a synagogue rabbi. Like all tools, it can be successful only if it is applied consistently and wisely. So considerable thought and preparation should go in the construction and message of the sermon.

I never write out my sermons, and I usually speak in a somewhat spontaneous style. However, I spend all week thinking about what I am going to say on Shabbat. Many times I have more than one thought on the subject that I have developed in my mind, and the decision as to what I am actually going to say often is not made until I am standing before my congregants in the pulpit. I know this method sounds a little haphazard, but over the years I have found that it works best for me.

I do not speak about current events, politics, diplomacy, or other "relevant" topics. I do not feel that people come to the synagogue to hear my opinions about Iran, the prime minister of Israel, or the president of the United States. They come to the synagogue for inspiration, strength, and faith. I try to speak about timeless ideas represented by Jewish values and Torah, and I also try to convey a broad historical perspective in which we can see ourselves as part of the great drama that is Jewish life. There is nothing as obsolete as being current, timely, and relevant.

This is a personal prejudice of mine and I know that many rabbis disagree with me. But I am very comfortable with my stance that a sermon is a lesson in Torah and not a book review, an op-ed opportunity, or a commentary on the human foibles of the past week.

Of course, there are momentous watershed events that warrant discussion. The Holocaust, the establishment of the State of Israel, the wars that Israel has been forced to fight over the decades – all are worthy of teachings and sermons. To me, Donald Trump is not such a subject.

So my speeches will be consistently more about Abraham, Isaac, and Jacob than about the hot personalities splashed across newspaper headlines. Synagogue rabbis should preach Judaism and Jewish values. Leave the social commentary to the media pundits who claim expertise in these matters.

Poetry

Judaism is a religion of words. The holy words of the Torah are the basis for all Jewish tradition. As we know, words can come in many forms – poetry, narrative prose, declamations, commands, essays, and statements. All of these combinations of words appear in the Torah. Though most rabbinic scholarship focused and concentrated on the statements and commandments of the Torah, the rabbis were always aware of the innate beauty of the poetry of the Hebrew language. This awareness was not limited to the actual poetic portions of the Torah such as the Song of Moses and Israel at the Red Sea or the blessings of Bilaam; even the more prosaic forms of the Torah, such as the blessings of Jacob and of Moses, were understood in their poetic meter and language. Thus from the infancy of Israel, poetry and an appreciation of language became an integral part of Jewish life and rabbinic study.

Certain books of the Bible are viewed as poetic works, foremost among them the book of Psalms. But the prose of Isaiah or Amos is also Hebraic poetry in its most exalted form. And since these books of the Bible became part of the synagogue service on a daily or weekly basis, the Jewish ear became attuned to the majesty of Hebrew poetic language. Poetry is a constant and important component of Jewish liturgy.

The Torah refers to its contents as *shirah* – poetry, song. Following this lead, all forms of poetry – liturgical, general, and personal – became common in Jewish life from the times of the Talmud onwards. The acknowledged master of liturgical poetry was Rabbi Elazar Hakalir, whose liturgical poems form the basis of many parts of Jewish prayer services even today. There are those who identify him as a scholar of the Mishnah (second-century Israel), while most scholars place him in seventh-century Babylonia or other Mediterranean communities.

In the Middle Ages, the use of poetry was common and became exalted in both the Sephardic and Ashkenazic Jewish communities. The gifted and renowned poets laureate of the Jewish people, such as Shlomo ibn Gavirol, Yehudah HaLevi, Moshe and Avraham ibn Ezra, Shimon of Mainz, all contributed to the development of Hebrew verse. Most of the poetry was devoted to prayers, such as *Selichot, Kinnot,* and *Piyutim* (penitential prayer, elegies, and liturgical poetry).

However, we do find a variety of general poetry as well, authored by these same illustrious wordsmiths. Yehudah HaLevi's "Songs of the Sea" remains a classic example of Hebrew poetry at its finest. Songs of nature and of love were widely popular in the Jewish world of Spain and North Africa; and the composition of unique poems to mark a special lifecycle event such as a marriage, circumcision, or funeral was the norm of good manners and proper etiquette.

Many rabbinic works over the centuries, even down to the twentieth century, contained introductions to the book written in poetic form. It seemed to be almost obligatory for rabbinic authors to try their hand at composing poetry in introducing their scholarly tomes.

In the nineteenth and twentieth centuries, Hebrew and Yiddish poetry regarding all aspects of life and literature became very popular. As the times changed rapidly, an entire genre of nostalgic poems appeared, rich in memory, pathos, and sadness. Concurrent with the rise of Zionism and nationalism, Hebrew poems describing the return to Zion and the nascent Jewish state abounded. Our generation is witness to an explosion of poetry regarding the Holocaust and the subsequent establishment of the State of Israel.

Most forms of prose speak to the brain and intellect of a person, while poetry speaks to one's heart and emotions. Since Judaism always deals with one's soul and the workings of one's inner spirit, it goes without saying that poetry deserves a place of high honor in Jewish life. Poetry reflects our inner longings and hopes, and it helps deflect our fears and trepidations. Perhaps this is why the Torah chose to describe itself as a poem – a poem of eternity and Godliness.

Alfred Joyce Kilmer, a famous poet, once wrote: "Poems are made by fools like me/But only God can make a tree." He was wrong. God also makes poetry.

Head Checks

The common practice in much of Jewish society is to issue and accept postdated checks – "head checks." Many pay their yeshiva tuitions in that fashion; some pay their charitable pledges that way as well. Personal debts and obligations are also funded in this fashion.

When I was a lawyer, I had a client who was substantially wealthy yet always paid his obligations with postdated checks. I informed him that technically that was not too legal, and since he had the necessary funds available, why did he insist on issuing postdated checks? His response was that when you give an individual or an institution a postdated check the receiver will undoubtedly pray for your continued good health and success – at least until the check finally clears the bank. There is a certain intuitive logic to that viewpoint.

In any event, issuing and/or accepting a head check is an act of faith and trust. The issuer is convinced that he will see that the check will be made good on the due date, and the acceptor of that check also demonstrates his faith in the issuer. Thus a more intimate relationship than usual is created between the two parties involved, governed by a feeling of mutual trust.

The God of Israel has issued us a number of long-term head checks. There is a head check regarding the Jewish people and the Land of Israel. There is another head check outstanding that promises a return of the people of Israel to a Torah way of life and to true service of God in their personal and national lives. There is a very large head check still outstanding regarding messianic times and the glory, peace, serenity, and independence that era will bring to Israel, and eventually to all of mankind. And there are numerous other head checks outstanding concerning universal peace and disarmament, a fair system of prosperity, and a unified recognition of God's sovereignty over all human affairs.

The rub of the matter is that these checks are undated. We do not know exactly when they can be presented for payment at the Heavenly bank. So the quality of faith and trust that always accompanies postdated checks is compounded in the case of God's commitments to us. Undated head checks are truly a matter of trust in the issuer. Over the long history of the Jewish people, our trust in the Issuer of those head checks has remained constant; we have trusted implicitly that they will all be paid in full. Only in our time have we begun to see that some of them are, perhaps, currently redeemable.

A dispute has raged in the Jewish world over the past two centuries whether these checks can be presented for payment even if the Issuer has not specifically informed us that the due date has arrived. This disagreement was (and is) marked by the contentious struggle over the Zionist movement and the establishment of the State of Israel. To a certain extent, we can all agree that partial payment on that head check has been made. The question is whether a head check can be redeemed in partial payments or whether the whole amount due must be paid at one shot.

We have no instruction on that matter, and the Issuer remains outwardly silent, which only adds to our lack of clarity. The head check regarding the ingathering of the Jewish exiles to the Land of Israel has in the main been cashed, even though millions of Jews voluntarily choose to remain in Diaspora lands.

So it seems that the checks will be paid piecemeal, and not in one fell swoop. Since the head checks were undated, we have no cause for complaint or despair. We hope and pray to see all of them fully redeemed soon, but until then we must retain our trust in the Issuer of the checks. And we must remain firm in our belief that the entire amount of those head checks will be paid to us with a full heart and open hand.